Martin Luther King and the Rhetoric of Freedom

Studies in Rhetoric and Religion 5

Cover Design by Steve Scholl, Waterstone Agency

Library of Congress Cataloging-in-Publication Data

Selby, Gary S.
  Martin Luther King and the rhetoric of freedom : the Exodus
narrative in America's struggle for civil rights / Gary S. Selby.
     p. cm. -- (Studies in rhetoric and religion ; 5)
  Includes bibliographical references and index.
  ISBN 978-1-60258-016-9 (pbk. : alk. paper)
  1. King, Martin Luther, Jr., 1929-1968--Oratory. 2. King, Martin
Luther, Jr., 1929-1968--Language. 3. Exodus, The--Sermons. 4.
Exodus, The. 5. Rhetoric--Religious aspects--Christianity--History--
20th century. 6. Rhetoric--Political aspects--United States--History-
-20th century. 7. Rhetoric--Social aspects--United States--History-
-20th century. 8. African Americans--Civil rights--History--20th
century. 9. Civil rights movements--Southern States--History--20th
century. 10. Civil rights movements--United States--History--20th
century. I. Title.
  E185.97.K5S45 2007
  323.092--dc22

                                    2007042670

Printed in the United States of America on acid-free paper with a
minimum of 30% pcw recycled content.

Martin Luther King and the Rhetoric of Freedom

The Exodus Narrative in America's Struggle for Civil Rights

GARY S. SELBY

BAYLOR UNIVERSITY PRESS

For my parents,

Fred and June Selby,

who taught me to hear the Word

CONTENTS

PREFACE

In the biblical story of the burning bush, when he realizes that he is on holy ground, Moses hides his face out of a sense of awe and of his own smallness in relation to God. In the writing of this book, as I have listened to the voices of the civil rights movement, I have often felt that sense of awe. I am struck by how small my own efforts to write about those years are when compared to the profound courage and sacrifice of those who lived them. I believe that our society is still far from the Promised Land of racial justice that Martin Luther King invited us all to imagine. Yet when I consider what those women and men did between 1955 and 1963, and how they did it, and against what odds, I find myself on holy ground.

I have written this book out of a conviction that a crucial part of studying social movements involves examining the processes through which people become caught up together in a feeling that they share common identity and purpose—and attending to the stories that are at the heart of that process. My hope is that this book makes a contribution to that enterprise. But I also hope that it contributes to our understanding of this particular movement. If racial healing is ever to come to our society, it will mean remembering and retelling our story of racial injustice and honoring the voices and the actions of those who stood against it. That has been the richest gain of this project for me, to stand in awe of the courage of those protesters and to find myself caught up in the optimism of Dr. King's vision of the beloved community.

I wish to say thank you to a number of people who, in one way or another, helped this project come to fruition: my teachers, David Roberts and Raymond Muncy, who inspired my love for history, and Robert Gaines, who guided my immersion in rhetoric; my students at

George Washington University and Pepperdine University, who graciously listened to my almost daily references to "Martin Luther King and the Exodus narrative"; my colleagues at both institutions and especially my GW mentor Clay Warren, for their constant encouragement; my friends at the Columbia Church of Christ, who nurtured my "other life" in academia; Maggie Earles, for her helpful comments on the earliest draft of this material; the office of the associate provost for research at Pepperdine, for released time from teaching responsibilities, which made this book possible; my reviewers, whose suggestions helped shape the project; Marty Medhurst and the folks at Baylor University Press, for being excited about my work; and finally, my wife, Tammy, and my sons, Joel and Tyler, for faithfully giving me support and good cheer along the way.

INTRODUCTION

On the evening of December 5, 1955, Martin Luther King, twenty-six years old and barely fifteen months into the first pastoral appointment of his career as minister for the Dexter Avenue Baptist Church in Montgomery, Alabama, stood before a gathering of some four thousand crowded into the auditorium and basement and spilling out onto the lawn of the Holt Street Baptist Church. The mass meeting, called to determine whether there was sufficient support for continuing a one-day boycott of the city's buses, opened with the singing of two hymns, followed by a prayer and a Bible reading. King then approached the podium and expressed his happiness at seeing the crowd of people who had come out that evening. He explained their purpose for assembling, to get the "bus situation in Montgomery" corrected, and he characterized Rosa Parks, arrested four days earlier for refusing to give up her seat on the bus to a white rider, as someone whom "nobody can call a disturbing factor," emphasizing that she was arrested "just because she refused to get up."[1] He complained that the buses had never set aside "a reserved section for Negroes," noting that "the law has never been clarified at this point." To this moment, King's tone had been subdued, almost prosaic, and his audience had responded to him with only an occasional, audible "amen," "yes," or "all right."

Suddenly, however, King began to give voice to the pent-up frustration his hearers felt toward their experience of the nation's legacy of racial oppression: "And you know, my friends, there comes a time when people get tired of being trampled over by the iron feet of oppression."[2] The audience erupted into thundering applause. King immediately fell into an emotion-filled, poetic expression of that outrage built on the repetition of the phrases "there comes a time" and "we are tired." His rhythmic chant, interrupted frequently by applause, ended with

1

this rousing proclamation: "We, the disinherited of this land, we who have been oppressed for so long, are tired of going through the long night of captivity. And now we are reaching out for the daybreak of freedom and justice and equality."

As he would repeatedly do throughout his career as the civil rights–movement spokesperson and icon, King called on the most salient story in the African American cultural tradition, the story of the Exodus, as he prophetically heralded a long-awaited moment: What had happened four thousand years earlier when God brought the nation of Israel out of slavery in Egypt, across the Red Sea, through the wilderness, and into the Promised Land of Canaan, was happening in their own day once again. Inspired by King's vision, the audience wholeheartedly endorsed a resolution that included a decision to "refrain from riding buses owned and operated in the city of Montgomery" until the bus company came to an agreement with the black community.[3]

AGAINST ALL ODDS

Although few in attendance that night could have realized it at the moment, that fateful meeting did more than mark the beginning of a boycott against the city's buses. It began a progression of large-scale, organized campaigns against segregation that would eventually become a movement of national and international significance, dramatically altering U.S. society even as it catapulted King into an iconic role as the symbol of resistance against racial oppression in the United States. Within one year, the boycott brought the bus company, the Montgomery City Lines, to the brink of financial collapse, demonstrating the economic and financial power that blacks could wield through collective action. Within a year and a half of that first mass meeting, King had become a national figure, appearing on nationally broadcast news programs as well as on the cover of *Time* magazine, and speaking to large audiences, many of them integrated, all over the nation.

In less than seven years, in early 1963, the movement that emerged from the initial protest against Montgomery's segregated seating policy would paralyze the entire economic and political structure of what was generally considered the country's most racially oppressive city: Birmingham, Alabama. The dignified perseverance of the Birmingham protesters, many of them children, juxtaposed against the incredible brutality of the police forces violently seeking to quell their campaign, would be captured by the international press, bringing the federal government into the struggle over racial injustice in the South in a way that had not happened since Reconstruction. One year later, Congress would pass the landmark Civil Rights Act of 1964 outlawing segregation in public places, prohibiting discrimination in companies that did business with the federal government and in educational institutions that received federal funding, creating the Equal Employment Commission. The following year, in 1965, Congress would pass the equally dramatic Voting Rights Act, which outlawed all poll taxes and literacy requirements for voting. By 1968, the number of blacks registered to vote in Mississippi, one of the South's most intractable states when it came to black suffrage, had almost reached 60 percent. That first mass meeting thus launched a movement that would change the political and cultural landscape of the United States forever.

The success of that initial protest and the movement that grew out of it is astounding when viewed within the social and political milieu in which it emerged, one in which the possibility of undertaking a successful campaign against racial injustice would have seemed utterly impossible to most blacks in the South. From the end of Reconstruction almost a century earlier, they had been beset by a pervasive sense of fear and powerlessness at the prospect of challenging racist social structures in any form. Writing about the barriers they faced in seeking the right to vote, for example, Morris pointed out that the majority "feared voting because it could get them killed or fired."[4] One episode from Mississippi's history poignantly demonstrates that this fear was well founded. In the early 1950s, Rev. George Lee, a minister and grocer in the small town of Belzoni, cofounded a local chapter of the National Association for the Advancement of Colored People (NAACP) and, despite constant harassment and intimidation, had convinced nearly a hundred black citizens to register to vote. On May 7, 1955, while driving home shortly before midnight, Lee's car was hit by three shotgun blasts from a passing car, killing Lee. Without investigating, the county sheriff ruled that his death was the result of a traffic accident and, when challenged by evidence of the gunfire, said that the lead pellets removed from Lee's face were dental fillings dislodged in the accident. The coroner's jury officially attributed his death to unknown causes, and no one was ever arrested for the murder.[5] This type of tragic episode was repeated many times over. Not surprisingly, blacks were so systematically excluded from the political process that most simply accepted voting as "white folks' business."[6]

This reluctance to challenge racial oppression was reinforced by a long tradition in the African American church of what Morris called a "religion of containment."[7] Black preaching often took a stance of accommodation toward social oppression, promising a heavenly reward to those who sought personal holiness and meekly endured oppression on earth.[8] As Eskew pointed out, in Birmingham, at least, the tendency for religious institutions to avoid confronting white power structures was encouraged by the economic arrangement through which some black churches were funded:

> For years, industrialists had kept black preachers on their payrolls, constructed churches for mill village employees, and promoted a fundamentalist view of individual salvation with its concomitant belief in social Darwinian damnation. Successful Negro ministers in Birmingham echoed these beliefs. The Reverends Luke Beard at Sixteenth Street Baptist Church and John W. Goodgame at Sixth Avenue Baptist Church accommodated the prevailing ideology by opposing unionization, the Communist Party, and other black radical grassroots movements to alter race relations.[9]

Although a tradition of activism did exist among a small number of churches in the South, much of African American Christianity was dominated by an otherworldly focus that, in Lischer's words, "permitted . . . a temporary escape from social and economic oppression and from the responsibility to do something about it."[10]

Throughout the movement's history, organizers also faced the problem of division in the black community. Even the initial gathering of Montgomery's black leaders, called the day after Rosa Parks's arrest to plan the initial one-day boycott, came dangerously close to dissolving into factional bickering, confirming the fears of many that "individual leaders would be unable to put aside their rivalries and desires for self-advancement long enough to agree on a unified community effort."[11] Later, King would speak of the "crippling factionalism" that persistently threatened the campaign, recalling how "it appeared . . . the tragic division in the Negro community could be cured only by some divine miracle"[12]

When the boycott extended beyond its first heady days of success, organizers faced the herculean challenge of sustaining a protest that brought severe hardships to its own participants, and doing so under constant pressure from the white establishment. Their attempts to negotiate with the city's political and economic leaders were met with a refusal to budge on the part of the bus company itself and later the city government that took campaign leaders by surprise. As the boycott continued and, later, in reaction to its successful resolution, blacks experienced a violent backlash from militant racists in the city, facing sniper fire, threatening and obscene phone calls, and the bombing of the homes of a number of their leaders and prominent white sympathizers. This kind of harassment and intimidation continued throughout the movement, reaching perhaps its worst point when members of the Ku Klux Klan bombed Birmingham's Sixteenth Street Baptist Church on Sunday morning, September 15, 1963, killing four young girls. Despite these enormous obstacles, blacks courageously persevered in their quest for a just society.

How do we account for this? How, after almost a century of racial oppression and against such overwhelming odds, were African Americans now able to join together in the kinds of sustained, mass protests that would force fundamental change in U.S. society? Certainly, part of the explanation lies in the charisma of King himself, a fact that, for all their tendency to overstate the importance of an individual actor, a number of King biographies have rightly emphasized. Stephen Oates, whose *Let the Trumpet Sound* recounts the development of the civil rights movement as an outgrowth of the story of King's own life, articulated that conviction this way: "King did more than any other leader in his generation to help make emancipation a political and social fact in the racially troubled South."[13] The support that John F. Kennedy gave to the cause of civil rights, he concluded, resulted in large part from King's own "personal crusade" to convert Kennedy "into a modern Lincoln."

At the same time, African American organizations, most of them closely connected to or extensions of the black church, played a crucial role in the movement. Reflecting this focus is David Garrow's magisterial study, *Bearing the Cross*, which recounts the history of the civil rights movement by tracing the history of local black organizations, such as the Montgomery Improvement Association (MIA) and the Alabama Christian Movement for Human Rights, as well as the broader Southern Christian Leadership Conference (SCLC).[14] From this perspective, the movement's success was not only the result of King's "sense of history, his brilliant oratory, [or] his defense of the moral example of American democratic principle,"[15] as Oates put it, but also reflected the logistical and managerial skill of those in the SCLC who, often outside of the public view, skillfully managed resources and organized people and events.[16] Aldon Morris particularly highlighted the organizational resources provided by the indigenous African American church. He argued that black church, with its organizational infrastructure, financial resources, as well as its "music, trenchant sermons, and challenging oratory," played the "central and overpowering role . . . in the movement."[17]

Still other explanations can be offered to help explain the dramatic change that the movement brought about in U.S. society. What began in December 1955 cannot be understood apart from attention to its continuity with the long tradition of localized struggles against racial oppression that extended back much earlier in the twentieth century.[18] Further, as Thornton argued, the cities in which the movement achieved its most dramatic successes had also undergone dramatic shifts in their municipal political structures, from systems dominated by local political machines to more populist structures. This "historic moment of political transition," as he described it, created an opportunity for progress in these cities that would have been impossible elsewhere.[19] Further, the attention given to the protests and demonstrations by the national media—from the Montgomery bus boycott in 1955, the lunch-counter sit-ins in 1960, and the Freedom Rides in 1961 to the confrontations with the Birmingham police in 1963 and the Alabama state troopers in Selma in 1965—clearly played a crucial role in mobilizing the support of the U.S. public and pressuring the Kennedy administration to propose sweeping civil rights legislation. As Lentz argued,

> In modern America, the nation's values—certainly its understanding of those values as associated with specific events and symbolic personages—increasingly have become the province of journalistic institutions. News reports, printed or broadcast, put flesh upon abstractions.

On this basis he concluded,

> What moved the nation to respond were the great moral dramas—
> Birmingham and Selma especially—in which the props were a police-
> man's club and his snarling dog, the characters violent segregationists
> and freedom-loving, nonviolent blacks, and the scenario one that could
> be easily sketched in starkly contrasting tones of good and evil.[20]

The press played a central role in the construction of this drama—
particularly, the growing medium of television, which brought scenes
of violent confrontation into the living rooms of Americans across the
nation.

Viewed from a still broader vantage point, the movement owed its
success, as well, to the influence within U.S. culture of the ideological
values of equality and freedom being marshaled to support the United
States's Cold War foreign policy. As Dudziak wrote,

> Domestic racism and civil rights protest led to international criticism of
> the U. S. government. International criticism led the federal government
> to respond, through placating foreign critics by reframing the narrative
> of race in America, and through promoting some level of social change.
> While civil rights reform in different eras has been motivated by a variety
> of factors, one element during the early Cold War years was the need for
> reform in order to make credible the government's argument about race
> and democracy.[21]

These various explanations underscore the complexity of causes
behind the civil rights movement. None of them, however, fully
accounts for what made the movement so revolutionary or successful—the fact that for the first time in U.S. history blacks were able to
unite in mass protest against racial oppression. Somehow the protesters found the courage, determination, and hope necessary to sustain
a united struggle in the face of unimaginable hardship. Despite the
fact that segregation had been an entrenched way of life for some four
generations, blacks somehow came to believe that change was possible.
They were able to overcome both fear of reprisal and division within
their own ranks. As it became clear what the campaigns might cost
them economically and physically, they responded with a willingness

to risk their very lives for the cause. Where did they find this courage and determination? For an answer, we turn to a tradition of religious discourse that they brought to the movement and to the way that King and other movement leaders were able to draw on that tradition to construct a perspective or frame of reference from which protesters could see themselves, their history and present circumstances, and their crusade to overcome U.S. apartheid. That tradition was grounded fundamentally in the biblical story of the Exodus.

The Exodus in the Rhetoric of Martin Luther King

King's reference to the "long night of captivity" made during his first boycott address is one example of what became his persistent practice of alluding to the ancient story in his civil rights rhetoric.[22] Indeed, months before the boycott even began, in his "Death of Evil on the Seashore" sermon, King was employing the Exodus narrative to account for the success of liberation movements of peoples of color worldwide and to explain the history of blacks in the United States. During the boycott itself, King frequently referred to the biblical narrative to exhort the protesters to continue their struggle. "This is the year God's gonna set his people free," he promised.[23] "You don't get to the promised land without going through the wilderness,"[24] he explained on another occasion. Protesters needed to continue their struggle because, he said, "we haven't reached the promised land, North or South."[25] Nevertheless, he assured them, "We can walk and never get weary, because we believe and know that there is a great camp meeting in the promised land of freedom and justice."[26]

King continued to use Exodus language as the movement developed beyond the local protest of segregated seating on Montgomery's buses. For example, on January 27, 1957, almost two months after the boycott had ended, he spoke to his congregation after a night of violence against Montgomery's black citizens in words that anticipated his famous, "I've Been to the Mountaintop" address, delivered a decade later: "If I had to die tomorrow morning I would die happy, because I've been to the mountain top and I've seen the promised land."[27] In May of that year, King urged a crowd of twenty thousand people gathered on the steps of the Lincoln Memorial for a "Prayer Pilgrimage for Freedom" to stand up for justice. (*Yes*) Sometimes it gets hard, but it is always difficult to get out of Egypt, for the Red Sea always stands before you with discouraging dimensions. (*Yes*) And even after you've crossed the Red Sea, you have to move through a wilderness with prodigious hilltops of evil (*Yes*) and gigantic mountains of opposition. (*Yes*) But I say to you this afternoon: Keep moving. (*Go on ahead*) Let nothing slow you up. (*Go on ahead*) Move on with dignity and honor and respectability. (*Yes*)[28]

The following October, King's wife, Coretta, read a statement on his behalf before a protest march in Washington, DC, supporting school integration, while King recovered from a stab wound inflicted by a would-be assassin, reminding the protesters, "We all know how Moses, inflamed by the oppression of his people, led the March of Egypt into the promised land."[29] When King and the other members of the SCLC brought their organization to the city of Birmingham, local leader Fred Shuttlesworth announced his arrival with these words: "Follow him to Jail. In the end, he will lead us to freedom."[30] King celebrated a particularly successful day of protest with these words: "We are moving on the freedom land." Two years later, after a successful march from Selma, Alabama, to the state capitol in Montgomery, King boldly proclaimed:

We are not about to turn around. (*Yes, sir*) We are on the move now. (*Yes, sir*) Yes, we are on the move and no wave of racism can stop us. (*Yes, sir*) We are on the move now. . . . Like an idea whose time has come, (*Yes, sir*) not even the marching of mighty armies can halt us. (*Yes, sir*) We are moving to the land of freedom. (*Yes, sir*)[31]

Of course, in the final speech of his life, delivered on April 3, 1968, King again took on the persona of Moses: "I've been to the mountaintop. . . . And I've looked over. And I've seen the promised land."[32]

As these examples show, the Exodus was a persistent theme in King's rhetoric throughout his career as spokesperson for the civil rights movement. Blacks were the chosen people of God, languishing in the Egypt of racial oppression. Significant events marking progress toward justice—the Supreme Court's landmark *Brown v. Board of Education* decision and the successful boycott of Montgomery's buses—were represented as the crossing of the Red Sea. The difficulties that blacks faced in pursuing racial equality were the travails of the wilderness, and the vision toward which they labored was the Promised Land of integration and brotherhood. From the beginning of his leadership to the final address of his life, King called on the ancient religious drama as a way of creating a symbolic context in which his hearers could experience their present circumstances, representing their campaign for racial justice as the enactment of a modern day Exodus.

Overview

The thesis of this book is that the development and ultimate success of the civil rights movement resulted, at least in part, from the way that movement leaders—Martin Luther King Jr. in particular—evoked this deeply held cultural narrative to create the sense that blacks were reliving the Exodus in their own day. This connection to that story provided them with a sense of identity as the people of God. It theologically legitimated their protest. It explained the successes they experienced, the problems they faced, and disappointments they suffered. It placed King in the undisputed role as the movement's leader, its Moses. The Exodus provided the symbolic context out of which the march emerged as the movement's principal means of mass protest, a form of demonstration whose meaning for the protesters was integrally related to the biblical story. Most of all, the Exodus story assured protesters that they would ultimately be successful in their journey to the Promised Land of racial justice.

This book explores the process through which the Exodus came to serve as the movement's archetypal narrative, focusing on five key "moments" in the movement's history, beginning with King's original "Death of Evil on the Seashore" sermon in July 1955 and continuing to what historians generally view as the climactic campaign of the civil rights movement, which took place in Birmingham in 1963. We begin in chapter 1 with a discussion of rhetoric and social movements. This chapter explains the study's fundamental theoretical perspective, which argues that social movements are more than just large-scale organizations, and that their creation and maintenance involve more than simply managing resources. Rather, social movements are as much ideas or states of consciousness as they are phenomena in the "real" world. They come into being when a collection of people begins to share a common identity and purpose—a sense of "going somewhere." The chapter further argues that rhetoric, and particularly narrative, plays a central role in the creation of that collective identity and purpose. Chapter 2 offers a brief overview of the biblical story of the Exodus and traces the use of that story within the African American cultural tradition, highlighting its prominent place in the black popular imagination. It underscores the Exodus as a dominant theme in African American oratory and a significant source of empowerment for blacks, and it suggests the ways that, because of their immersion in this body of social knowledge, King's hearers might have been expected to respond to him.

Chapters 3 through 7 trace the process through which the rhetorical use of the Exodus developed across the movement's rhetorical tradition. Chapter 3 analyzes King's "Death of Evil on the Seashore" sermon, delivered in July 1955, five months before the start of the Montgomery bus boycott, as an attempt to create among his hearers a consciousness that a movement had already begun. Chapter 4 focuses on King's use of the Exodus in the mass rally speeches he gave during and shortly after the Montgomery bus boycott, highlighting the alterations in form and content that the narrative underwent as it was applied to an actual, organized protest. Chapter 5 analyzes what was, in many ways, the complete, paradigmatic presentation of the Exodus applied to the movement, found in King's "Birth of a New Nation" sermon, delivered in April 1957. Chapter 6 traces the process through which King took on the persona of Moses, the uniquely ordained prophet chosen by God to lead God's people to the Promised Land, a process that began in the boycott and continued during the years immediately following its successful conclusion. Chapter 7 analyzes the rhetoric surrounding the climactic 1963 Birmingham campaign. It highlights the way that the use of the Exodus became concentrated on the theme of "movement," a shift that coincided with the emergence of the march as the movement's principal mode of collective action. The book concludes with a reflection on the implications of this study for contemporary understandings of King, the civil rights movement, and the study of social movements in general.

CHAPTER 1

RHETORIC AND SOCIAL MOVEMENTS

In his provocative essay " 'Social Movement': Phenomenon or Meaning?" Michael Calvin McGee forcefully argued that the label "social movement" essentially reflected a shared set of meanings within human consciousness—an "organizing of social facts which can be objectivated only in linguistic usage"—rather than an objective phenomenon. From this perspective, he asserted, the "rhetoric of social movements" was more than merely an element existing within the context of the objective phenomenon but was itself the ground out of which the consciousness emerged.[1] Although his primary aim was to sharpen the conceptual assumptions underlying scholars' use of the label—a critique not universally welcomed[2]—McGee's study nevertheless highlighted what rhetorical scholars have long emphasized, that persuasive discourse is the primary agency through which social movements "transform perceptions of reality, enhance the ego of protestors, attain a degree of legitimacy, prescribe and sell courses of action, mobilize the disaffected, and sustain the movement over time."[3] Scholars working from this perspective see social movements as "more than collectively organized actions: They also consist of collectively constructed and shared meanings, interpretations, rituals, and identities."[4] In other words, central to the emergence of a social movement is the discursively created, shared consciousness among individuals engaged in collective action, that a movement exists and that they share a common identity as "members" of it.

Many sociologists have come to share this view, reflecting a shift from a traditional focus on structural and organizational dimensions of collective action to one that views "collective action . . . as an interactive, symbolically defined and negotiated process among participants, opponents, and bystanders."[5] Klandermans reflected this orientation when he observed that previous approaches failed to take into account the "mediating processes through which people attribute meaning to events and interpret situations. Scholars of social movements have become increasingly aware that individuals behave according to a *perceived* reality." Social movements, he continued, are "involved in a symbolic struggle over meaning and interpretation."[6] Thus as Gamson put it, "One can view social movement actors as engaged in a symbolic contest over which meaning will prevail."[7]

Movement actors create these symbolic meanings through what have been termed *interpretive frames*, which they use to "fashion meaningful accounts of themselves and the issues at hand in order to motivate and legitimate their efforts."[8] As Klandermans put it, "Social movements frame—that is, assign meaning to and interpret—relevant events and conditions in ways that are intended to mobilize potential adherents and constituents, garner bystander support, and demobilize antagonists."[9] These interpretive frames help to create the sense of collective identity through which "the 'we' involved in collective action is elaborated and given meaning."[10] They make it possible for social movements to transform perceptions of the past and the present and to "portray a vision of the future that instills a sense of urgency in audiences to organize and do something *now*." Finally, they enable social movements to sustain themselves by offering "believable explanations for setbacks or the lack of meaningful gains or victories" and by convincing followers "that victory is near or inevitable, if all is done correctly and members remain steadfast in their commitment."[11]

Narrative, whether conveyed in speech or song or enacted through ritual, is crucial to this process of meaning creation among social-movement actors, going "to the heart," Davis argued, "of the very cultural and ideational processes" that social-movement scholars have identified as being essential to movement development. Narratives make events in human experience meaningful by structuring them within temporal and causal sequences, configuring the past in a way that explains the present and predicts the future. They place events within a moral universe, revealing characters' motives and attributing guilt or innocence to their actions. Through processes of identification, a narrative's hearers come to experience a common identity, "a 'we' that involves some degree of affective bond and a sense of solidarity: told and retold, 'my story' becomes 'our story.'"[12] Narrative thus uniquely fulfills what McGee identified as the impulse behind defining certain forms of collective behavior as "movement"—the impulse to see the human environment as an "ordered progression of mutually salient episodes" in which social actions are imbued with morality, purpose, and destiny.[13] Central to the rhetoric through which Martin Luther King framed the experience of African Americans was one particular story, the Exodus. From his speech on the first night of the Montgomery bus boycott in December 1955, down to his "Mountaintop" address in Memphis, Tennessee, on April 3, 1968, the night before he was assassinated, King found in the ancient biblical story an inventional resource for addressing a variety of different rhetorical needs, from creating a collective identity for his audience to providing theological legitimacy to the act of protesting; from explaining why circumstances seemed to get worse rather than better after some initial successes to bolstering his own ethos as the movement's leader. As I shall argue later in this book, the language of the Exodus also pervaded much of the movement's music. Finally, at the height of the movement's success, the Exodus provided a framework of meaning for what became the movement's principal means of collective action, the march. Essential to an analysis of the discourse of the civil rights movement, then, is an understanding of narrative as a form of persuasion, which this chapter offers in three parts. It begins by exploring the theoretical conception out of which the contemporary focus among rhetorical scholars on narrative as rhetoric first emerged: Kenneth Burke's articulation of the psychology of form. Next, it explores the ways that contemporary rhetorical scholars have analyzed narrative within public discourse, with particular focus on the function of character and plot as the central features through which stories achieve their persuasive effect. The chapter concludes by extending this theoretical understanding to include ritual as a unique form of symbolic activity through which social-movement actors participate in the stories that give rise to their movement not simply by hearing them within the oratory of the leaders, but by enacting them through bodily performance.

KENNETH BURKE AND THE PSYCHOLOGY OF FORM

The attention to narrative among rhetorical scholars grew out of Kenneth Burke's writings on the psychology of form and his emphasis on the dramatistic nature of human discourse.[14] Burke theorized that human beings possess an innate appreciation for processes of arrangement or development within an artistic work such as crescendo, balance, repetition, and series. He observed, for example, that the formality of beginnings and endings, "such procedures as the greeting of the New Year, the ceremony of laying cornerstones, the 'housewarming,' the funeral," all pointed to a human mind that was "prone to feel beginnings and endings as such."[15]

Artistic form plays on this intrinsic appreciation for structure and arrangement by creating and then satisfying "an appetite in the mind of the auditor," as when an audience experiences emotions of suspense and relief when watching a dramatic production, emotions that arise from

> the suspense of certain forces gathering to produce a certain response. It is the suspense of a rubber band which we see being tautened. We know that it will be snapped—there is no ignorance of the outcome; our satisfaction arises from our participation in the process; from the fact that the beginnings of the dialogue lead us to feel the logic of its close.[16]

Building on this observation, he argued that form does far more than merely embellish content; rather, it readily awakens

> an attitude of collaborative expectancy in us. For instance, imagine a passage built about a set of oppositions ("we do this, but they on the other hand do that; we stay here, but they go there; we look up, but they look down," etc.). Once you grasp the trend of the form, it invites participation regardless of the subject matter. Formally, you will find yourself swinging along with the succession of antitheses, even though you may not agree with the proposition being presented in this form.[17]

By drawing an audience into "participation," form thus invites assent to content, or at least, "prepares for assent to the matter identified with it." In other words, what makes discourse compelling or persuasive is not simply its correspondence to truth or to the "real world," but also its ability to arouse and then satisfy this appetite or desire in the listener by means of its internal aesthetic qualities.

Burke's conception of dramatism built on that fundamental conception by suggesting that narrative or dramatic form was embedded in virtually all human discourse, from historical and sociological accounts of human behavior to "typical news reports of people's actions, predicaments, and expressions."[18] A central way that humans use language to make sense of their world, in other words, is by employing the elements of story—character, plot, setting, and so forth—to situate their experiences within coherent narratives. For this reason, narrative and drama play a potent role in the construction of social reality.

NARRATIVE AND PERSUASION

One of the primary trajectories of Burke's conception of the psychology of form has been a substantial body of rhetorical scholarship focused on narrative as rhetoric. Spurred by Walter Fisher's declaration that narrative was the "paradigm" of human communication, rhetorical scholars have come to share an appreciation for both the pervasiveness and the force of narrative in human communication, prompting many to explore the uses and functions of narrative in a variety of discursive settings.[19] Some have explored the role narrative plays in public argument,[20] in cultural formation,[21] and in the construction of national identity.[22] Others have sought to offer functional accounts of specific types of narrative, such as parables,[23] conversion stories,[24] and autobiographies.[25] Still others have focused on narrative as a tool of social control in families,[26] organizations,[27] and society at large.[28] Although diverse in their specific applications, these studies share a common conviction that narrative is more than simply a rhetorical device used to embellish rational argument. To the contrary, narrative is "a fundamental form of human understanding that directs perception, judgment, and knowledge"[29]

Although stories can be analyzed in terms of a number of different constituent elements, the persuasive power of narrative derives principally from two features, the first of which is character development. Stories are peopled by actors—heroes, villains, victims, bystanders—whose acts unfold in relation to the actions of others and in response to external events that occur in the story. Through particular techniques of disclosure, stories provoke audiences to be attracted to or repelled by these characters or to experience varying degrees of identification or "sympathy" with them. In his classic work, *The Rhetoric of Fiction*, Wayne Booth explored a number of these techniques; for example, portraying a virtuous character as being isolated and alone, facing "helplessness in a chaotic, friendless world," or in the case of a less virtuous character, by unfolding the story through the character's own eyes. At the heart of

this process lies the power of an omniscient narrator to make authoritative pronouncements about his or her characters, revealing "the precise
quality of every heart, . . . who dies innocent and who guilty, who [is]
foolish and who wise." [30]

Although most studies of the rhetoric of narrative assume the
importance of character development, a handful have actually undertaken to offer a precise account of the process by which character
portrayals contribute to a narrative's persuasive power. For example,
Bishop noted the way that media accounts of the growing social phenomenon of collecting antiques and memorabilia place the act of collecting within a narrative frame that highlights the motivations behind
the activity. These motivational attributions provide coherent explanations for actors' behaviors and invite a moral evaluation of those behaviors. The true "collector" in this narrative is motivated by a passion for
collecting that has little to do with any interest in the collectibles' monetary value, whereas the story's "villains" are "just in it for the money"
and view collecting "as an industry, rather than an avocation." This
contrast in motivations thus provides the basis for the story's underlying moral, that "love, not money, should draw one to collecting." [31]
Similarly, Kenny explored the techniques with which renowned ethicist
Peter Singer, in the story with which he opens his treatise *Rethinking Life
and Death*, creates a main character who is patently despicable, and how
that mode of character development encourages the audience to adopt
a particular moral stance in relation to the story. The story revolves
around the heroic efforts of a hospital to keep a woman who is legally
dead as a result of a gunshot wound on life support until her unborn
child can be delivered. Through a series of strategic disclosures—that
she was shot while trying to rob a disabled, elderly man, that she had
alcohol and cocaine in her bloodstream, that her four other children
were in foster care and that her boyfriend, another important character in the narrative, turned out not to be the father of the child she
was carrying—the narrator portrays her as "the worst sort of social
parasite," and he casts those who heroically attempt to keep her alive
as fools. The result, Kenny argued, is an ironic narrative in which the
audience, experiencing "varying degrees of contempt for every character" in the story,[32] is left with no choice but to reject the fundamental
ethical principle on which the heroic attempt to save the fetus's life was
based on the first place—an impact intended to support the particular
ethical position that Singer argued in his book. In this way, an aesthetic

feature of the narrative, in this case a particular portrayal of character, functions as a powerful rhetorical proof that subverts an audience's
ability to engage in rational deliberation.

Finally, Osborn and Bakke explored the way that the Memphis
press framed the 1968 Memphis sanitation workers' strike in terms of
a melodramatic narrative that pitted evil villains, in the form of union
bosses, especially a union official named P. J. Ciampa, against a virtuous
hero, Mayor Henry Loeb. Central to the development of both characters were the motives that the paper ascribed to each, with Ciampa
cast as an "outside agitator," an opportunist preying on a vulnerable
Memphis to expand the power of the union, and Loeb, a man whose
principles and convictions would not allow him to "cave in" to union
demands. By portraying the strike as a contest between these one-
dimensional characters, the press framed the dispute within a "good
versus evil" story that diverted attention away from the plight of the
sanitation workers themselves, who were largely invisible in the early
coverage of the strike. Melodrama, as a potent form of narrative rhetoric, thus derives its power primarily from its depiction of characters
who represent moral absolutes: "Melodramatic characters are pure
representations of goodness, evil, self-sacrifice, and victimage. The
melodramatic hero has no tragic flaws, the villain possesses no redeem-
ing qualities, and the martyr is not complicated by self-interest." This
presentation of characters in "simple and oppositional forms" simpli-
fies the audience's decision-making process by "posing choices in two-
valued, either-or, black-or-white terms."[33]

These studies emphasize that character development plays a crucial role in the rhetoric of narrative, illuminating the way that narrators
imbue actors in a story with certain traits by revealing or implying connections between the actors' internal states of thought and feeling and
their actions, in a way that ascribes to those actions a motive or intent.
This connection of internal states of cognition, emotion, or volition to
an actor's behavior are what give the actor "character," not simply as
a structural element of narrative but as an ethical category—character
as a moral trait. Exposed to these revelations, hearers come to feel compassion or antipathy to characters in a story, to applaud or condemn or
excuse their actions, to desire their good or ill fortune, and even to place
themselves imaginatively within the characters' circumstances.

The second crucial dimension, of course, is plot, the formal structure through which "a diversity of events or incidents" are sequentially

arranged or organized into a "meaningful story."[34] As numerous literary theorists have noted, this sequential configuration is primarily chronological, with a story's events or episodes placed within some kind of temporal order (e.g., A then B). As Bakhtin argued in his discussion of what he termed the "chronotope" (literally, "time space"), however, the sequential arrangements of plot are also often spatial. Bakhtin described this "intrinsic connectedness of temporal and spatial relationships" in this way:

> In the literary artistic chronotope, spatial and temporal indicators are fused into one carefully thought-out, concrete whole. Time, as it were, thickens, takes on flesh, becomes artistically visible; likewise, space becomes charged and responsive to the movements of time, plot, and history.[35]

Plot thus combines spatial references with time sequences in a way that provides not only a temporal organization but also a "spatial map" within which the story's events unfold.[36]

Because it builds on what Burke described as the human appreciation for form, this process of configuring events within a temporal and spatial framework is central to a narrative's power to engage hearers, arousing through its beginnings the expectation of certain endings, transforming, as Boje put it, "chronological time into storied and teleological time"[37] and leading hearers toward an experience of closure. Even when the story lacks a formal ending, as is often the case with the narratives that are embedded in public discourse, this lack of closure exploits formal expectations of an ending to achieve its rhetorical effect.[38] Such narratives, Lucaites and Condit pointed out, offer a "vivid vision of what an appropriate resolution [to the story] *might* be" (emphasis added) and then prescribe the course of action that the audience must take to achieve that ending.[39] The expectation of closure, aroused by the story's plot, thus functions rhetorically even in narratives that have no formal ending.

Plot also makes events in a story meaningful by positing causal relationships between them, explaining not only the temporal order in which they occur, but accounting for *why* they occur. Novelist E. M. Forster argued that the imposition of causality is the essential function of plot, a claim captured in his famous comparison of the following two sentences: 1) The king died, and then the queen died; 2) The king died, and then the queen died of grief.[40]

The second, he argued, represents a plot in its most basic form because it links two separate events not only chronologically, but also causally. Plot thus gives a story its "capacity to be followed," which Ricoeur described in this way:

> To follow a story is to move forward in the midst of contingencies and *peripeteia* under the guidance of an expectation that finds its fulfillment in the "conclusion" of the story. This conclusion . . . gives the story an "end point," which, in turn, furnishes the point of view from which the story can be perceived as forming a whole. To understand the story is to understand how and why the successive episodes led to this conclusion.[41]

Placed within the temporal, spatial, and causal framework provided by the story's plot, particular events within the story are imbued with meaning and significance.

As Ricoeur's statement suggests, the actions of characters, configured within an unfolding plot, lead to an "end" that is not simply a logical culmination of those events but is also an "end" in a moral sense, a function that Hayden White expressed in his famous dictum: "Where in any account of reality, narrativity is present, we can be sure that morality or a moralizing impulse is present too."[42] One of the ways that stories invite moral judgment is in their development of characters as agents who face events and make choices, and by revealing the cognitive, emotional, and volitional states out of which they make those choices. Thus Lewis observes, "Narrative form shapes morality by placing characters and events within a context where moral judgment is a necessary part of making sense of the action."[43] But narrative also posits morality in the sense that by leading to an "end," it invites its audience to derive a "moral" from the story in the sense of "a 'point,' a 'theme,' that provides its rationale as a unitary whole and for which, to some important degree, the story is told."[44] White argued that this element of the moral end was fundamentally what separated narrative from annals or chronicles, which merely recount a temporal (albeit selective and therefore rhetorical) succession of events. It is the narrative's "moralism which alone permits the work to end or, rather, to *conclude*."[45] By following the action of the characters through to the story's end, in other words, the audience "learns" what consequences come of particular moral choices.

Through their depiction of character and their configuration of events within plot, narratives function epistemologically as frames through which audiences come to "know" the world. They "help us impose order on the flow of experience so that we can make sense of events and actions in our lives. They allow us to interpret reality because they help us decide what an experience 'is about' and how the various elements of our experience are connected."[46] Stories direct attention toward some events and away from others, explaining what happened and why, and ascribing actions to choices in a way that invites moral judgment. They evoke particular emotions—sympathy, fear, surprise, disgust, anger, hope—in ways that provide powerful motivations for acting. Rhetorically, then, narratives are, in Burke's words, "proverbs writ large."[47]

What is crucial to note is that narrative achieves its rhetorical potency not simply, or even primarily, through its correspondence with the real world, but rather by means of its internal aesthetics, an insight anticipated in Burke's discussion of the psychology of form. Of course, stories must ring true to be compelling; that is, they must accord with "the social formations through which individuals, as members of an interpretive community, understand the world they inhabit."[48] This is the conception behind Fisher's notion of narrative fidelity and what others have termed *verisimilitude*, the idea that believable stories are grounded in the social knowledge or common sense of the communities in which they are told,[49] a requirement Lewis described in this way: "If the story is not true, it must be true-to-life; if it did not actually happen, it must be evident that it could have happened or that, given the way things are, it should have happened."[50] But even more importantly, stories are compelling when they possess the *internal* coherence that Fisher called narrative probability, which has to do with "whether a story 'hangs together,'" whether its plot possesses structural coherence—in Burke's words, whether the "beginnings" of the narrative "lead us to feel the logic of its close"[51]—as well as characterological consistency, such that a character's "actional tendencies" remain consistent across the story.[52] When narratives possess this internal coherence, they take on a quality of persuasiveness driven by the aesthetics of the story itself, regardless of how truthfully the story represents a state of conditions or facts in the world. Lewis thus noted that narrative form "shapes ontology by making meaningfulness a product of consistent relationships between situations, subjects, and events and by making truth a property that refers primarily to narratives and only secondarily to propositions."[53] Indeed, the fact that stories owe their persuasiveness as much to these aesthetic qualities as to any faithful representation of reality has led some scholars to warn of their potential for subverting the process of logical reasoning.[54] At the least, narrative's alternative epistemology points to the possibility that "emotion and imagination—as well as intellection are not merely unavoidable but legitimate and valuable in public debate."[55]

This study assumes that narrative is a potent force in the discourse of movements that coalesce around a desire for social change, providing movement participants with what Rosteck called "interpretive contexts for social action."[56] Griffin underscored this point when he argued that

> whether they appear in the form of histories, autobiographies, novels, dramatic productions, formal addresses by skilled orators or the informal personal narratives of rank and file members, the stories a movement tells *to* and *about* itself embody its moral appeal to the world.[57]

The analysis of narrative form within social-movement rhetoric, then, can reveal the internal dynamic through which individual constituents come to share a collective, social identity and see themselves as engaged in purposive actions that are "going somewhere," that are imbued with the sense of direction inherent in the designation "movement."

NARRATIVE AND RITUAL

One form of symbolic behavior in which this capacity for narrative or drama to construct social reality is particularly significant for social-movement participants is the communicative activity that Roy Rappaport called "humanity's basic social act," the ritual.[58] As Rappaport defined it, ritual involves "the performance of more or less invariant sequences of formal acts and utterances not entirely encoded by the performers." Rituals thus communicate something of the performers themselves even as they also invoke broader social and cultural motifs that do not originate with the performers. Those broader motifs,

moreover, are often dramatistic, whether they take the form of reenacted cultural myths or reflect what Victor Turner described as the
"distanced and generalized reduplication of the agonistic process of
the social drama."[59] In either case, rituals possess a unique power to
reinforce the symbolic imposition of narrative on experience.

This unique potency derives from ritual's singular capacity to give
bodily form to symbolic representation, thereby adding a dimension
to the communicative action that linguistically encoded messages by
themselves cannot produce.[60] Although that bodily form may not be
fully congruent with the thought processes accompanying the behaviors, the unique relationship that ritual creates between the message
being performed and the act of performing can potentially transcend
this distinction to produce an "experiential unity of thought and
actions."[61] Thus, as Clifford Geertz emphasized in his discussion of
religion and culture, it is in the "consecrated behavior" of ritual that
the "conviction that religious conceptions are veridical and that religious directives are sound is somehow generated."[62] Catherine Bell,
in her analysis of ritual and power, likewise asserted that through "a
series of physical movements" ritual practices "spatially and temporally construct an environment according to the schemes of privileged
opposition."[63] Rappaport similarly explained that the "act of performance" is what brings the "substance" of ritual into being or makes it
real. In ritual, he stated, performers are "not merely transmitting messages they find encoded in the canon. They are participating in—that
is, becoming part of—the order in which their own bodies and breath
give life."[64] As an example, he noted the practice in many parts of
the world of ritually enacting subordination through the use of bodily
postures such as kneeling or prostration:

> It would seem that the messages transmitted by such displays could be
> adequately rendered verbally as "I submit to you" or something of the
> sort. But since such messages are often transmitted by physical display
> rather than speech it is plausible to assume that the display indicates
> more, or other, than what the corresponding words would say, or indi-
> cates it more clearly. By kneeling or prostrating himself, a man seems to
> be doing more than *stating* his subordination to an order. He is *actually
> subordinating himself* to that order.[65]

Ritual is thus, par excellence, a communicative action through which
individuals are invited to give assent to content by means of their

participation in form, along the lines Burke suggested. Except, as Rappaport pointed out, the effect of such participation is not only conventional, but material: "The act brings into being not only an institutional fact but a correlated 'brute' or physical fact, as 'palpable'—while it lasts—as water or wind or rock." In ritual the performer incarnates the message, gives it bodily substance, creating a symbolic representation in which "the cosmic, social, psychic and physical become . . . fused."

This will become particularly important for understanding the meaning, within the civil rights movement's larger narrative framework, of what became its principal means of collective action, the protest march. Of course, this study emphasizes the way that Exodus language pervaded the public discourse of the movement throughout its history. At the same time, it will argue that when the march emerged in 1963 as the dominant mode of collective action, it did so within a symbolic context that persistently connected the campaign for civil rights with the spatial-temporal plot of the Exodus story. In this way, the protest march itself simply continued the discursive tradition of framing the movement within the biblical narrative, but in a new form that came to offer something like the "fusion" that Rappaport described, one in which bodily action gave form to cultural myth.

CONCLUSION

The purpose of this chapter has been to provide a theoretical grounding in the rhetoric of narrative as a prelude to the analysis of civil rights–movement discourse that follows. I have argued that social movements, if not exclusively states of consciousness as McGee suggested, are at least constituted and energized by rhetoric, often in the form of narrative. By placing actors and events within the temporal-spatial framework of plot, and by constructing characters in the form of heroes and villains, victims and bystanders, these stories provide movement participants with a sense of identity, an explanation for how their present circumstances came to be, and a compelling vision of their movement's "destiny" or "end," which they can attain by committing themselves faithfully to the cause. This understanding of narrative provides a perspective for examining the way that King drew on a long tradition in African American cultural history of invoking the Exodus for just such strategic ends.

CHAPTER 2

LET MY PEOPLE GO
The Exodus in African American Cultural History

When, on the first night of the Montgomery bus boycott, King spoke of the "long night of captivity,"[1] when almost a year later he proclaimed, "The Red Sea has opened,"[2] when he invited his audience to imagine the "great camp meeting in the promised land of freedom and justice,"[3] and when he urged his hearers, "We've got to keep moving" because "we've got to get to Canaan,"[4] he joined a long tradition in African American culture of viewing life through the lens of the Exodus.[5] As Miller observed, "African Americans composed songs, preached sermons, and wrote tracts about the Exodus because no other story proved more sublimely expressive of the theme of deliverance."[6] When King used that biblical language, therefore, he was not simply quoting the Bible but was invoking a cultural myth that had been developed and transmitted over the more than 150 years in which that story was told and retold by African Americans. The place it held as sacred social knowledge presented him with both promise and risk.

This chapter explores the Exodus tradition from which King drew so pervasively. It begins with a discussion of social knowledge as a crucial element in the rhetoric of narrative. Then, it offers a brief account of the story as it was recorded in the Bible, followed by a survey of the way it was used in African American discourse. The chapter concludes by noting how, because of the recurring patterns with which elements of the Exodus myth had been used across the years, King's audiences might have been expected to "hear" the story, in a way that presented King with possibilities and challenges as he sought to articulate a vision of social reform.

Narrative and Social Knowledge

Narratives are compelling, in part because they evoke previously held myths, recognizable characters, and paradigmatic or even archetypal themes and plot lines among their hearers, and because they accord with the values and presuppositions—the social reality—of the communities in which they are told. Gronbeck emphasized this dimension of narrative as rhetoric when he argued that a narrative

> is not simply a story told by a narrator to someone else, but rather is a complex, that is, multi-layered, series of action-sequences, all of which depend for their meaningfulness upon knowledges shared by the teller and the told-to. A narrative does not somehow *un*fold, for its intelligibility depends upon the action-sequences which are already *en*folded in commonly held stocks of knowledge.[7]

A narrative thus depends on an audience's "preknowledge" to achieve salience with that audience.

As a number of scholars have argued, this preknowledge can represent a significant inventional resource for the rhetor. For example, Lewis emphasized that Ronald Reagan persistently drew on one familiar and easily-stated story line: "America is a chosen nation, grounded in its families and neighborhoods, and driven inevitably forward by its heroic working people toward a world of freedom and economic progress unless blocked by moral or military weakness." The themes of Reagan's presidency—the "moral imperative of work, the priority of economic advancement, the domestic evil of taxes and government regulation, and the necessity of maintaining military strength"—achieved their resonance, Lewis asserted, because they were consistently grounded in a social reality that fulfilled all of the requirements of myth: it was "widely believed, generally unquestioned, and clearly pedagogical."[8] Similarly, Browne argued that the narratives embedded in accounts of the British treatment of the colonies, accounts that inflamed anticolonial passions by plotting "a sustained conflict between freedom and tyranny," exploited previously held myths of Saxon political rights that were "known to all literate colonists" and that constituted "a powerful source of collective pride." These accounts also evoked the powerful myth of "America's errand into the wilderness, a composite narrative of daring, courage, and entitlement that remains intact and familiar even now as sanctioning a collective political and social identity."[9] In both cases, the social knowledge in which these narratives were grounded helps to explain why they were persuasive.

Scholars have also pointed out, however, that the familiar myths and stories that comprise a community's shared knowledge can severely limit the options with which the members of that community view events or problems. As Ehrenhaus argued, for example, in the years following the Vietnam War, the political opposition of Vietnam veterans to U.S. military policy became configured within a popular narrative that emphasized "psychological dysfunction, emotional fragility, healing, and personal redemption," thereby effectively silencing "the voice of the veteran as a source of legitimate knowledge about the nature of contemporary warfare."[10] Murphy likewise observed the way that collective memory in the United States frequently positions "heroes" who have struggled against social injustice within popular narratives that highlight "individual, conciliatory, and apolitical acts of volunteerism." He cited as an example the popular conception of Rosa Parks, whose refusal to yield her seat on a city bus to a white rider is typically viewed as a "spontaneous act of defiance and courage" by an isolated heroic citizen who "had simply had enough and would no longer stand idly by," a narrative that undermines the social value of "collective action, strategies of political agency, and collaboration with associations which support active critique and contestation of systemic problems."[11] These examples point to the possibility that a culture's narratives can exercise what Ehrenhaus referred to as a "tyrannizing power" over that culture's ability to envision alternative interpretive frameworks for viewing social issues.[12]

King clearly faced both possibilities when he evoked the familiar story of the Exodus. On the one hand, it offered a rich and salient inventional resource for crafting his own oratory in the form of a narrative that his hearers would immediately recognize and readily identify with. At the same time, it represented a patterned form of social knowledge that was deeply ingrained within African American culture, with a life of its own, so that it possessed its own potential tyranny over King's efforts to invite his audience to see new, creative possibilities for resisting racial oppression.

The Exodus in the Biblical Narrative

Although Israel's liberation from Egyptian slavery and entrance into the Promised Land provide the overall framework for most of the Pentateuch and the book of Joshua, the events that constituted the Exodus story in the African American popular imagination were actually a small part of a larger and far more complicated biblical narrative.[13] The "liberation narrative" itself, recorded in Exodus 1–15, begins with Israel, "fruitful and prolific" (1:7),[14] having multiplied and filled the land of Egypt, so that they pose a threat to Egyptian power. In response, the Egyptians

> set taskmasters over them to oppress them with forced labor. They built supply cities, Pithom and Rameses, for Pharaoh. But the more they were oppressed, the more they multiplied and spread, so that the Egyptians came to dread the Israelites. The Egyptians became ruthless in imposing tasks on the Israelites, and made their lives bitter with hard service in mortar and brick and in every kind of field labor. (1:11-14)

The Israelites, however, continue to thrive, so Pharaoh institutes a program of infanticide in reaction to the growing threat, the event that provides the setting for Moses' birth, his "miraculous" deliverance, and his upbringing in the household of the king.

The narrative abruptly shifts to Moses as an adult, recounting how he comes upon an Egyptian mistreating a Hebrew, kills the Egyptian, and then buries his body. When Pharaoh learns of it, Moses is forced to flee to Midian, where he spends the next forty years herding sheep for his father-in-law, Jethro. There, he encounters the burning bush, out of which Yahweh, the God of Abraham, Isaac, and Jacob, speaks to him:

> I have observed the misery of my people who are in Egypt; I have heard their cry on account of their taskmasters. Indeed, I know their sufferings, and I have come down to deliver them from the Egyptians, and to bring them up out of that land to a good and broad land, a land flowing with milk and honey, to the country of the Canaanites, the Hittites, the Amorites, the Perizzites, the Hivites, and the Jebusites. The cry of the Israelites has now come to me; I have also seen how the Egyptians oppress them. So come, I will send you to Pharaoh to bring my people, the Israelites, out of Egypt. (3:7-10)

Moses is reluctant to accept Yahweh's call and, in a lengthy process of negotiation (3:7–4:17), he offers a series of reasons why he should be relieved of this responsibility. Yahweh responds by giving Moses a series of miraculous signs that establish his authority and by appointing his brother, Aaron, to be a spokesperson for Moses. In this way, Yahweh prevails and Moses returns to Egypt.

What follows is an epic contest between Yahweh and Pharaoh, unfolded in a series of ten plagues, in which Pharaoh alternatively hardens his heart against Yahweh's claims (e.g., 8:15, 32) or has his heart hardened by Yahweh himself (e.g., 10:1). As the contest progresses, prospects for deliverance grow dim and life becomes increasingly oppressive for Israel, as when their Egyptian taskmasters stop providing the straw needed for making bricks but demand the same quota of bricks from the Israelite slaves, who must now forage for straw on their own (5:10-21). As the narrative makes clear, however, this turn of events reflects God's design:

> Then the Lord said to Moses, "Go to Pharaoh; for I have hardened his heart and the heart of his officials, in order that I may show these signs of mine among them, and that you may tell your children and grandchildren how I have made fools of the Egyptians and what signs I have done among them—so that you may know that I am the Lord." (10:1-2)

Finally, with the tenth plague—the killing of the firstborn of Egypt by Yahweh himself—Pharaoh sends the Israelites away from Egypt.

No sooner do they leave when Yahweh hardens Pharaoh's heart once more, this time prompting him to muster his army to recapture the Israelites, who are camped at the edge of the Red Sea. As Yahweh tells Moses, "I will harden Pharaoh's heart, and he will pursue them, so that I will gain glory for myself over Pharaoh and all his army; and the Egyptians shall know that I am the Lord" (14:4). When Israel sees the Egyptian army approaching, they cry out in fear, but Moses assures them that Yahweh will fight for them. Moses then stretches his hand over the sea, and Yahweh sends a strong wind to divide the waters so that the Israelites cross on dry land. The Egyptians attempt to follow, but Yahweh throws the Egyptian army into a panic. As the narrator puts it, Yahweh "clogged their chariot wheels so that they turned with difficulty. The Egyptians said, 'Let us flee from the Israelites, for the Lord is fighting for them against Egypt' " (14:25). When the Israelites are safely across, Moses stretches out his hand over the sea once again and the waters rush back, drowning Pharaoh and his army. In this way, the narrative says, "The LORD tossed the Egyptians into the sea" (14:27). The Israelites exult in the dramatic overthrow of their enemies with singing and celebration, reveling in how the Egyptians "sank like lead in the mighty waters" (15:10) as they proclaim Yahweh to be their God:

> The LORD is my strength and my might,
>   and he has become my salvation;
> this is my God, and I will praise him,
>   my father's God, and I will exalt him. . . .
> Who is like you, O LORD, among the gods?
>   Who is like you, majestic in holiness,
>   awesome in splendor, doing wonders? (15:2, 11)

With Egypt behind them, Israel is now prepared to continue its journey toward the Promised Land.

Much of the rest of the story is taken up with the Israelites' sojourn at Mount Sinai, where they ratify their covenant with Yahweh and receive the Ten Commandments, along with extensive instructions for building a tabernacle for worship (Exodus 19–40) and stipulations for worship and ritual purity (Leviticus 1–27). When the Israelites depart Sinai and arrive at Canaan, they fail in their first attempt to enter the land and are sentenced by Yahweh to wander in the wilderness for forty years, which leads them to the edge of the Promised Land once again (Numbers 1–36). There, they hear a restatement of the law, given in the form of a farewell address by Moses that occupies most of the book of Deuteronomy, at the end of which Moses dies and is buried by Yahweh himself. Only in the book of Joshua do the Israelites cross the Jordan and begin the conquest of Canaan.

As even this brief summary indicates, the biblical account, taken as a whole, is complex, multilayered, and often problematic. Meyers captured this complexity when she wrote,

> The dramatic flow of the narrative . . . belies the diversity of its liter-
> ary genres as well as the complexity of the text and the problem of its
> relation to the emergence of the people of Israel in the eastern Mediter-
> ranean thousands of years ago. The appealing universality of many of

its themes masks the moral ambiguities of an account that celebrates the freedom of one people amidst the suffering of others. And its canonical authority tends to privilege social constructs that were pioneering in the Iron Age but are less compelling in the twenty-first century. Moreover, so well known are the outlines of this master narrative of escape to freedom and establishment of community that the various shadings and nuances of the dramatic picture are overlooked.[15]

Moses, for example, is a complex character in the narrative, murdering an Egyptian (Exod 2:11-12), resisting Yahweh's call to return to Egypt (4:13), and needing the advice of his father-in-law to keep from being overrun by the demands of adjudicating disputes among the Israelites (18:14-23). In one particularly bizarre episode (4:24-26) Moses himself narrowly escapes being killed by Yahweh and is only rescued through the quick action of his non-Israelite wife, Zipporah, who performs the ritual of circumcision on their son, an episode from which Brueggemann drew this implication:

> Yahweh is set loose for the sake of Israel, but Yahweh is also set loose by the narrator in savage ways against Pharaoh and (here at least) in savage ways against Moses. The larger narrative is not solely about liberation. It concerns, rather, the claim that all parties, Israelite as well as Egyptian, must live in the presence of unleashed, unlimited holiness. There are provisional strategies for safety in the face of holiness, but none that will finally tame this dangerous God.[16]

Aaron, Moses' helper, is likewise a problematic character, particularly in his collusion with the Israelites in their orgiastic worship of the golden calf (32:1-35)—an episode in which Yahweh sends a plague on Israel (32:35). That event, moreover, epitomizes Israel's inconsistent faith in Yahweh, complaining about the lack of food (16:3) and water (17:2-3), rebelling against Moses and Aaron when the spies sent to the Promised Land return with a report about the formidable nations occupying the land (Num 14)—the action for which they are cursed to wander in the wilderness for forty years until all of the adults of that generation have died (Num 14:32-35). Equally problematic is the slaying of Egypt's firstborn children, presented as the climactic element in Yahweh's miraculous triumph over Pharaoh and deliverance of Israel, as also are Israel's gloating over their vanquished enemies and their conquest of the Promised Land itself, which, in the narrative, involves either subjugating or outright exterminating the peoples who already live in the land.

All of this underscores the canonical narrative's multifaceted and mysterious character, conveying a complexity of meanings about Israel's identity and relationship to Yahweh beyond the simple outline of the deliverance from Egypt, the Red Sea crossing, the journey through the wilderness, and the arrival in the Promised Land. Not surprisingly, as the Exodus was taken up and appropriated within African American discourse, it took on a much more selective form, one that strategically exploited elements from the story to make meaningful the experiences of racially oppressed blacks in the United States. For example, as Sundquist observed, African American portrayals

> often idealized the leadership of Moses (in the biblical account, God's intervention is decisive, while Moses is a reluctant hero, and hence a marginal figure in the Passover observance) and his delivery of his people into the Promised Land (the biblical Moses did not live to see the conquest of Canaan achieved by Joshua) . . . [Many] simply deploy the story as a symbolic shorthand for political resistance and envisioned liberation.[17]

Certainly, the biblical account of the Exodus never ceased being an important part of the backdrop to King's rhetoric. But as we shall see, King most often drew from this idealized version held in the African American popular imagination. More importantly, it was through the filter of this cultural version that his audience most readily heard his references to the canonical narrative.

THE EXODUS TRADITION IN AFRICAN AMERICAN CULTURE

Although the precise point in history at which African Americans began appropriating the Exodus is unknown, the tradition extends at least as far back as the time of African slaves, who developed a profound identification with the biblical narrative.[18] Genovese, for example, recounted the wry observation of an ex-slave living in South Carolina named Savilla Burrell, who attended his gravely ill former master: "I see the lines of sorrow had plowed on dat old face and I 'membered he'd been a captain on hoss back in dat war. It come into my 'membrance de Song of Moses: 'de Lord had triumphed glorily and de hoss and his rider have been throwed into de sea.'"[19] Hughes and Bontemps, in their anthology of African American folklore, record an unnamed former slave's recollection of a dominant theme of slave preaching: "The children of Israel was four hundred years under bondage and God looked down and seen the suffering of the striving Israelites and brought them out of bondage."[20] Another former slave, a Ms. Holmes, recalled slaves' reaction to a locust plague: "You couldn't walk on the ground for the locust shells, and couldn't hear your ears for them hollowing 'Pharoah' [*sic*]. They hollowed 'Pharoah' for the old Pharoah plague."[21]

Especially prominent in slaves' use of the Exodus narrative was the figure of Moses. As Thomas Wentworth Higginson, a white officer who served among black troops for a time during the Civil War put it, "The blacks spoke and sang incessantly of Moses and associated him with all the great events of history, including the most recent."[22] Elizabeth Keckley, a slave who had served the Lincoln family in the White House, reflected the way that slaves assigned that persona to Abraham Lincoln when she wrote, after his death: "The Moses of my people had fallen in the hour of his triumph."[23] According to W. G. Kiphant, a Union army chaplain attached to a unit of freedman in Alabama,

> There is no part of the Bible with which they are so familiar as the story of the deliverance of the children of Israel. Moses is their *ideal* of all that is high, and noble, and perfect, in man. I think they have been accustomed to regard Christ not so much in the light of a spiritual Deliverer, as that of a second Moses who would eventually lead *them* out of their prison-house of bondage.[24]

Indeed, as Asante observed, "The name of Moses grew as important in Africans' minds as the person had been in Israel's eyes, and dominated the future of blacks as Moses had dominated the history of Jews."[25]

Among the earliest and clearest examples of connecting black experience with the Exodus were the Negro spirituals, which frequently spoke of Egypt, the Red Sea, Pharaoh, Canaan, and, of course, Moses.[26] As one former slave recalled,

> Some of them old slaves composed the songs we sing now like "I am bound for the promised land," "No more, no more, I'll never turn back no more," [and] "Moses smote the water and the children they crossed over, Moses smote the water and the sea gave way."[27]

Brown noted that the spirituals were deeply connected to the experi-ence of physical bondage and the desire for freedom:

> It required no stretch of imagination to see the trials of the Israelites as
> paralleling the trials of the slaves, Pharaoh and his army as oppressors,
> and Egyptland as the South. "Go Down, Moses" was a censored song,
> according to fugitive slaves. "O Mary don't you weep, don't you mourn;
> Pharaoh's army got drowned, O Mary don't you weep" is less direct, but
> expresses the same central idea.[28]

Reflecting that connection, one such spiritual proclaimed, "I'm bound
for Canaan land."[29] Another evoked the image of the Egyptians
drowning in the Red Sea:

> Didn't old Pharaoh get los', get los', get los',
> Didn't old Pharaoh get los',
> In the Red Sea.[30]

Slaves sang in the voice of God, charging Moses with his mission of
seeking the deliverance of Israel:

> Go down Moses
> Way down in Egyptland
> Tell old Pharaoh
> To let my people go.
>
> When Israel was in Egyptland
> Let my people go
> Oppressed so hard they could not stand
> Let my people go
>
> Go down Moses
> Way down in Egyptland
> Tell old Pharaoh
> "Let my people go."
>
> "Thus saith the Lord," bold Moses said,
> "Let my people go;
> If not, I'll smite your firstborn dead
> Let my people go."[31]

Another spiritual challenged the slaves to

> Wade in the water,
> Wade in the water, children,
> Wade in the water,
> God's a-going to trouble the water.[32]

Sanger observed that these songs "provided slaves with one way to reclaim rhetorical power in their lives, communicating among themselves an affirming and positive self definition." By singing them, slaves constituted themselves as "God's chosen," portrayed God as friend and confidant, and retained some sense of agency by emphasizing the role that humans played in the divine story—Moses speaking for God or Joshua fighting the battle of Jericho. In particular, Sanger highlighted the theme of movement as a ubiquitous motif in the spirituals:

> When slaves sang of movement, tentative or bold, they sang of moving away from the place of their slavery. The essential message was one of determination and inevitability. They sang, "I can't stay behind," asked "who will rise and go with me," warned "no man can hinder me," promised "I ain't got long to stay here," and "I don't expect to stay much longer here." The message was "I'm bound to go." Slaves proclaimed themselves willing, according to their songs, to travel under difficult conditions: "we'll cross the mighty river," "we'll run and never tire," "we'll walk in the miry road," and "go in the wilderness." They identified their goal, ostensibly, as Heaven. They sang, "I want to go to Canaan," "my soul feels heavenly bound," "I'm bound for the Promised Land," and "I want to climb up Jacob's ladder."

Slaves thus "made their spirituals an act of rhetorical resistance. With song, they constituted themselves as members of a valued community, as fully human in their desire and ability to create, as chosen for spiritual notice by God, and as capable of acting on their own behalf."[33]

The Exodus was also a pervasive theme in African American oratory. One of the earliest and most extensive recorded examples is a sermon by Absalom Jones, delivered in Philadelphia on January 1, 1808. Jones's sermon, built entirely around the Exodus story, began by elaborately describing the Jews' affliction in Egypt but also noting that God had, "for wise reasons . . . delayed to appear on their behalf for

several hundred years, yet he was not indifferent to their sufferings."
He then told of how God, moved by the cries of the people, "rises
from his throne—not to issue a command to the armies of angels that
surrounded him to fly to the relief of his suffering people—but to
come down from heaven in his own person, in order to deliver them
out of the hands of the Egyptians." In the same way, Jones assured his
audience, God "who is as unchangeable in his nature and character as
he is in his wisdom and power," has

> heard the prayers that have ascended from the hearts of his people; and
> he has, as in the case of his ancient and chosen people, the Jews, *come
> down to deliver* our suffering countrymen from the hands of their oppres-
> sors. He *came down* into the United States, when they declared, in the
> constitution which they framed in 1788, that the trade in our African
> fellowmen should cease in the year 1808: He *came down* into the British
> Parliament, when they passed a law to put an end to the same iniquitous
> trade in May, 1807: He *came down* into the Congress of the United States,
> the last winter, when they passed a similar law, the operation of which
> commences on this happy day.[34]

Using similar language, Austin Steward, speaking at a celebration of
emancipation in New York in 1827, said this of slaves: "Like the people of God in Egypt, you have been afflicted; but like them too, you
have been redeemed."[35] At the conclusion of her speech, delivered at
the fourth anniversary meeting of the New York Anti-Slavery Society
in 1857, Frances Ellen Watkins issued this rousing call to join the abolition cause:

> Will you not resolve that you will abate neither heart nor hope till you hear
> the death-knell of human bondage sounded, and over the black ocean
> of slavery shall be heard a song, more exulting than the song of Miriam
> when it floated o'er Egypt's dark sea, the requiem of Egypt's ruined hosts
> and the anthem of the deliverance of Israel's captive people?[36]

In an 1865 speech decrying the policies of Andrew Johnson, Lewis
Hayden condemned Johnson for his failure to fulfill the promise he
had made in a speech the year before to be a "Moses" for freed blacks.
In that earlier speech, Johnson had spoken to his audience of his

hope that "as in the days of old," a Moses might arise "to lead them safely to their Promised Land of freedom and happiness." The audience thereupon cried, "You are our Moses!" Johnson responded: "Humble and unworthy as I am, if no better shall be found, I will indeed be your Moses, and lead you through the Red Sea of war and bondage to a fairer future of liberty and peace."[37]

Hayden countered that "although he [Johnson] was to be our Moses to lead us to liberty, . . . instead . . . I fear he will prove to be the Pharaoh of our day." He concluded with a prayer that the "Lord . . . deliver us from such a Moses."[38]

In the years during and after the Civil War, African Americans found in the Exodus an abundant source of language and imagery to describe national events or advocate for causes aimed at improving their economic and social conditions. Most notably, they saw in the Civil War the possibility for reaching the Promised Land of freedom. As one former slave put it,

> The war progressed, fair fields had been stained with blood, thousands of brave men had fallen, and thousands of eyes were weeping for the fallen at home. There were desolate hearthstones in the South as well as in the North, and as the people of my race watched the sanguinary struggle, the ebb and flow of the tide of battle, they lifted their faces Zionward, as if they hoped to catch a glimpse of the Promised Land beyond the sulphureous clouds of smoke which shifted now and then but to reveal ghastly rows of new made graves.[39]

Thirteen years after the war ended, the preface to the *Narrative of Sojourner Truth* asserted that God had swallowed up slavery "in a Red Sea of blood," delivered blacks from the "Egypt of their captivity," and brought them through the "dark wilderness of oppression by the 'pillar of cloud and of fire.'" Her race, it proclaimed, now stood

> on the Pisgah of freedom, looking into the promised land, where the culture which has so long been denied them can, by their own efforts, be obtained. "The Lord executeth righteousness and judgment for all that are oppressed." "O give thanks unto the Lord; for he is good; for his mercy endureth forever." "Sing ye to the Lord, for he hath triumphed gloriously." "Who is like unto thee, O Lord? who is like thee, glorious in holiness, fearful in praises, doing wonders?"[40]

The following year, in 1879, Robert Harlan, a prominent black leader (and half brother to U.S. Supreme Court justice John Marshall Harlan), urged a gathering of the National Conference of Colored Men of the United States to undertake a mass migration from the South to Kansas and areas of the West, couching his exhortation in the language of the biblical story:

> If the leading men of the South will make another Egypt of these bright and sunny valleys, then must the oppressed go forth into the promised land of liberty, into the Western States and Territories, where the people are at peace and the soil is free, and where every man can secure a home for himself and a family with none to molest him or make him afraid.[41]

Similarly, in his 1887 call to blacks in Selma, Alabama, to join together with other oppressed peoples in a united labor movement, M. Edward Bryant evoked the wilderness experience of Israel: "Colored men of America, we have made great advances, but we have not reached Canaan. We must still contend against the Amalekites, Hittites, Hivites, and Philistines. May the God who presides over the destinies of nations help us to work out our destiny."[42] In 1889, William Bishop Johnson called on blacks to defend themselves against "Southern outrages," even "if every inch must be converted into a fort with Winchester and Gatling guns to keep off the wildcats and the crows. Israel remained in Egypt and mourned, and God told them to come forth, but they passed through many bloody struggles before they reached Canaan."[43]

This persistent identification of blacks with the Exodus story continued into the twentieth century. In his account of African American history, for example, W. E. B. Du Bois used the language of the Exodus to recount how blacks had pinned their hopes of improvement on the pursuit of learning: "Here at last seemed to have been discovered the mountain path to Canaan."[44] But like so many such hopes, this one proved futile: "To the tired climbers, the horizon was ever dark, the mists were often cold, the Canaan was always dim and far away." Ware and Linkugel argued that a central element of the appeal of Marcus Garvey in the early twentieth century was his adoption of the Moses persona, becoming a "prototype Moses for Harlem blacks who were fervently awaiting a deliverer."[45] Describing the status of blacks five decades after the Emancipation Proclamation, L. J. Coppin proclaimed, "Fifty years brings us to the border of the Promised Land. The Canaan of our citizenship is just before us and is infested with enemies who deny our right to enter."[46] In his sermon "Moses at the Red Sea," delivered in the mid-1950s, prominent black preacher C. L. Franklin reminded his hearers of the faithfulness of God in every crisis they had faced:

> In every crisis God raises up a Moses. His name may not be Moses but the character of the role that he plays is always the same. His name may be Moses or his name may be Joshua or his name may be David, or his name, you understand, may be Abraham Lincoln or Frederick Douglass or George Washington Carver, but in every crisis God raises up a Moses, especially where the destiny of his people is concerned.[47]

As these examples show, the Exodus functioned as an archetypal event not only for the slaves, but also within African American rhetoric up to the time when King emerged as leader of the civil rights movement.[48] Blacks identified with the plight of the Israelites, God's chosen people who suffered under the harsh rule of Pharaoh, and they awaited the time when God would raise up a Moses who would deliver them from their oppression. Describing the slaves' profound symbolic identification with the Exodus story, Miller noted that their discourse "telescoped history, replacing chronological time with a form of sacred time," enabling

> Old Testament characters to become slaves' immediate predecessors and contemporaries as they freely mingled their own experiences with those of Daniel, Ezekiel, Jonah, Joshua, and Moses. Slaves could vividly project Old Testament figures into the present because their expansive universe encompassed both heaven and earth and merged the Biblical past with the present.[49]

This sense of connection with the biblical story went beyond that of explicitly identifying, by means of analogy, the elements of correspondence between their situation and that of ancient Israel—offering a hope "embalmed in detached, lifeless sermons." Rather, their songs and sermons emotionally transported them into experiences that transcended the boundaries of geography and chronology. As Miller put it, "Preachers initiated a powerful electric charge that surged back and forth between pulpit and pew. . . . Black homilists routinely and visibly aroused churchgoers from their lethargy, drained their anguish, and revitalized their spirits with the intoxicating elixir of the gospel."[50]

Harris confirmed the potency of that experience in his study of religion and political activism among African Americans, arguing that the black church offered much more than a ready-made organizational structure for the collective protests of the civil rights movement. Rather, it provided what he termed a "religiously inspired political efficacy," the feeling of empowerment that was crucial to the process of mobilization. In support of this assertion Harris cited the testimony of participants in protest actions who reported experiencing "a feeling of divinely granted protection" that sustained their courage. He recounted, for example, the story of a woman named Bee Jenkins, who had been involved in a store boycott in Holmes County, Mississippi, and who described her experience in this way:

> The law enforcements 'n' highway patrol was allgather up there—you name 'em, they was there. I wasn't afraid. Because I know *I had somebody there who was on my side*. And that was Jesus; he was able to take care of me. *That who I can depend on and put my trust in.*

Harris concluded that these discursively created religious experiences played a crucial role in sustaining the protest:

> The feelings of self-worth and personal efficacy inspired by a commitment to religious faith served as a critical psychological resource for some blacks during the civil rights movement. Religion helped many activists face the threats of material and physical sanctions leveled against them by white supremacists.

The Exodus story, of course, was a primary source of this religious faith, with "its stress on the oppression of the chosen people, their material weakness, and their need to rely on God's help in the imbalance of power within which they find themselves."[51]

The Exodus as an Inventional Resource: Possibilities and Challenges

A number of scholars have emphasized that African American preaching was historically rooted in a "profoundly oral pulpit tradition" in which preachers circulated and employed themes, turns of phrase, passages, and even entire sermons that had been passed on to them from others in the tradition. The black preacher's voice was thus

> the voice of earlier speakers. The voice and the identity of the preacher converge with those of sanctified predecessors who have previously articulated these popular homilies. Preachers create a voice and a self by merging their identities with other representatives of a well-known, authoritative tradition.[52]

Certainly, this was true of King, who had received from that tradition a "body of titles, outlines, and formulas from other preachers."[53] The centrality of this practice in black preaching, combined with the sacred place that the Exodus story held in African American cultural history, assured the biblical story's prominence within King's rhetoric. In particular, King would find significant sources of appeal in several recurring patterns in that tradition.

Most obvious was blacks' historical identification with the Israelites. Viewed from the perspective of the Exodus, they were God's chosen people who suffered unjustly in their own Egypt of slavery and apartheid. The story also emphasized that God was aware of their suffering and, even though God might delay action on their behalf, they had not been forgotten. Just as God delivered Israel, God would deliver them. This history of self-identification provided a source of social knowledge that King could exploit to evoke the kind of collective identity that theorists have insisted is essential for a social movement to exist, as well as a basis for his appeals to unity in the black community. By symbolically framing their experiences within a deeply held religious myth—one that had been traditionally used to create expectations for social change—he could offer a theological justification for engaging in collective action. He needed simply to convince blacks that they were reenacting the biblical story in their own day.

The central figure in that tradition, of course, was Moses. At every point in their history, African Americans had eagerly awaited a Moses who would deliver them from bondage, an expectation captured in the penetrating questions raised by Sojourner Truth a decade after the Civil War had ended:

> Would a Moses appear to remove the bands from wrist and ankle, and with uplifted finger pointing to the pillar of cloud and of promise, lead

them forth from this sea of troubles and plant their weary feet upon the Canaan of their desires? Would manna descend from heaven to feed this multitude, who were morally, physically, and intellectually destitute?[54]

Indeed, so eager were they for this deliverer that one black leader, noting the problems that frequent migrations posed for efforts to improve education among African Americans, complained that they were ready to follow "every little politician, every crank," who "constituted himself a Moses to lead the Negro somewhere."[55] Given this emphasis on the person of Moses in the African American rhetorical tradition, when King emerged as the leader and spokesperson for the civil rights movement, his hearers would naturally have viewed him in that role, as the divinely appointed prophetic figure who would lead them to freedom's land.

King would find in this tradition, as well, a history of viewing significant national events through the lens of the biblical story. The most striking example of this was blacks' identification of the Civil War with the Exodus, and particularly, with the Red Sea crossing, an identification poignantly captured in the claim, made in the preface to Sojourner Truth's autobiography, that "slavery had been swallowed up in a Red Sea of blood."[56] But African American orators also connected it with other events. Henry Highland Garnett, in a sermon commemorating the passage of the Thirteenth Amendment, proclaimed that "the nation has begun its exodus from worse than Egyptian bondage; and I beseech you that you say to the people that they go forward."[57] Absalom Jones depicted laws abolishing the slave trade in Britain and later in the United States as examples of when God "*came down*" to deliver "our suffering countrymen from the hands of their oppressors," as he had done for "his ancient and chosen people."[58] When King evoked the story to explain the significance of events in his audience's experience, then, he was continuing that longstanding tradition.

At particular points in the tradition, finally, African American rhetors called attention to Israel's journey through the wilderness, a strategy that King would use extensively in his speeches and sermons. William Bishop Johnson reflected this identification when he urged blacks to arm themselves in preparation for defending their lives and land by reminding them that Israel "passed through many bloody struggles before they reached Canaan."[59] In language that King would echo almost ninety years later, M. Edward Bryant warned of the "Amalekites, Hittites, Hivites, and Philistines," who stood between blacks and their Promised Land.[60] As the civil rights movement developed, particularly when conditions seemed to deteriorate rather than improve, King would likewise remind his hearers that, like Israel, they had to endure the travails of the wilderness before they reached Canaan.

Clearly, the Exodus story, as a prominent element of African American cultural history, was a significant asset for King. At the same time, invoking the Exodus to explain blacks' circumstances and motivate them to engage in collective action against racial oppression was not without risks or challenges. Indeed, King's discourse is at times poignant in its glaring omission of potentially salient connections between the experience of Israel and that of blacks in the United States; for example, Egypt's pervasive fear that the Israelites would one day grow powerful enough to seize control of the country. At other points, King is at great pains to minimize familiar elements of the story that his hearers might readily have employed as frames for seeing themselves or their opponents, a fact underscoring his awareness of the potential the story held for undermining his vision of reform. Three such risks were of particular significance.

One had to do with the way that the story would have naturally invited blacks to see whites, who were cast in the role of the "Egyptians." The original story emphasizes God as personally acting to bring about the destruction of the Egyptian army when it pursues the Israelites into the Red Sea. In the biblical account, the Israelites exult as they watch the Egyptian army perish in the raging waters of the Red Sea. Although their song of celebration proclaims God's power and sovereignty over the nations of the earth, it nevertheless also contains repeated expressions of delight at the overthrow of their enemies:

> I will sing to the LORD, for he
> > has triumphed gloriously;
> > horse and rider he has thrown into the sea. . . .
> Pharaoh's chariots and his army
> > he cast into the sea;
> > his picked officers were sunk in the Red Sea.
> The floods covered them;
> > they went down into the depths
> > > like a stone. (Exod 15:1, 4-5)

As the "song of Moses" continues, the Israelites take particular enjoyment in the fact that the destruction of the Egyptians reflects such a dramatic reversal in fortune, through which the cruel and arrogant are brought low:

> The enemy said, "I will pursue, I
>   will overtake,
>   I will divide the spoil, . . .
>   I will draw my sword, my hand
>   shall destroy them."
> You blew with your wind, the sea
>   covered them;
> They sank like lead in the
>   mighty waters. (Exod 15:9-10)

The African American tradition of applying the Exodus to U.S. racial oppression contains clear echoes of this element of the original story. The slave spiritual recalled how Pharaoh was lost in the Red Sea. Savilla Burrell told of remembering the "song of Moses" about the overthrow of Pharaoh as he saw his former master's suffering, and Frances Ellen Watkins anticipated the day when blacks would join in a "song, more exulting than the song of Miriam when it floated o'er Egypt's dark sea, the requiem of Egypt's ruined hosts."[61]

When King employed the Exodus in his own rhetoric, then, he potentially evoked a predictable identification not only between his hearers and righteous Israel, but between whites and the cruel Egyptians as well. Indeed, the biblical narrative might have even been expected to encourage blacks to see their white opponents in melodramatic terms, as one-dimensional caricatures of evil. The natural response to such villains, if not outright animosity and a desire for revenge, would at least have been the hope for similar reversal of fortune. Given that symbolic framework provided them by the Exodus, when successes in their struggle against racial oppression did occur, it would have been difficult for African Americans to avoid taking delight in watching the mighty in their own social hierarchy brought low.

The second challenge has to do with the role of God's agency in the deliverance of Israel. The original biblical account, of course, emphasizes God's direct and miraculous intervention on Israel's behalf. Indeed, one of the biblical narrative's overarching themes has to do with Israel as the trusting but passive recipient of God's gracious act of deliverance, a theme captured in the closing verse of Exodus 14: "Israel saw the great work that the LORD did against the Egyptians. So the people feared the LORD and believed in the LORD and in his servant Moses" (v. 31). This theme is reflected in Absalom Jones's sermon, which ascribed actions that others had taken on blacks' behalf, apart from any agency of their own, to the direct action of the God who had "come down" on their behalf. The tendency for African Americans, prompted by the biblical narrative, to adopt a position of passivity with regard to racial oppression may have been behind Garnett's challenge to the expectation of a dramatic, miraculous deliverance from their own Egypt. In his famous 1843 "Address to the Slaves of the United States of America," Garnett called slaves to "Arise! Strike for your lives and liberties," and then confronted their expectation of a dramatic deliverance: "If you must bleed, let it all come at once—rather *die as freemen than live to be slaves*. It is impossible, like the children of Israel, to make a grand exodus from the land of bondage. The Pharaohs are on both sides of the blood-red waters!"[62] In a similar way, because the story positioned Israel as the passive recipient of God's dramatic action, King's references to the Exodus risked encouraging his hearers to remain in a stance of helplessness and passivity as they patiently waited for God to act on their behalf.[63]

The third challenge King faced when he employed the Exodus narrative concerns the theme of movement. The plot of the biblical narrative involved both spatial and temporal dimensions, with the story revolving around the motif of the journey. As noted, this was a particularly pervasive element in the African American cultural tradition of the Exodus as well. For slaves, the Exodus symbolized an escape from bondage that demanded a literal journey to the free North or to Canada. In the years after slavery, the Exodus was linked to migrations, so that African Americans enacted the original story by literally leaving one location and moving to another. Thus, for example, Robert Harlan in 1879 invoked the Exodus to encourage freed slaves to migrate from the South to the West.[64] William Crogman decried the frequent appearances of "little politicians" and "cranks" who, in the guise of Moses, would call blacks to follow: "One cried, 'On to Arkansas!' and other 'On to Texas!' and another 'On to Africa!' and each one had a following more or less."[65] Marcus Garvey couched his call to blacks to migrate to Africa in the language of the Exodus, as in this speech delivered on March 16, 1924:

As children of captivity we look forward to a new day and a new, yet ever old, land of our fathers, the land of refuge, the land of the Prophets, the land of the Saints, and the land of God's crowning glory. We shall gather together our children, our treasures and our loved ones, and, as the children of Israel, by the command of God, face the promised land, so in time we shall also stretch forth our hands and bless our country.[66]

A year later, he urged his followers from an Atlanta prison that "we who have struggled in the wilderness for all this time shall surely see the promised land."[67]

In each case, the theme of movement involved a symbolic use of the original narrative, but in a way that applied that narrative to a literal change in location. This potentially lent a certain plausibility to the rhetorical claim that, through their collective action, blacks were reenacting the Exodus. Like ancient Israel, they were literally *going somewhere*. King's use of a story that had originally unfolded spatially and that had often been used by African Americans to signify literal migrations certainly problematized the use of the Exodus journey as a metaphor for blacks' collective action by raising it to a higher level of abstraction than it had often been used before. For his hearers, the Promised Land was not a different place, but rather, an alteration in the social configuration where they now lived. By applying the Exodus to his hearers' circumstances, even as he stood in a venerable tradition of African American rhetoric, he also faced a challenge of establishing the plausibility of his claim that the "journey" from Egypt to Canaan was occurring once more in his people's history. As we shall see in chapter 7, this ambiguity in the application of the narrative found its ultimate resolution in the emergence of the march as the movement's primary means of protest.

The Exodus myth, so significant in African American cultural history, thus offered King a body of traditional material to draw on to imbue events in his own hearers' lives with sacred meaning. Much more, it provided a reservoir of emotion that could be tapped to supply the motivation that would be needed to sustain the protest. At the same time, elements in the story itself and patterns in its traditional usage could easily have led King's hearers to adopt attitudes or expectations that ran counter to his vision of social change. Negotiating this tension between potential and risk would be a significant element throughout King's civil rights rhetoric.

Conclusion

The Exodus was among the most pervasive themes in African American cultural history, providing a remarkably malleable interpretive frame through which blacks made sense of a variety of different events and experiences, from a locust infestation to the Civil War itself. More importantly, it was a significant source of empowerment, enabling slaves to retain some kind of dignity and agency in what were otherwise hopeless circumstances, offering a source of motivational appeal for black rhetors in the years following emancipation, and providing inspiration to African Americans themselves in their attempts to seek better lives within a racially oppressive culture. King's emergence as the movement's leader and icon resulted, at least in part, from his ability to exploit this myth, developed and nurtured within African American churches and communities in the 150 years before the movement started.

As this chapter has argued, however, invoking the Exodus also posed a number of potential problems for King. It risked encouraging blacks to look at whites with hostility and vengefulness. The story's emphasis on God's dramatic, miraculous action on behalf of Israel had the potential to undermine calls for direct, organized action against racial oppression. Finally, the traditional association of the Exodus with literal movement, whether in the form of escape to Canada or migration to locales that seemed more favorable to enjoying the privileges of citizenship, presented King with the challenge of making his application of the story to efforts at reforming existing society believable to his audiences.

King employed the Exodus within the parameters created by this important body of social knowledge, exploiting it as a rhetorical asset, but also working within the constraints that it placed on him. We find him creatively negotiating that tension from his earliest attempt to apply the ancient story to the lives of his hearers, in his "Death of Evil on the Seashore" sermon. To this text we now turn.

CHAPTER 3

THE RED SEA HAS OPENED
King's "Death of Evil on the Seashore" Sermon

On Sunday, July 21, 1955, just twenty-five years old and nine months into his first year as pastor of Montgomery, Alabama's, Dexter Avenue Baptist Church, King stepped into the pulpit and read from Exodus 14:30, his chosen text for that morning's sermon: "And Israel saw the Egyptians dead upon the seashore." With these words, he began what would become one of the most significant speeches of his early career as spokesperson for the civil rights movement.[1] Less than one year later, on May 17, 1956, he would deliver the same sermon before a New York City audience of some 12,000 gathered to commemorate the second anniversary of the Supreme Court's *Brown v. Board of Education* decision, an occasion that would signal King's emergence as a national figure.[2] Additionally, the speech was published in a leading denominational magazine, disseminated in pamphlet form, and included in his first volume of published sermons, *Strength to Love*.[3] It thus enjoyed wide circulation and influence, and King himself clearly saw it as one of his most significant early addresses. Most importantly for this study, "The Death of Evil on the Seashore" is the earliest programmatic example of what would become a persistent pattern in King's rhetoric, that of invoking the Exodus story as a symbolic framework for viewing blacks' struggle for justice in the United States.

King had arrived in Montgomery the previous summer, officially taking over his duties as Dexter Avenue's pastor on September 1, 1954, at the age of twenty-four. His first year had been devoted to meeting the demands of preparing and preaching a sermon each Sunday, implementing plans for reorganizing the congregation, and completing his doctoral dissertation, which he successfully defended in the spring of 1955. Although he encouraged voter registration among his congregants and appointed a new committee in the church to focus on social and political action, charging it with keeping "before the congregation the importance of the NAACP," King was only minimally involved in local political efforts to improve conditions for blacks in Montgomery.[4] Nevertheless, racial oppression occupied King's thinking during this period. As Ralph Abernathy, with whom King had become close friends since arriving in the city, later recalled, the Kings and the Abernathys would often spend evenings together talking about race. Said Abernathy,

> We had no particular program in mind when we talked about the social ills of society . . . except for the fact that Dr. King felt his training demanded that he bring to the Dexter Avenue congregation the greatest social gospel and action program it had ever experienced.[5]

King's "Death of Evil" sermon not only demonstrates that conviction, but it also reflects King's attempt to create the kind of symbolic, interpretive framework for addressing those social ills that would be a crucial element in the emergence of the movement—and this, months before any organized collective action had even begun.

This chapter explores King's "Death of Evil on the Seashore" sermon, initially delivered five months before the start of the Montgomery bus boycott, which began in December 1955. Building on the theoretical foundation from chapter 1, which views social movements as discursively constructed states of consciousness, it examines the sermon as King's effort to create what we might call "movement consciousness" in an audience by applying this powerfully salient cultural narrative to the experience of African Americans in the South. It argues that by exploiting the narrative processes of identification, emplotment, and causality, King invited his hearers to participate in a collective identity as the people of God miraculously set free from the Egypt of racial oppression. By manipulating the character of the story's protagonists, he attempted to proscribe his audience's attitudes toward their white oppressors, depicting his black hearers as compassionate witnesses to the overthrow of their enemies. Most importantly, by placing them where he did in the plot of the biblical story, at the far side of the Red Sea, he sought to convince his hearers, for whom the prospects of change seemed bleak, that the journey toward freedom had *already* begun and that they were participating in a dramatic social transformation *already* in progress. This transformed a future hope into a past event, symbolically establishing the reality of a "movement" months before, by any empirical measure, a movement existed.

OVERVIEW

The entire sermon was built around one overarching premise, offered as a fundamental law of the universe that good ultimately triumphs over evil, which King unfolded in three major sections followed by a hortatory conclusion. In the first part of the sermon, he pointed to the reality of evil in the world: "It projects its nagging, prehensile tentacles into every level of human existence." He noted the Bible's affirmation of this reality, pictured in the biblical story of the fall, in the parable of the tares sown among the wheat, and in the crucifixion of Jesus himself. King next addressed the reality of evil in his audience's experience: "We have seen it walk the streets of Montgomery." As evidence, he presented a litany of "sins" that began with the personal and "private" offenses that his audience would likely have expected him to address, such evils as drunkenness, lust, and "inordinate ambition." But then King broadened his enumeration of evils to include sins in the political realm, in the form of "vociferous politicians [who] are willing to sacrifice truth on the altars of their self-interest," and even on the world stage: "We have seen it in imperialistic nations crushing other nations by the iron feet of oppression." Although they would have been more accustomed to a focus on personal morality, King's hearers would likely have assented to his description of "the reality of evil," impelled by his repetition of the phrase "we have seen it," as well as by their own experience of both personal and societal ills. With this blend of the personal and political, King offered an early articulation of what would become a crucial strategy in his later rhetoric, that of placing political issues within a moral and theological framework, so that actively seeking political change became as much a legitimate cause for the church as seeking personal holiness.[6]

Nevertheless, he asserted, "in the endless struggle between good and evil, good always emerges as the victor." As a "beautiful example" of this universal principle, King offered a creative retelling of the Exodus story:[7]

Egypt was the symbol of evil in the form of humiliating oppression, ungodly exploitation, and crushing domination. The Israelites symbolized goodness in the form of devotion and dedication to the God of

Abraham, Isaac, and Jacob. These two forces were in a continual struggle against each other. Egypt struggling to maintain her oppressive yoke and Israel struggling to gain freedom from this yoke. Finally, however, these Israelites, through the providence of God, were able to cross the Red Sea, and thereby get out of the hands of Egyptian rule. The Egyptians, in a desperate attempt to prevent the Israelites from escaping, had their armies to go in the Red Sea behind them. But as soon as the Egyptians got into the Red Sea the parted waves swept back upon them, and the rushing waters of the sea soon drowned all of them. As the Israelites looked back all they could see was here and there a poor drowned body beaten upon the bank.

For the Israelites, this signaled "the end of a frightful period in their history. It was a joyous daybreak that had come to end the long night of their captivity."

In the second major division of the speech, King turned to successful freedom movements elsewhere in the world through which exploited peoples had gained their independence from colonial powers. In these freedom movements, he said, "we are seeing freedom and justice emerging victoriously out of some Red Sea only to look back and see the forces of oppression and domination dead upon the seashore." In support of this claim, King gave an extended statistical account of people worldwide who had overthrown colonial powers, asserting that "the great struggle of the twentieth century has been between these exploited masses questing for freedom and the colonial powers seeking to maintain their domination."[8]

There are 2,400,000,000 people in the world today. Of this number, 1,600,000,000 are colored. So you can see that the vast majority of the peoples of the world are colored. Fifty years ago most of these 1,600,000,000 colored people were dominated and exploited by some western power. There were 400,000,000 million [sic] colored people in India under the iron feet of British rule. There were 600,000,000 persons in China under the gripping yoke of British, Dutch, and French rule. There were 100,000,000 persons in Indonesia under the oppressive hands of Dutch rule. There were 200,000,000 in Africa dominated and exploited by the British, French, and Dutch. . . . What we have seen in this struggle is the gradual victory of the forces of freedom and justice. Today, 1,300,000,000 of the 1,600,000,000 colored people have won their freedom from the Egypt of colonialism.

These exploited masses, he said, "are now free to move toward the promised land of economic security and cultural development. As they look back they clearly see the evils of colonialism and imperialism dead upon the seashore."

To this point in the sermon, King had articulated the principle that good triumphs over evil, emphasizing particularly the inevitability of that triumph in the face of all appearances to the contrary and offering as the paradigm of that principle the story of the Exodus, which he called "a glaring symbol of the ultimate doom of evil in its struggle against good." In this second division of the sermon, King provided empirical evidence of that inevitable victory in the form of these vast numbers of people who had won their own independence. He thus brought the story into the contemporary scene in a way that made its application to events in modern history plausible, fulfilling what Fisher identified as the crucial dimension of narrative fidelity, which has to do with the way that "individual components of stories . . . represent accurate assertions about social reality and thereby constitute good reasons for belief or action."[9] In this way, King's litany of statistics underscored the "truth of . . . [the] text" in a way that prepared his hearers to accept its direct application to their own lives.

In the third major division of the sermon, King applied the principle to his present audience, pointing them to the Supreme Court's overthrow of the "separate but equal" doctrine as the dramatic event signaling the "death of evil" in their own experience:

> Many years ago we were thrown into the Egypt of segregation, and our great struggle has been to free ourselves from the crippling restrictions and paralising [sic] effects of this vicious system. For years it looked like we would never get out of this Egypt. The Red Sea always stood before us with discouraging dimensions. But one day, through a worldshaking decree by the Supreme Court of America and an awakened moral conscience of many white people, backed up by the Providence of God, the Red Sea was opened, and freedom and justice marched through to the other side. As we look back we see segregation and discrimination caught in the mighty rushing waters of historical fate.

Expressing something like empathy for the overthrown "Egyptians," he observed that "to be in the midst of rushing water is a frustrating experience." He could imagine that "those Egyptians struggled hard to survive in the Red Sea. They probably saw a log here and even a straw there, and I can imagine them reaching desperately for something as light as a straw trying to survive." In the same way, segregation was "caught in the midst of a mighty Read [*sic*] Sea, and its advocators are reaching out for every little straw in an attempt to survive." This explained why "so many absurd laws" had been passed by southern legislatures. Nevertheless, he said, "We need not worry, . . . for the passing of such laws is indicative of the fact that the advocators of segregation have their backs against the wall. Segregation is drowning today in the rushing waters of historical necessity." Blacks could thus be assured that as happened to Israel and to exploited peoples elsewhere in the world, his hearers would experience victory, because "death upon the seashore is the ultimate doom of every Egypt."

King concluded the sermon by turning "the spotlight of this text from social relation to our own personal lives," because "there is not only an Egypt in the world, but there are Egyptians in our souls." He offered once more an extended recounting of the Exodus story, his third of the sermon, again highlighting the "truth of the text," but this time applying it to personal sin:

> Years, years ago you became its captive. Perhaps you cannot at all remember when. Perhaps, like so many of the Hebrew children, you were born into this captivity. It probably started with your father or father's father before you. When you first came to know yourself its chains were wraped [*sic*] around you. You know you were a slave to it, but you never ceased to struggle against it. Many times, however, you came to feel that the struggle was hopeless; you felt that this evil habit had captured you to such a degree that it could never be defeated. You could imagine yourself an old man still struggling against this Egyptian that had been your master for so many years. But then one day the conviction broke out within you like a burning fire that this Egyptian could be conquered; that it could pass out of existence, finally dying upon the seashore.

As with the sermon's other renditions of the story, he emphasized the intractability of the enslavement and the hopelessness and despair of the oppressed, and their miraculous, almost unexpected liberation. Whatever sin his hearers faced, that dramatic experience of hope could sustain them in their struggle against the "Egyptians" in their own souls. Thus he exhorted them, "My friends, get out of Egypt! Get something done! Realize that your life is not made to be dominated by

evil Egyptians [*sic*] Go out and leave your Egyptian dead. Your ultimate destiny is the promised land."

This shift in the sermon's conclusion, from a social and political
focus to a personal and private one, is predictable, given the fact that
at this point no large-scale movement yet existed to which King could
exhort his audience to give their allegiance. In later versions, King
would end the sermon by pleading with his hearers to have "the vision
and the will to be . . . [God's] co-workers," transforming society into
one "where all men will live together as brothers, and where every
man recognizes the dignity and worth of all human personality."[10] But
the shift may also have reflected his sensitivity to the resistance his
audience would likely have felt toward this nascent vision of social
revolution and, particularly, his attempt to support it theologically.
King mitigated that resistance by placing the vision of radical social
change within a sermon that begins and ends on the familiar notes of
personal holiness, employing for its overall structure an "ABBA" pattern of reverse parallelism:

A: Articulation of the basic theme of evil in the personal and
political realms; statement of the central claim, that good
inevitably triumphs over evil, as seen in the biblical narrative.
(Part one)

B: "Political" example: Worldwide liberation of peoples from the
Egypt of colonialism. (Part two)

B: "Political" example: The Supreme Court's *Brown v. Board. of
Education* ruling. (Part three)

A: "Personal" example and call to "get out of Egypt." (Conclusion)

Within that overall structure, the conviction on which his early civil
rights-movement rhetoric would be based—that the end of racial
oppression in society was not only possible, but inevitable, and that
segregation was doomed to destruction in "the rushing waters of
historical necessity"—was also the one that, on its face, King's audience would have heard with greatest skepticism. King's response was
to envelope that argument within a set of passages that his audience
would have found much more compelling—the familiar biblical story,

the use of that story to explain concrete, empirical instances of dramatic social change elsewhere in the world, and the application of the story to the lives of his hearers in ways that would have evoked their own experiences of personal transformation. In this way, even the ending of the sermon, with its focus on the personal and private reform, helped to reinforce King's claim that a dramatic social transformation had begun.

THE EXODUS NARRATIVE AND MOVEMENT CONSCIOUSNESS

The "Death of Evil on the Seashore" sermon, initially delivered before there was anything that might be called a civil rights *movement*, represents one of King's earliest efforts to frame the struggle for racial justice in the United States using the Exodus story. A truly comprehensive explication of the Exodus paradigm in King's rhetoric would not come until just over two years later, in his "Birth of a New Nation" address.[11] At this point King had yet to work out the full implications of the biblical narrative for his contemporary audience. The theme of personal liberation, for example, occupies far more space in the sermon than that of political or social change. His sermon contains no mention of the wilderness, which would become a prominent element in his later attempts to use the Exodus to explain the protestors' experience of setbacks and increasing tensions in their relations with whites. His use of the Red Sea crossing to explain the present situation risked evoking the identification his hearers would naturally have made between racist whites and the Egyptians who drowned in the Red Sea's torrent, an identification that would have undermined his call to adopt a compassionate stance toward their opponents. Although he clearly adapted the story to avoid that possibility, his efforts to do so would become much more deliberate in his later addresses. As might be expected in a sermon delivered before any organized protest had begun, King gave no calls for collective action against racial oppression.

Nevertheless, by using the Exodus narrative as he did, King offered his hearers at least a first glimpse of a radically changed way of seeing their present circumstances. To a people who had as yet experienced no practical change in their lives, who as yet possessed little in the way of collective identity as participants within a campaign for change, it announced that a divinely ordained movement had *already begun*. For a people who felt isolated and helpless and who despaired of ever seeing progress, the sermon proclaimed that by God's power the Red Sea had *already* opened, that they had *already* passed through on dry land, and that segregation was *already* dead. Although King deftly employed a number of different persuasive strategies in his sermon, three features of narrative rhetoric are particularly helpful for illuminating his effort to use the biblical story to create a sense that, like the ancient Hebrews, his audience stood at the watershed moment in their own history.

NARRATIVE IDENTIFICATION

As noted in chapter 1, one of the principal ways that narratives engage audiences is by evoking what literary theorists have traditionally called "sympathy" with the story's characters. By presenting these characters in certain ways or from particular perspectives, or simply through the authoritative pronouncement of an omniscient narrator, the story reveals, as Booth put it, "the precise quality of every heart, . . . who dies innocent and who guilty, who [is] foolish and who wise."[12] These techniques of character development encourage audiences to associate themselves with some characters and distance themselves from others, to feel compassion for some and animosity toward others, and to desire good fortune for some and wish ill for others. King's "Death of Evil" sermon exploited the familiar tradition among African Americans of identifying with characters in the Exodus story, yet in a way that also shifted the moral character of the figures in the narrative with whom the audience was invited to identify. In doing so, King urged his hearers to take on the disposition of the story's protagonists, especially in regard to their enemies.

In the first section of the speech, King depicted the Israelites as righteous, innocent sufferers. He recounted how the "children of Israel were reduced to the bondage of physical slavery under the gripping yoke of Egyptian rule," conditions that paralleled the horrors of U.S. slavery and segregation and the powerlessness most blacks felt to overcome racial injustice. He asserted that "the Israelites symbolized goodness, in the form of devotion and dedication to . . . God," evoking blacks' self-identity as righteous sufferers. Given the history of blacks' persistent identification with the Exodus story, combined with this characterization of the Hebrews as righteous victims of Egyptian cruelty, King's hearers would naturally have placed themselves in the story as God's chosen people suffering in Egyptian slavery.

Having initially established this connection between his audience and the enslaved Israelites, King began to highlight the specific attitudes and emotions that his audience would need to possess if they were truly to play their role as the modern incarnation of the ancient people of God. After briefly narrating the Red Sea crossing, he described how the Israelites looked back to see "here and there a poor drowned body beaten up upon the bank," inviting his audience to survey the scene through the eyes of characters who feel sympathy toward the suffering of the Egyptians.[13] The event thus symbolized not the destruction of Israel's personal enemies but rather, the "death of evil," the "death of inhuman oppression and crushing exploitation." This shifted the significance of the Red Sea from its original meaning in the biblical narrative—the triumph of God over the enemies of Israel—to the defeat of an abstract "system" or "force" of evil. He emphasized the essential humanity of the enemy, depicting them as victims caught up in that same system. Having already committed themselves to identifying with the righteous Hebrews both as innocent victims of suffering and as symbols of goodness, King's hearers were thus compelled by the narrative to fulfill that identification by adopting a similarly compassionate disposition as people who bore no malice toward their own enemies.

King continued this process of narrative identification in the second major division of the speech, where he applied the story to oppressed peoples elsewhere in the world who had "won their freedom from the Egypt of colonialism." Although King did not emphasize the elements of the protagonists' character as explicitly as in the opening section, several features reinforced that depiction here as well. As with his characterization of the Hebrews, these contemporary victims were "dominated and exploited by some western power." King emphasized not the death of individual Egyptians, but rather, the death of an abstraction: evil "in the form of oppression and colonialism." Indeed, what he said "we see emerging victoriously from the Red Sea" are not the liberated people themselves, but the principles of "freedom and justice." When he did emphasize the masses of people themselves, he noted that they gained their freedom not from individual oppressors, but from faceless "colonial powers seeking to maintain their domination." These depictions, although not explicitly highlighting the sympathy of the liberated toward their erstwhile oppressors, did minimize the impulse to seek personal vengeance toward them.

What King most emphasized in the second part of the sermon, however, was simply the sheer number of people who had been enslaved and who had found freedom, which he highlighted by using historical examples and statistical details: 400,000,000 people in India, 600,000,000 in China, 100,000,000 in Indonesia, 200,000,000 in Africa. King's use of these vast numbers helped to evoke both the sense of hopelessness at the prospect of social change, which he had emphasized in his original telling of the Exodus, and the magnitude of this worldwide liberation. The unlikelihood that these oppressed peoples could ever have gained freedom from colonial powers made their liberation that much more dramatic and miraculous. That he could point to contemporary historical examples as evidence of the Exodus principle raised at least the possibility that his own hearers, who felt the same hopelessness, might witness such dramatic, world-shaking events in their own day.

King's enumeration of freedom movements elsewhere in the world as modern-day examples of the ancient story also served as a crucial bridge between the ancient story, narrated in the sermon's first section, and its application to his audience, which occupied the sermon's third section. In the first section of the speech, he told the story in a way that created identification between his audience and his hearers, but only implicitly, by highlighting characteristics of Israel with which African Americans had traditionally identified, such as Israel's devotion to God or their status as righteous sufferers. In the second part of the speech, he extended that process of identification by evoking two different associations, one explicit and the other implicit. King explicitly identified oppressed, colored peoples elsewhere in the world with suffering Israel by using the language of the Exodus to describe those peoples. After languishing in the "Egypt of colonialism," they, too, had crossed the Red Sea, they could look back and see "the forces of oppression and domination dead upon the seashore," and they were now moving toward the "promised land of economic security and cultural development." At the same time, he evoked an implicit identification between his immediate audience and those liberated peoples elsewhere in the world, calling them "colored peoples," even though only a fraction were of African descent, and emphasizing their domination and exploitation by Western powers. Rhetorically, this moved his immediate hearers a step closer to their ultimate identity within the story as *liberated* Israel by associating them with the colored peoples elsewhere in the world who in turn represented a concrete, contemporary incarnation of the ancient people of God. All of this led to the third section of the sermon, where King applied the Exodus directly to his hearers' own history.

To this point, then, he had rhetorically constructed the identity of the ancient Hebrews as righteous sufferers who responded to the defeat of their enemies with compassion, and he had portrayed the victims of colonialism as modern examples of righteous sufferers rescued from the Egypt of oppression. Now, in the third major division of the sermon, he continued that process of identification by explicitly placing his hearers in the story. He reminded them of how "we were thrown into the Egypt of segregation," despairing of ever getting out of Egypt and facing a daunting Red Sea "with discouraging dimensions." As with his characterization of the ancient Hebrews, King invited his audience to see themselves as the beneficiaries of the "Providence of God," demonstrated in the parting of the waters through which "freedom and justice marched . . . to the other side." But he also portrayed them as accepting the essential humanity of those who have historically exploited them. The Supreme Court's "worldshaking decree" had been brought about, in part, by the "awakened moral conscience of many white people." Those who now opposed them were simply acting out of desperation and frustration, "reaching out for every little straw in an attempt to survive." They deserved not hatred but pity.

Taken together, these elements of narrative characterization reflect King's attempt to evoke a profound connection between his hearers and the biblical story, but in a way that deftly responded to the demands of his rhetorical situation. He first exploited his audience's traditional identification with the Israelites whom God dramatically rescued from the cruel Egyptians, but then, once the identification was established, he depicted the story's protagonists as sympathetic toward their vanquished enemies. Next, he invited them to identify with peoples elsewhere in the world who, like the Israelites, had successfully crossed the Red Sea, lending plausibility to his assertion that the fundamental principle behind the ancient story held true in the modern age. Finally, he explicitly cast U.S. blacks as the people of God for whom the Red Sea had opened and who now looked back to see, not their enemies, but rather, the evil system of segregation dead on the seashore. King's hearers fulfilled their "role" in the story by taking on the same attitude toward their enemies as the Hebrews did in

King's rendition of the story—one of compassion and sympathy. This process of identification thus prepared them for the direct calls to graciousness toward the oppressor that would become a central part of King's civil rights–movement rhetoric, a call that King would explicitly make in the version of the same sermon that he gave in New York the following May:

> Let us remember that as we struggle against Egypt, we must have love, compassion and understanding goodwill for those against whom we struggle, helping them to realize that as we seek to defeat the evils of Egypt we are not seeking to defeat them but to help them, as well as ourselves.[14]

EMPLOTMENT

The second element of narrative rhetoric at work in King's use of the Exodus is what literary scholars call *emplotment*, the process through which, as Ricoeur put it, "a diversity of events or incidents" are transformed into a "meaningful story."[15] Plot is the element of organization within narrative through which events are unfolded in chronological sequence (A, then B) and often, concurrently, within a spatial sequence, so that the story moves from episode to episode (or place to place) toward some end or destination.[16] This process of organization, Ricoeur said, gives a story its "capacity to be followed."[17] Theorists have noted particularly that narrative plot engages an audience by building on its appreciation for processes of formal arrangement and their expectations about causality, order, and meaning, as well as in their connection both to familiar stories and deeper, archetypal story lines.[18] Emplotment thus works closely with narrative identification in such a way that even as listeners are identifying with characters in the story, they also grasp the narrative logic through which specific events in the lives of the characters are temporally and causally related, and the particular configuration of these elements leads them to experience satisfaction, the sense of "closure," when the story concludes in a particular way.

In the "Death of Evil" sermon, King attempted to make sense of blacks' experiences by employing the Exodus in a way that reflected an even deeper, archetypal story line: Good and evil are locked in a struggle, and then, through the intervention of divine agency, good triumphs over evil. The morality of the Hebrews' triumph over Egypt was thus transferred to blacks' "escape" from racial oppression. What is significant about King's "Death of Evil" sermon is that this basic story line gets fleshed out in just one episode of the larger Exodus story, the crossing of the Red Sea, so that this one event becomes a self-contained narrative.

After articulating the basic story line in the opening of his speech, that "in the endless struggle between good and evil, good always emerges as the victor," King called his hearers' attention to a "beautiful example" of this principle in the history of the nation of Israel. He then told the story of the Red Sea crossing in five stages. The narrative began with the Israelites "reduced to the bondage of physical slavery under the gripping yoke of Egyptian rule." Through the providence of God, however, the Israelites were able to cross the Red Sea and "thereby get out of the hands of Egyptian rule." In the third stage, the Egyptians attempted to prevent the Israelites from escaping and sent their armies into the sea after them. Once the Egyptians were in the sea, the "parted waters swept back upon them, and the rushing waters of the sea soon drowned all of them." The story concluded with the Israelites looking back across the Red Sea where they saw "here and there a poor drowned body beaten upon the bank." Although clearly envisioned as one step in the larger Exodus, it is told as a self-contained narrative that culminates with the Israelites looking back to see the "system" of oppression, represented by Egypt, so thoroughly decimated that all that remains is a handful of bodies scattered on the shore. Viewed from the perspective of plot, the story contains its own *telos*, its own sense of closure.

King then pointed to the repetition of that plot structure elsewhere in the world, as "freedom and justice" had emerged "victoriously out of some Red Sea, only to look back and see the forces of oppression and colonialism dead upon the seashore." These freedom movements thus proceeded through the same basic sequence of events toward a similar moment of closure. Finally, King imposed this plot structure on the experiences of blacks in the South. Like the Israelites before them, blacks had been "thrown into the Egypt of segregation," struggling to free themselves "from the crippling restrictions and paralising [*sic*] effects of this vicious system." But then, with *Brown v. Board of Education*, the "Red Sea was opened, and freedom and justice marched through to the other side." Although not explicitly recounting the pursuit of the Egyptians into the sea, his account assumes this as it skips to the story's "end": "As we look back we see segregation and discrimination caught in the mighty rushing waters of historical fate." Although his account also assumes the larger, familiar story culminating in the arrival of God's people in the Promised Land, he applied the Red Sea story to his audience as a self-contained narrative with its own sense of closure, as blacks looked back on a system of oppression that had already been brought to "doom and destruction" by the "Red Sea" of history. Although his hearers were still a long way from their journey's end, King's manipulation of the original story's plot proclaimed that the movement had already started, that the historic moment had already occurred.

Narrative Causality

An essential function of plot is the establishment of causality. In other words, the coherence that plot brings to its sequential arrangement of events or places is fundamentally causal, explaining why things have happened. Plot, then, not only carries an audience along successive episodes or locations, but much more, makes the succession meaningful by explaining the causality behind it. When he imposed the story of the Exodus on blacks' experiences in the United States, therefore, King not only placed those experiences within a coherent time-space sequence, he also explained the agency behind those events: They represented the work of God. Remarkably, however, he did so in a way that starkly depersonalized God's agency, so that the events represented not so much God's personal judgment on the enemies of God's people but rather, the effect of impersonal moral laws that God had built into the universe.

In the opening of the speech, when King initially established the "good versus evil" duality, he framed that duality using a grammatical form analogous to what, in some languages, is called the "middle voice," where the subject participates in the results of an action performed by an agent who is not directly identified. He simply stated that "evil is ultimately doomed," that "Good Friday . . . ultimately . . . must give way to the triumphal beat of the drums of Easter," and that "truth crushed to the earth will rise again." Only when he pointed to the liberation of the Hebrews from Egyptian bondage as a "beautiful example" of this truth did he identify the agency behind this inevitable process—what he called the "providence of God." This choice of phrase distances God from direct responsibility for the calamity that follows. Instead, God's action is mediated through the impersonal force of "providence."[19] When King described the drowning of the Egyptians, he did so as if it had resulted from some kind of natural calamity: "As soon as the Egyptians got into the Red Sea the parted waves swept back upon them, and the rushing waters of the sea soon drowned all of them." When he identified the symbolic value of the drowning of the Egyptians, "the death of inhuman oppression and ungodly exploitation," he similarly attributed that liberation to impersonal forces that existed within the structure of the universe: "There is something in the very nature of the universe which is on the side of Israel in its sturggle [sic] with every Egypt. There is something in the very nature of the universe which ultimately comes to the aid of goodness in its perenial [sic] wrestle with evil."

In the second section of the speech, where King discussed freedom movements elsewhere in the world as examples of this universal principle, he said almost nothing about agency, but instead assumed that the remarkable overthrow of colonialism worldwide was simply another example of the "truth of this text" whereby "good, in the form of freedom and justice," overcomes "evil, in the form of oppression and colonialism." As portrayed by King, worldwide successes were not so much the result of the efforts of the oppressed people themselves as they were the manifestation of larger, transcendent forces or laws. With what almost seems like a sense of surprise, these oppressed peoples found themselves emerging from their own Red Seas, only to discover that the "forces of oppression and domination" lay dead on the seashore.

King continued this attribution of divine causality in the final section of the speech, where he applied the Exodus story to the experience of blacks in the United States. He first emphasized the helplessness and paralysis they experienced in the "vicious system" of segregation, evoking the despair many in his audience felt, that they "would never get out of this Egypt." This prepared his audience for the dramatic reversal of events reflected in the "worldshaking decree by the Supreme Court of America" through which in their own experience, "the Red Sea was opened and freedom and justice marched through to the other side." The agency behind this miraculous event, he said once more, was the "Providence of God." Under the control of these

universal forces God had built into the structure of the universe, segregation and discrimination were now "caught in the mighty rushing
waters of historical fate." As King told their story, God was ultimately
responsible for these dramatic events, but not directly involved in them.
Like the traditional deists' view of God as the clockmaker who creates
the clock but then allows it to run on its own, God created a cosmos
governed by moral and physical laws and then allowed those laws to
rule the course of human events.

At first glance this depersonalization of God's agency might seem
to represent the language of a theological liberalism that rejected a
conception of God as personal and active in the world. However an
examination of the later version of the sermon clearly shows that King
possessed such theological language as a persuasive resource. As King
came to the conclusion in that version, he shifted the audience's primary vantage point, that of looking back to see the "death of evil,"
to one that overwhelmingly looked forward toward his vision of the
beloved community. People could be "lifted from the valley of hate to
the high mountain of love" to experience a "world where all men live
together as brothers, and where every man recognizes the dignity and
worth of all human personality."[20] At this point in the sermon, when
King articulated a positive, future vision of community, God became a
personal presence in his rhetoric. King urged his audience not to lose
faith in God, and he reminded them that through the "grace of God"
people could change:

> God has a great plan for his world. His purpose is to achieve a world
> where all men will live together as brothers. . . . He is seeking at every
> moment of His existence to lift men from the bondage of some evil
> Egypt, carrying them through the wilderness of discipline, and finally to
> the promised land of personal and social integration.

King thus exhorted them to "pray that we gain the vision and the will
to be His co-workers in this struggle."

This suggests that although King certainly had at his disposal the
language for portraying God as present and active in the world, he
chose not to use such language in his account of the destruction of
Israel's oppressors. Instead, he carefully employed theological language to portray a God who, although ultimately responsible, was not
personally involved in the overthrow of Egypt. On the one hand, this

posited a clear causal explanation for the dramatic social transformation he claims his hearers had witnessed. God had "acted" on their
behalf without their even realizing it. On the other hand, the overthrow of oppression, as he described it, had not come about through
the direct action of a God who personally metes out vengeance on
the enemies of God's people, but rather, was the result of impersonal
laws of righteousness and justice, administered through the agency of
divine "providence." King thus provided theological support for resisting racial oppression and a conviction that social change was inevitable, a matter of "historical fate." But by avoiding the portrayal of
God as an angry deity personally involved in destroying their enemies,
his account also constructed a theological framework in which it was
consistent for blacks to look on their oppressors with compassion and
goodwill even as they celebrated the death of evil on the seashore.

CONCLUSION

This chapter has explored the way that in his "Death of Evil on the
Seashore" sermon, King adapted a deeply held cultural myth, the
biblical story of the Exodus, to create what might be called a "movement consciousness" among his hearers. He exploited a long tradition
among blacks of identifying with the story's protagonists, the Israelites, but then altered the protagonists' character such that they became
compassionate witnesses to the overthrow of their enemies. King initially created this identification implicitly. Then, in the second part of
the speech, he associated his hearers with freed peoples elsewhere in
the world who represented concrete, contemporary examples of the
story's recurrence. Finally, he explicitly recounted their own history in
North America through the lens of the Exodus. Through this process
of narrative identification, he encouraged blacks to see themselves as
God's chosen people, now set free from the Egypt of racial oppression.
At the same time, he portrayed them as gracious and compassionate
toward their own vanquished oppressors. By manipulating elements in
the original story's plot, he offered hearers a construction of their own
story that placed them on the far side of the Red Sea, looking back on
the overthrow of the nation's system of racial apartheid. Finally, in his
depiction of God as the author of moral laws that destined the overthrow of oppression, King was able to assure them that God was on

their side without portraying God angrily punishing their enemies. He offered a causal explanation for how blacks found themselves on the far shore of a symbolic Red Sea in a way that theologically legitimized the formation of a protest movement without encouraging personal vengeance toward whites.

This analysis points to the way that King exploited this rich, preexisting body of social knowledge, the Exodus story, but then adapted it in a way that addressed a complex set of competing rhetorical demands. To people who were not accustomed to engaging in political action, much less to viewing such action as arising out of their Christian commitment, it offered the beginning of a theological framework for viewing collective action. To an often-fragmented black community for whom the prospects of achieving racial justice seemed hopeless, his narrative proclaimed that the long-anticipated liberation had already occurred. Certainly, at this point in blacks' history, King could not with any plausibility have spoken of reaching the Promised Land. But by rhetorically framing the *Brown v. Board of Education* ruling within an abbreviated form of the original story, he could at least place his audience on the far side of the Red Sea. Indeed, his depiction of the Israelites as almost surprised to find themselves looking back from the far side of the Red Sea seems to have been calculated to evoke a similar feeling of surprise in his audience as they experienced a dramatic, symbolic reconfiguring of their own circumstances. At the same time, King was also mindful of the deep resentment blacks felt toward whites, was aware that civil protest could easily become violent and destructive, and was determined that, whatever form it took, the "social gospel and action program" aimed at ending racial oppression occur within the parameters of Christianity's demand to love one's enemies. Because of the nature of the original story and because of the use to which it had at times been historically put by African Americans, the Exodus might easily have evoked a different attitude toward whites—one of animosity and a desire for vengeance. Faced with that possibility, King adapted the story in a way that negotiated the tension between creating a powerful sense of urgency and rejecting violence as a means for securing social and economic justice.

Viewed from a broader perspective, King's "Death of Evil" sermon provides a concrete historical example of McGee's assertion that rhetoric is the ground out of which social movements emerge. King's sermon symbolically established his hearers' collective identity and placed them on the far side of the turning point in their history—all of this, months before they would engage in any organized, large-scale collective action. To the degree that they accepted his account of their story, blacks who joined the organized protest five months later were simply acting out of an identity they already possessed and were participating in a transformation of U.S. society already in progress.

CHAPTER 4

BROKEN ALOOSE FROM EGYPT
The Exodus in King's Montgomery Bus Boycott Rhetoric

On February 21, 1956, almost three months into the Montgomery bus boycott—a protest most thought would be over in days or, at most, a couple of weeks—King and eighty-nine other boycott leaders were indicted for violating Alabama's antiboycott law. A month later, on March 22, King was convicted and fined five hundred dollars. His conviction represented just one in a succession of efforts by the city to put down the protest. King and other boycott leaders were subjected to acts of harassment and intimidation ranging from capricious surveillance and citations from city police to obscene and threatening letters and phone calls. One month earlier, on January 30, King's house had been bombed. To this point in the protest, the city's white business and political leadership had been utterly unyielding in its refusal to negotiate with the city's black leaders.

On the night of his conviction, King spoke to a mass rally at the Holt Street Baptist Church, the same church where a crowded audience had voted to launch the boycott in the first place the previous December. Before King spoke, the congregation joined together in singing such hymns as "We Shall Not Be Moved," "Go, Send Me Oh Lord," and "Walk Together, Children." In his address, King proclaimed, "The protest is still on." Echoing a constant theme from his early speeches, he reaffirmed his conviction that God would lead them to success: "We believe in God, and we believe that God controls the destiny of the universe, and Evil can't triumph in this universe. This is our hope. This is the thing that keeps us going." But then he warned his audience of what lay ahead:

> Whenever there is any great movement toward freedom, there will inevitably be some tension. Somebody will have to have the courage to sacrifice. You don't get to the promised land without going through the

wilderness. Though we may not get to see the promised land, we know
it's coming because God is for it. So don't worry about some of the things
we have to go through. They are just a part of the great movement that
we are making toward freedom. [1]

As he had done in his original "Death of Evil on the Seashore" sermon, King called on the familiar story of the Exodus in an attempt to
make sense of what he and his hearers were experiencing.

Now, however, King faced a vastly different set of circumstances
from those of the original sermon. The existence of a movement was
no longer simply a rhetorical construction. For the first time in U.S.
history, blacks in a major southern city had united in a campaign of
collective action against racial injustice and were now struggling to
sustain a mass protest that had brought risk and hardship to their lives
and meeting stubborn and sometimes violent resistance to their efforts.
Instead of delivering a Sunday sermon before his home congregation,
he needed to convince a throng of protesters, many of them weary
and discouraged, that their cause was just and that it would succeed.
Not surprisingly, King's use of the biblical story underwent a dramatic
transformation in response to this new and daunting situation.

This chapter explores that transformation by analyzing King's
speeches and sermons from the period during and just after the Montgomery bus boycott, which ran from December 5, 1955, until December 21, 1956, exploring the ways he adapted his initial formulation of
the story in his "Death of Evil on the Seashore" sermon, given five
months before the boycott had started, to address this new set of challenges. The chapter begins by tracing the early history of the boycott
and offering an overview of the passages in King's speeches from this
period that employ the Exodus motif. Next, it analyzes ways that King
altered his use of the story in both content and form in response to
these challenges. Finally, it explains how, by using the biblical story,
King constructed a symbolic framework for explaining the setbacks
and disappointments protesters faced as the campaign wore on, even
as he challenged them to remain faithful to the cause.

THE MONTGOMERY BUS BOYCOTT: SUCCESS AND SETBACK

As noted in the Introduction of this book, a number of long-standing
obstacles had made the possibility of undertaking collective action

against the southern system of apartheid a highly unlikely prospect. Among them were the pervasive sense of fear and powerlessness many African Americans felt in the face of the racist social structure, a religious tradition that urged accommodation instead of protest, and the problem of division and rivalry within the black community itself. When the boycott extended beyond the first heady days of success, organizers also confronted a set of daunting challenges that grew out of the particular political and social setting in which their campaign emerged.

Part of the challenge involved organizing a workable system of transportation that would serve as an alternative to the buses. Describing their initially chaotic efforts to organize a carpool system, Branch stated, "Every day's transportation brought slightly less chaos but more strain and fatigue." By the time the boycott was but a month old, he continued,

> Transportation chairman Rufus Lewis had dragooned nearly every Negro-owned vehicle into the car pool—between 275 and 350 a day—and there were no replacements for those who wanted to drop out. The MIA treasury was exhausted, which meant that Lewis relied increasingly on goodwill, and the inspiration of the mass meetings was wearing down under the hardships of another day's resistance.[2]

The task of maintaining morale and organization grew still more daunting as campaign organizers were forced to admit that they had vastly underestimated the length of time it would take to achieve success. As Jo Ann Robinson, an original boycott leader, put it, "We felt that in a week's time, the city would give in. . . . That was the longest, we thought." Ralph Abernathy similarly recalled expecting that "this would all be over in three or four days."[3] Instead, their attempts to negotiate a settlement to the boycott were met with a stubborn refusal to compromise that left campaign organizers puzzled and dismayed.

Resistance at first came from the bus company itself. The MIA's initial demands, remarkably modest by later standards, called for a seating policy that would replace designated black and white sections with one in which blacks would board from back-to-front and whites from front-to-back, a policy that was already in use in several Alabama cities. Bus company officials, however, refused to negotiate, claiming that they were "merely 'obeying the law.'"[4] One week into the boycott, the company responded to low ridership in black sections of the city by simply canceling routes, and as the boycott moved into its third week in early January 1956, officials sought to avert financial disaster by raising fares by 50 percent. Only when they faced imminent collapse, more than two months into the protest, did they show any willingness to accept the MIA's demands.

By far, however, the staunchest refusal to negotiate came from Montgomery's city government. City officials were unrelenting in their attempts to block the protest at every turn. On the first day of the boycott, the city's black taxi drivers had agreed to transport passengers for the same price as the bus fare, ten cents. Three days later, city police commissioner Clyde Sellers responded by threatening to arrest any drivers who charged less than the minimum fare stipulated in a city ordinance. When the MIA organized its carpool system, police threatened to halt any "overloaded private autos."[5] At one point two motorcycle officers trailed King's car for several blocks and then arrested him for driving 30 mph in a 25-mph zone. In late January 1956, Montgomery's mayor, W. A. Gayle, met secretly with three of the city's black ministers not involved in the protest and then announced to the press that they had reached a settlement with the protesters. When those tactics did not work, the city resorted to taking legal action against the movement's leaders, first indicting MIA attorney Fred Gray on a procedural matter and then, on February 21, indicting almost one hundred MIA members for violating the state's antiboycott law. On the very day that the Supreme Court upheld a lower-court decision ruling segregation on Montgomery's buses unconstitutional, November 13, King was in court for a hearing on the city's request to ban the carpool as an illegal attempt to undercut the city's bus system.

In addition to facing resistance from the white political establishment, protesters also encountered a violent backlash from angry whites in Montgomery almost from the start of the boycott. Within the first week of the campaign, assailants fired on several near-empty buses and into the home of a black police officer. Boycott leaders received a constant barrage of obscene and threatening phone calls. Cars were vandalized. The homes of King and other leaders were bombed. Within days of the boycott's successful conclusion, on December 23, 1956, at 1:30 a.m., someone fired a shotgun into King's house. Five days later, on December 28, snipers fired on two buses, and a third was struck the following day.

King and movement leaders thus faced the challenge of sustaining a protest that extended long beyond the point that any expected and that brought severe hardships to its own participants—and doing so under constant pressure from the city government and with the constant threat of injury or death at the hands of those who would stop at nothing in their determination, as Police Commissioner Sellers put it, "at all cost . . . to preserve our way of life."[6] In a way that was anticipated in his "Death of Evil on the Seashore" sermon, King addressed those challenges by employing the time-honored tradition of invoking the story of Israel's miraculous liberation from Egyptian slavery, strategically adapting that story to explain the particular circumstances of his hearers and to exhort them to continue the protest.

KING'S BOYCOTT RHETORIC

In contrast to his "Death of Evil on the Seashore" address, which was structured entirely around the Exodus narrative, most of King's speeches and public statements during the boycott itself offered only brief allusions to the story, but did so in ways that echoed the longer sermon. Although only a fraction of the many addresses King gave during this period have been preserved, those that have been almost universally make reference to the Exodus.[7] King typically delivered these addresses at campaign "mass meetings," those emotionally charged revival services that became so vital to the movement's existence. These gatherings, held in the city's black churches, were led by local ministers, and their programs usually included hymns, prayers, and readings from the Bible along with the addresses by King, Abernathy, and others.[8] At the beginning of the boycott, they took place two nights per week, on Mondays and Thursdays. Before the protest had even been in place for two months, however, organizers decided to expand that number to six nights per week, as Garrow put it, to "keep up the spirits of boycott supporters."[9] King's frequent references to the Exodus thus achieved their potency not only because they appealed to a deeply held cultural tradition, but also because they occurred in the context of these religious gatherings.

As he had done in his original "Death of Evil on the Seashore" sermon, King frequently used the Exodus story to explain the experience of blacks in the United States, representing racial oppression as Egyptian slavery and efforts to challenge that oppression as the first steps toward obtaining the long-awaited release from captivity. At the boycott's initial mass meeting, for example, King described the significance of their gathering with these words: "We, the disinherited of this land, we who have been oppressed so long, are tired of going through the long night of captivity. And now we are reaching out for the daybreak of freedom and justice and equality."[10] In another address from the period, he stated that the *Brown v. Board of Education* ruling represented to "all men of goodwill . . . a joyous daybreak to end the long night of human captivity"; it was "a beacon of hope to the colored peoples throughout the world who had had a dim vision of the promised land."[11] In a speech delivered shortly after the end of the boycott, King offered a more fully developed account of the "Egypt" of racial oppression that reflected, almost verbatim, the language of the "Death of Evil" sermon:

> Back in 1896, the Supreme Court of this nation established the doctrine of "separate but equal" as the law of the land. And as a result of this doctrine we were thrown and left in the Egypt of segregation. At every moment there was always some pharaoh with a hardened heart who, amid the cry of every Moses, would not allow us to get out of Egypt. There was always a Red Sea before us with its glaring dimensions.[12]

King also used the Exodus to explain freedom movements elsewhere in the world, recounting how these oppressed peoples had "broken loose from the Egypt of Colonialism and Imperialism."[13]

King's boycott speeches also portrayed important successes in the overthrow of racial injustice as reenactments of the Red Sea crossing. As in the earlier sermon, that pivotal event was most often the *Brown v. Board of Education* ruling, which he described to one audience in this way: "One day through the providence of God and the decision of the Supreme Court—May seventeen, 1954—the Red Sea opened."[14] On at least one occasion, however, King depicted a different movement success as a Red Sea crossing. Addressing an audience on November 14, 1956, one day after word came that the Supreme Court had ruled Montgomery's policy of segregating buses unconstitutional, King drew on the language of his "Death of Evil" sermon to announce to a cheering crowd that "the Red Sea has opened for us, we have crossed the banks, we are moving now, and as we look back we see the Egyptian system of segregation drowned upon the seashore."[15]

King often emphasized that the movement was unfolding, as he put it four months after the boycott ended, "through the providence of God."[16] For example, King's conviction on March 22, 1956, for violating the state's antiboycott law was seen as a setback for the movement, raising doubts as to whether the protest would continue. That night King addressed a gathering of several thousand protesters packed into the Holt Street Baptist Church, declaring that "this is the year God's gonna set his people free, and we want no cowards in our crowd."[17] He confidently proclaimed that the Promised Land was coming, "because God is for it."[18] King similarly promised an audience at the American Baptist Assembly in July of 1956, midway through the boycott, that they would succeed because, as he put it, "We have the strange feeling down in Montgomery that in our struggle for justice we have cosmic companionship. And so, we can walk and never get weary, because we believe that there is a great camp meeting in the promised land of freedom and justice."[19]

Finally, as these passages suggest, King invoked the Exodus to describe the campaign's goal, "the promised land of cultural integration."[20] Indeed, this conviction provided protesters with the motivation to endure the hardships of the boycott, as he told the national convention of the NAACP on June 27, 1956: "We believe that, and that is what keeps us going. That is why we can walk and never get weary because we know there is a great camp meeting in the promised land of freedom and equality."[21] Even though he was clear that the movement still had a long way to go—"We are far from the promised land, both north and south"[22]—he nevertheless assured his hearers that it would surely happen. As he told his followers early in the campaign, "Though we may not get to see the promised land, we know it's coming."[23]

These examples show King frequently drawing on the Exodus story in ways that echo his "Death of Evil on the Seashore" sermon, applying key elements of the story in familiar ways to events in African Americans' experience: They were the people of God, freed from the Egypt of racial oppression through God's providence. They had already passed through the Red Sea, the turning point in their history, and now they were confidently making their way to the Promised Land. However his use of the Exodus narrative also underwent several significant adaptations in both content and form that are clearly tied both to the settings in which he was most often speaking, the mass meetings that soon became an almost nightly event, and to the unique challenges confronting the protesters in their attempts to seek even modest change against overwhelming odds.

THEMATIC DEVELOPMENTS

The first thematic development that emerges in King's boycott rhetoric has to do with the agency responsible for bringing about racial justice. In his "Death of Evil" sermon, King clearly attributed the dramatic "Red Sea crossing" event, identified as the Supreme Court's *Brown v. Board of Education* decision, to the agency of God, mediated through what he called God's "providence." As King described it, God created a moral universe in which justice inevitably prevails. His account of the Exodus portrayed the Israelites as being almost surprised to find themselves on the far side of the Red Sea, the recipients of action on their behalf to which they had contributed nothing—a depiction that may have been intended to mitigate the incredulity King's hearers would have felt at his claim that they, too, had experienced the watershed moment of their own history without even realizing it. During the boycott, however, that emphasis changed significantly.

Although King continued to depict God as ultimately orchestrating the social changes that blacks were witnessing, his rhetoric during this period also began to emphasize the crucial role of human agency in the quest for social justice. In his address to the campaign's initial mass meeting, he attributed the success of their first day's boycott to the fact that his hearers, "tired of going through the long night of captivity," were now "reaching out for the daybreak of freedom and justice and equality."[24] Almost exactly one year later, he used strikingly similar language to explain the dramatic rise of movements for racial justice throughout the world:

> But there comes a time when people get tired. There comes a time when people get tired of being trampled over by the iron feet of oppression. There comes a time when people get tired of being plunged across the abyss of exploitation where they experience the bleakness of nagging despair.[25]

Midway through the boycott, in his NAACP convention speech, he described the "story of Montgomery" as the "story of fifty thousand

Negroes who are tired of oppression and injustice"[26] Although he could proclaim that "historical necessity" guaranteed their success, he nevertheless asserted that the force assuring the inevitability of triumph was the perseverance of the protesters who were "willing to substitute tired feet for tired souls, and walk and walk and walk until the sagging walls of injustice have been crushed by the battering rams of historical necessity." In an earlier mass-meeting address, after assuring his hearers that the Promised Land was coming "because God is for it," King two lines later urged protesters to "continue with the same spirit, with the same orderliness, with the same discipline, with the same Christian approach."[27]

In this way, even as he continued to assure his hearers of their ultimate success—their cause was, after all, in God's hands—he nevertheless also emphasized the imperative of persevering in their efforts. Perhaps no passage better captures the dialectical tension between these two themes than one from King's St. Louis, Missouri, freedom-rally speech on April 10, 1957. The address ends with a stirring call for the development of black leadership, a call that emphasizes the need for human effort even as it ascribes ultimate authority to God. His plea is both a prayer to God and a powerful exhortation for his hearers to accept their responsibility to their people:

> God grant that ministers, and lay leaders, and civic leaders, and business-men, and professional people all over the nation will rise up and use the talent and the finances that God had given them, and lead the people on toward the Promised Land of freedom with rational, calm, and nonviolent means. This is the great challenge of the hour.[28]

Even as they lived with the assurance that the campaign for justice was unfolding according to the providence of God, success also demanded that blacks take courageous and determined action in their pursuit of the Promised Land. Much more, with his emphasis on the need for action, King introduced a new level of "dramatic significance" to his hearers' sense of their place in the historic moment by highlighting the crucial role they had been called to play in bringing about this social transformation.[29]

The second thematic development in King's boycott rhetoric is the emergence of the wilderness as a prominent stage in the movement toward racial justice. The earliest version of his "Death of Evil" sermon, delivered in July 1955, contains no mention of the wilderness whatsoever. As the Montgomery protest unfolds, that begins to change dramatically, with King frequently invoking the wilderness experience of the Hebrews in connection with protesters' experiences of tension and opposition. In his address quoted in the introduction to this chapter, delivered to a mass meeting following his conviction for violating Alabama's antiboycott law, he warned his hearers that "you don't get to the promised land without going through the wilderness."[30] What obstacles they faced in that journey, he assured them, were "just a necessary part of the great movement we are making toward freedom." When he delivered the later version of his "Death of Evil" sermon on May 17, 1956, he altered the ending to include the wilderness, telling his hearers that God "is seeking at every moment of His existence to lift men from the bondage of some evil Egypt, carrying them through the wilderness of discipline, and finally to the promised land of personal and social integration."[31] He gave the same assurance to a mass meeting on November 14, 1956, one night after the Supreme Court's ruling that Montgomery's system of segregated buses was unconstitutional. The news, while clearly cause for celebration, came in the midst of an intense legal battle against the city's efforts to win a temporary restraining order halting the campaign's carpool. Although elated by the news, the protesters also feared an intense backlash from angry whites—and with good reason. The night before, forty carloads of Ku Klux Klan members had driven through Montgomery's black neighborhoods, offering a clear threat to those who attempted to challenge the city's social structure. Calling to mind the challenges God's people faced in the wilderness, King warned his audience of what lay ahead:

> Some days will be dark and dreary, but we will keep going. Prodigious hilltops of opposition will rise before us, but we will keep going. (*Yes*) Oh, we have been in Egypt long enough (*Well*), and now we've gotten orders from headquarters. The Red Sea has opened for us, we have crossed the banks, we are moving now, and as we look back we see the Egyptian system of segregation drowned upon the seashore. (*Yes*) We know that the Midianites are still ahead. We see the beckoning call of the evil forces of the Amorites. We see the Hittites all around us but, but we are going on because we've got to get to Canaan. (*Yes*) We can't afford to stop. (*Yes*) We've got to keep moving.[32]

When King described freedom movements elsewhere in the world, he similarly depicted them as having passed into the wilderness. In his "Facing the Challenge of a New Age" address, delivered on December 3, 1956, King detailed the results of worldwide anticolonial movements:

> More than one billion three hundred million . . . of the colored peoples of the world are free today. They have their own governments, their own economic system, and their own educational system. They have broken loose from the Egypt of Colonialism and Imperialism, and they are now moving through the wilderness of adjustment toward the promised land of cultural integration. As they look back they see the old order of Colonialism and Imperialism passing away and the new order of freedom and justice coming into being.[33]

He used almost identical language in his address to the St. Louis freedom rally four months later, proclaiming that oppressed peoples throughout the world had "broken aloose from the Egypt of colonialism" and were "now moving through the wilderness of adjustment toward the Promised Land of cultural integration."[34]

King continued to develop the theme of the wilderness in the months following the boycott's successful conclusion, a period marked by violent reactions from angry whites. In his address to the Prayer Pilgrimage for Freedom (May 17, 1957), delivered five months after the boycott had ended, King urged blacks to

> stand up for justice. (*Yes*) Sometimes it gets hard. But it is always difficult to get out of Egypt; the Red Sea always stands before you with discouraging dimensions. (*Yes*) And even after you've crossed the Red Sea, you have to move through a wilderness with prodigious hilltops of evil, (*Yes*) and gigantic mountains of opposition. [*Laughter*] But I say to you this afternoon: Keep moving. (*Go on ahead*) Let nothing slow you up.[35]

Several months later, in a sermon to his home congregation, King decried the response of those who were tempted to give up by comparing them to the Hebrews who sought to return to Egypt rather than face the harsh difficulties of the wilderness:

> Another way is to acquiesce and to give in, to resign yourself to the oppression. Some people do that. They discover the difficulties of the

wilderness moving into the promised land, and they would rather go back to the despots of Egypt because it's difficult to get in the promised land. And so they resign themselves to the fate of oppression; they somehow acquiesce to this thing.[36]

Only by enduring the travails of the wilderness could blacks experience the liberation of the Promised Land.

SHIFTS IN FORM

King's use of the Exodus story during the boycott also underwent several important shifts in form from that of his original "Death of Evil" sermon, the most obvious of which had to do with the length of his citations. The sermon, of course, was structured entirely around the narrative, beginning with a somewhat complete telling of the story, moving to an explicit application of the story to freedom movements elsewhere in the world, and concluding with a final application of the story to his hearers. In his boycott rhetoric, King's references to the Exodus take the form of a "code" through which a brief passage, often a phrase or a single word—*captivity, Egypt, Pharaoh, Red Sea, wilderness, Promised Land*—is used to evoke the larger story. Further, although King used this "code" language at a variety of points in his speeches during this period, the highest concentration occurs in the conclusions, at the point when he would move into an emotionally charged climax. An example is, again, his March 22 address. He began by ironically describing, in general terms, the "sins" of which he was "guilty": being born a Negro, being subjected to the "battering rams of segregation and oppression," and having the "moral courage to stand up and express our weariness of this oppression."[37] He explained the judgment handed down earlier that day and then launched into an extended, somewhat rambling passage articulating the core principles of the movement, among them nonviolent protest, faith in democracy, and a commitment to Christian principles, all leading up to his pronouncement, "The protest is still on." King then proclaimed, as he had often done before, his conviction that success was inevitable, giving a prescient warning about the impact of racism on U.S. international standing:

God is speaking to his children today and saying, "Don't play with me. For if you keep playing with me, I'll break the backbone of your power and knock you out of the orbits of your international and national prestige. I am going to be God in this universe." We want the world to know that we believe in God, and we believe that God controls the destiny of the universe, and Evil can't triumph in this universe. This is our hope. This is the thing that keeps us going.

Having expressed that confidence, however, he concluded with a rousing call to courage and sacrifice that contained several brief references to the Exodus:

> You don't get to the promised land without going through the wilderness. Though we may not get to see the promised land, we know it's coming because God is for it. So don't worry about some of the things we have to go through. They are just a necessary part of the great movement that we are making toward freedom. There can never be growth without growing pains. Let us continue with the same spirit, with the same orderliness, with the same discipline, with the same Christian approach. I believe that God is using Montgomery as his proving ground. It may be that here in the capital of the Confederacy, the birth of the ideal of freedom in America and in the Southland can be born. God be praised for you, for your loyalty, for your determination. God bless you and keep you, and may God be with us as we go on.

King's speech of November 14, 1956, also illustrates this pattern. On the previous day, the Supreme Court had ruled that segregation on the city's buses was unconstitutional and in response, carloads of Klan members had driven menacingly through black neighborhoods. That night, King delivered a lengthy address before another mass rally at the Holt Street Baptist Church. Much of it was taken up with recounting how, for the past eleven months, they had carried out the protest "with high moral standards," with "methods and techniques . . . rooted in the deep soils of the Christian faith," and buoyed by the faith that "in our struggle we have cosmic companionship, and that, at bottom, the universe is on the side of justice."[38] He described the previous day's Supreme Court ruling as "a revelation of the eternal validity of this faith." King next communicated the MIA's recommendation that the end of the boycott only take place after the federal mandate demanding desegregation on the city's buses had been delivered to the district court for final implementation, which they expected within days, a recommendation the audience affirmed unanimously. King urged his hearers to approach this monumental success with grace and respect toward whites and to remain nonviolent regardless of what happened to them when they returned to the buses. As he came to the end of his address, he began to exhort his hearers to "keep on moving," to "keep on moving and keep on keeping on." Quoting Langston Hughes's poem, "Mother to Son," with its ending line, "For I'se still climbin', I'se still goin', and life for me ain't been no crystal stair," King offered this final, stirring exhortation:

> Well, life for none of us has been a crystal stair, but we've got to keep going. We'll keep going through the sunshine and the rain. Some days will be dark and dreary, but we will keep going. Prodigious hilltops of opposition will rise before us, but we will keep going. (*Yes*) Oh, we have been in Egypt long enough (*Well*), and now we've gotten orders from headquarters. The Red Sea has opened for us, we have crossed the banks, we are moving now, and as we look back we see the Egyptian system of segregation drowned upon the seashore. (*Yes*) We know that the Midianites are still ahead. We see the beckoning call of the evil forces of the Amorites. We see the Hittites all around us but, but we are going on because we've got to get to Canaan. (*Yes*) We can't afford to stop. (*Yes*) We've got to keep moving.

As these examples show, rather than telling the story at length as he had done in the "Death of Evil" sermon, King's typical strategy during the boycott was to reinforce his exhortations with brief, codelike allusions to the larger, shared story.

King shifted his use of the Exodus in another, more subtle and potentially significant way, during this period, from a self-conscious use of the story as example or illustration to a form that rhetorically situated his audience within the drama itself. In his original "Death of Evil" sermon, King cited the story as an extended analogy, asking his hearers to consciously consider the ways that the ancient story was "like" their own. In the opening of the sermon, after articulating the fundamental principle that "in the endless struggle between good and evil, good always emerges as the victor," he stated that "a beautiful example of this is found in the early history of the Hebrew people."[39] He next invited the audience to recall the story: "You will remember that at a very early stage in her history, the children of Israel were reduced to the bondage of physical slavery under the gripping yoke of Egyptian rule." He described Egypt as the "symbol of evil" contrasted with Israel, which "symbolized goodness," and he recounted the story, highlighting once again its illustrative value as "a glaring symbol of the ultimate doom of evil in its struggle against good." His use of the Exodus was explicit and self-conscious, placing his audience outside the narrative and inviting them to consider its application to their present situation.

In his "code" usage of the Exodus, by contrast, King compressed the narrative and employed "literal" language to evoke it, so that the story now took on the character of a metaphor with the potential to provoke what Osborn and Ehninger described as "a ready, almost automatic, response" in his hearers.[40] Instead of inviting them to consider the ways that their situation was "like" that of ancient Israel, these brief references gave the protesters, in Kirkwood's words, "a brief experience of nonrational awareness, directly halting the otherwise incessant flow of their own intellectualizing."[41] With a phrase or even a single word, King placed them *in* the story: The Red Sea *has* opened; *we are* moving through the wilderness; *we are* marching toward the Promised Land.

These shifts in form were rhetorically important for King in several ways. On the most basic level, King's use of words and phrases as code for the larger story had the potential to create in his hearers a powerful sense of identification with him and with one another. Davis described this as one of the more significant dimensions of narrative as a social transaction in which a storyteller creates a relationship with an audience by engaging their "narrativity," their "ability to fill in the connections that are required to make sense of the characters and events in the story."[42] Citing reader-response theorist Wolfgang Iser's contention that "inevitable omissions" give a story its "dynamism," Davis observed, "These omissions are crucial because they give us the opportunity to 'bring into play our own faculty for establishing connections—for filling in the gaps left by the text itself.'" In King's case, what the audience was invited to "fill in" was essentially the story as a whole, creating the sense that he and his hearers were insiders to a set of meanings held so deeply in common that they could be evoked with a mere word or phrase. At the same time, King's shift from analogy to metaphor in his code references to the Exodus allowed his hearers to participate in the narrative at a deeper, nonrational level, not simply observing the story from the outside but, rather, enjoying what Kirkwood described as "a fleeting experience of a given mood or state of awareness" of their identity as the chosen people of God.[43] His hearers could place themselves imaginatively and emotionally within the drama at a deeper, more personal and experiential level than had been possible in the earlier sermon.

A SYMBOLIC FRAMEWORK FOR COLLECTIVE ACTION

As the foregoing analysis shows, King followed a clear pattern of strategically invoking the Exodus narrative from the beginning of his leadership in the Montgomery bus boycott. His mass-rally speeches and public statements repeatedly framed the struggle from the perspective of this deeply held religious drama, typically calling to mind a powerful set of shared meanings and emotional associations with a mere phrase or even a single word. King's language symbolically placed his hearers within the drama, inviting them to imagine that they were, literally, the children of God enacting the Exodus in their present experience: "The Red Sea has opened up for us, we have crossed the banks, we are moving now. . . . We are going on because we've got to get to Canaan."[44] The effect, as Levine pointed out, was to collapse history, "extending the world . . . temporally backward so that the paradigmatic acts of the gods and mythical ancestors can be continually re-enacted and infinitely recoverable."[45] That effect was heightened by the way King typically invoked the Exodus narrative during the final moments of his speeches—that part of the sermon that produced what Du Bois had called "the Frenzy."[46] As Lischer put it, this was the climactic moment in a sermon when "the *experience* of God replaces *talk about* God."[47] Speaking in the persona of the biblical prophet, King thus created an intensely emotional experience of identification with the biblical narrative through which his hearers relived the drama of deliverance.

At the same time, during this period King adapted the story's content in ways that strategically addressed various problems and obstacles faced by the participants in the boycott. In the biblical account, the Israelites arrive at the border of Canaan within weeks of crossing the Red Sea. Overwhelmed with fear at the strength of the nations who already occupy the land, they rebel against Moses and make plans to appoint a new leader who will take them back to Egypt. God punishes their lack of faith by forcing them to wander in the wilderness for forty years, after which a new generation of Israelites enters the Promised Land successfully.

King's boycott speeches offer an alternative plot structure that begins with the Israelites suffering in Egyptian captivity, moves to their miraculous crossing of the Red Sea, proceeds immediately through an "inevitable" wilderness period, and looks forward to their arrival at the Promised Land. Further, by superimposing this simplified plot structure on the Montgomery campaign, he situated the protesters at predictable points within the story to account for whatever circumstances they were facing at the moment. In his earliest boycott speeches, King placed his audience in the "Egypt" of slavery, segregation and colonialism, yet poised on the verge of deliverance: "We are reaching out for the daybreak of freedom and justice and equality."[48] When the Supreme Court ruled that Montgomery's system of segregated buses was unconstitutional eleven months later, King announced that they had crossed the Red Sea: "The Red Sea has opened for us, we have crossed the banks, we are moving now, and as we look back we see the Egyptian system of segregation drowned upon the seashore."[49] In a particularly significant development of the story, King encompassed the failure of the movement to achieve rapid success, along with the heightened racial tensions that the protesters faced as the boycott wore on, by situating them within the wilderness, an inevitable part in the journey preceding their arrival at the Promised Land. He could thus exult with them that they had crossed the Red Sea—they had witnessed the turning point in their history—while also warning them of the arduous journey that lay ahead. Always, of course, his narrative persistently pointed protesters to their journey's destination, "the promised land of freedom and justice."[50]

King also adapted the agency behind the dramatic events unfolding around them, bringing the imperative of human action into dialectical tension with the providence of God. In his original formulation, God's providence alone assured the inevitability that racial justice would be achieved. As the boycott developed, that outcome became contingent on whether the protesters fulfilled their role in the story because "freedom doesn't come on the silver platter." Instead, the transformation of society they sought had begun because they had finally become "tired of being trampled" and were willing to "stand up for justice," to "walk and walk," to "keep on moving." At the same time, this human action occurred within a larger framework of providence and "historical necessity." King's development of the Exodus narrative as a framework for viewing the protest thus maintained a delicate balance between human action and divine providence. This balance was particularly significant for the movement because it created a structure of meaning in which the call for nonviolent protest—"passive resistance" as he called it—made sense. Without the continued call for action, of course, blacks might easily have fallen back into a stance of acquiescence in response to the overwhelming tide of resistance to their calls for social change. A protest movement based on human effort alone, on the other hand, could just as easily have degenerated into violence driven by the sense that they were on their own and had to use whatever means necessary to achieve liberation.[51] The genius of King's formulation of the Exodus is that it provided a third path, one in which they were actors in the social drama and yet in another sense "passive" before the leading of God. Within the story, they were simply responding to events that God had initiated and following resolutely the path that God had laid out for them, as he had done centuries previously for his people, Israel. They could be confident that if they simply continued the journey, they would reach the Promised Land.

CONCLUSION

King's references to the Exodus during the boycott offered protesters a rhetorical vision that developed out of his original formulation of social change as the reenactment of the Exodus, but one that was transmitted not in a full account of the story but rather, in the form of a "rhetorical code" that powerfully evoked the ideas and the emotions surrounding this crucial part of African Americans' cultural heritage. This vision, as I shall argue in chapter 6, implicitly cast him in the role of Moses, the prophet chosen by God to lead the people to the Promised Land. It theologically legitimated the protest, reinforcing the emerging commitment to nonviolence and providing strong motivation to continue engaging in collective action against racial injustice. It also addressed the particular obstacles Montgomery's black citizens faced in their attempts to organize and sustain the boycott. By persistently subsuming their local struggle within the worldwide deliverance of oppressed peoples from "the Egypt of colonialism," King spoke to the fear and impotence of his hearers. In their protest, they now joined the great flow of history through which racial injustice and oppression inevitably gave way to freedom and equality, a process that began when the Jews marched out of Egypt some thirty-five centuries earlier. By framing the protest within the biblical narrative, moreover, King gave the protesters a theologically sanctioned justification for their actions. Morris hinted at this process when he asserted that "by giving contemporary relevance to familiar biblical struggles through spellbinding oratory and by defining such religious heroes as Jesus and Moses as revolutionaries, King had begun to refocus the content of black religion."[52] Indeed, by bringing human agency into dialectical tension with divine providence, the vision placed protesters under obligation to act in response to miraculous events initiated through the agency of God. God had parted the Red Sea; they had no choice but to march across. When the protest march emerged in 1963 as the movement's principal mode of collective action, this emphasis on human agency would become the basis for King's strident call to "keep moving."

This rhetorical vision also helped to reinforce among blacks the sense of collective identity that social-movement theorists have pointed to as an essential element of movement formation, an identity transcending the fragmentation that had characterized African American communities since Reconstruction. In reality, King's hearers participated in a rigid caste system that stratified black society on the basis of education, income, dialect, and complexion. In the symbolic world of King's discourse, however, his hearers were the united people of God, long oppressed by Egypt, but now set free from their long night of captivity by God's mighty hand. King stylistically underscored this identity by his persistent use of the pronoun "we": "We, the disinherited of this land, we who have been oppressed for so long, are tired of going through the long night of captivity. And now we are reaching out for the daybreak of freedom and justice and equality."[53] King also reinforced this unity by evoking the Exodus in the form of a code, which engaged the audience in the process of supplying the larger narrative evoked by a word or phrase and positioned rhetor and audience together as insiders to the deeply held, shared biblical story.

Finally, the Exodus narrative, with the introduction of the wilderness as a crucial element in the story's plot, provided King with a discourse for addressing the continuing tensions that blacks faced in Montgomery as the boycott wore on and for responding to the backlash they experienced when the Supreme Court ruled in their favor.

From one perspective—one shared by many—it appeared that racial tensions had grown worse rather than better, that society had become more polarized, and that the movement was further from its goal of integration and racial harmony than when it had started. Placed within the narrative logic of the Exodus, however, these tensions and setbacks were not only understandable, they were to be predicted, for they represented the travails of God's people in the wilderness. Their troubles actually became a source of narrative fidelity, providing empirical evidence that they had crossed the Red Sea and were moving toward Canaan.

CHAPTER 5

REACHING OUT FOR CANAAN
King's "Birth of a New Nation" Sermon

In March of 1957, barely two months after the boycott had ended, King traveled to the West African country of Ghana at the invitation of the country's prime minister designate, Kwame Nkrumah, to attend the celebration of its transition from a colony under British rule (known as the Gold Coast) to an independent country. The transfer of power, which officially took place on March 17, 1957, was remarkably peaceful, coming at the end of several years of nonviolent protest and agitation led by the American-educated African leader. The event had a deep impact on King, confirming his emphasis on the worldwide nature of the struggle against oppression and demonstrating the effectiveness of nonviolent protest as a strategy for achieving that goal. His invitation to attend the event also signaled his status as "a symbol of liberation for an international constituency."[1]

Exactly one month after Ghana's independence, on April 7, 1957, King recounted his experience in a sermon at the Dexter Avenue Baptist Church in Montgomery titled, "The Birth of a New Nation." Employing the same strategy he had used in his original "Death of Evil on the Seashore" sermon and in his boycott rhetoric, King placed the Ghanaians' struggle for independence within a larger narrative framework provided by the Exodus story, briefly pointing his hearers to the story itself, applying that story to a successful struggle for freedom elsewhere in the world, and finally, drawing the lessons from the worldwide struggle, seen through the lens of the Exodus, for his own movement. In fact, the sermon presents the most complete, paradigmatic application of the Exodus story to the struggle for racial justice of King's career. At the same time, the address, delivered in response to a new and complex rhetorical situation, reflected King's continuing program of adapting the cultural myth to changing circumstances.

91

This chapter analyzes the way that King, in his "Birth of a New Nation" sermon, offered a construction of the history of Ghana's exploitation and liberation, framed within the symbolic context of the Exodus, as a response to this new rhetorical situation. It traces the continuing evolution of his use of the biblical narrative, noting particularly the way that King configured both the myth and the "history" within a "hermeneutic circle," one that highlighted the mythical significance of the "history" while at the same time providing "empirical" evidence for the myth. In so doing, King found the resources to address the demands of his immediate situation even as he sought to lift the vision of his hearers so that they would see themselves as part of a dramatic, global revolution in the fortunes of persons of color. The chapter begins with an overview of the rhetorical situation King faced as he addressed his congregation that morning, followed by a summary of the sermon as a whole, an account of the particular ways that King continued the Exodus tradition, and an explanation of his strategy of configuring myth and history in a reciprocal interpretive relationship. It concludes by detailing the ways that this strategy enabled King to address the challenges he faced as leader of the newly emerging civil rights movement.

Post-Boycott: International Prestige and Local Disillusionment

In the fourteen months following the start of the Montgomery bus boycott in December 1955, King's leadership of the campaign had catapulted him onto the national and even the international stage. In the closing months of 1956 and into 1957, King was highly sought after as a speaker, making more than fifty speaking appearances during the spring and summer of 1957. On February 10, 1957, he was a featured guest on NBC's nationally broadcast Sunday television program, *The Open Mind*. Eight days later his photograph filled the cover of *Time* magazine's February 18, 1957 edition, and on February 10, the date set by the National Council of Churches for the thirty-fifth annual observance of Race Relations Sunday, a message he penned was read from pulpits all across the nation.

This broad exposure reflected not only King's popularity as a civil rights leader, but also his vision for the movement. What had started inauspiciously as a local protest demanding a more predictable but still racially segregated seating arrangement on the city's buses had evolved into a movement for racial equality that received national and international attention. King highlighted that wider focus in a speech he gave on December 3 titled "Facing the Challenge of a New Age," delivered at the opening of what became an annual "Institute on Non-violence and Social Change," before an overflow crowd at the Holt Street Baptist Church. He recalled the meeting that had occurred in that same church a year earlier and expressed his amazement at how far they had come:

> Little did we know on that night that we were starting a movement that would rise to international proportions; a movement whose lofty echos [*sic*] would ring in the ears of people of every nation; a movement that would stagger and astound the imagination of the oppressor, while leaving a glittering star of hope etched in the midnight skies of the oppressed. Little did we know that night that we were starting a movement that would gain the admiration of men of goodwill all over the world.[2]

That larger vision was also reflected practically in the development of a new organization, the SCLC, which grew out of a series of meetings in the opening months of 1957. Designed to support and coordinate civil rights activity in local organizations, particular in southern black churches, the SCLC sought to gather up local protests into a truly regional and even national movement, bringing "the Negro masses into the freedom struggle by expanding 'the Montgomery way' across the south."[3]

Ironically, at the same time that both King and his movement were shifting to a national stage, the audience that he faced that morning at Dexter Avenue, along with the city's other black citizens, had faced violent reactions to the successful boycott. As Oates put it,

> On December 28, a reign of terror erupted in Montgomery, as armed whites opened fire on buses all over town, shot a pregnant Negro woman in both legs, and pummeled a teenage Negro girl. The Klan marched in full regalia, and fiery crosses lit up the night sky.[4]

In response, the city's police commissioner ordered the bus service halted, and the next morning the city commissioners, while reinstating limited public transportation, imposed a 5:00 p.m. curfew on the buses, a move that undermined the victory blacks had achieved through the boycott. Less than a week later, whites distributed leaflets allegedly signed by blacks claiming that King and his associates "ride high, eat good, stay warm and pilfer the funds. . . . Wake up! Mess is His Business. Run Him Out of Town!"

This reign of terror continued into the early months of 1957. On January 10, 1957, within the space of one hour, the home of a white supporter of the movement, the parsonage where Ralph Abernathy lived, and four of the city's black churches were rocked by bomb blasts, and on January 27, ten sticks of dynamite were discovered under the front porch of King's house by a Montgomery police officer. In response to the violence, city commissioners again suspended bus service indefinitely. As Garrow wrote, "The black community was angry at the bombings and fearful that the commission might use the violence as an excuse for permanently halting bus service, thus denying the MIA the victory it had won."[5] Although the bus service was soon restored, the commissioners again imposed a 5:00 p.m. curfew on the buses, which remained in effect until almost mid-February. When King began his journey to Ghana in early March of that year, then, the gains of the boycott seemed overshadowed by this backlash and by the city's continued determination to resist granting the rights that blacks had been guaranteed by the Supreme Court.

Complicating King's situation still further, the national and international attention he was receiving, along with the worsening circumstances for blacks in Montgomery, combined to fuel an already-deep resentment toward King among some of the city's other black leaders. Chief among his antagonists was longtime local black leader E. D. Nixon, who was bitter toward King for taking the credit for what be believed had initially been his idea. As Garrow noted, however, Nixon was not alone in his resentment toward King. Many in the organization complained that the MIA had become, in the words of an MIA official, "a closed operation," and that if "people outside had been aware of what was going on . . . they could have found all kinds of things to criticize." Rosa Parks was reportedly bitter and disgruntled because the MIA had refused to put her on its payroll after she had lost her job as a seamstress. Finally, many in the black community responded coolly to King's appearance on the cover of *Time*, reflecting, in the words of one black reporter, "an element of resentment and jealousy, a feeling that the article gave King too much credit at the expense of other leaders."[6]

When he stood before his congregation that Sunday morning, April 7, King thus faced a rhetorical challenge since the fortunes of many blacks in Montgomery seemed worse rather than better and, especially, where blacks had gone from experiencing an uneasy stability in their dealings with whites to being victims of outright hostility and violence. Further, he faced resentment and rivalry from several key figures in the local movement. King thus needed to craft a discourse that would explain the setbacks facing the local campaign, enhance his ethos as the movement's leader, and shore up blacks' commitment to continue working together to achieve racial justice, even as he sought to place the local movement within the global campaign against colonialism. In his "Birth of a New Nation" sermon King responded to those challenges, as he had done so often during the past year and a half, by calling on the familiar themes of the ancient biblical story.

OVERVIEW

King began by announcing the title of his address and his plan to structure the sermon around the story of the Exodus, beginning with "the flight of the Hebrew people from the bondage of Egypt, through the wilderness, and finally, to the promised land." As if to emphasize the story's timelessness, he told of having recently seen the movie *The Ten Commandments*, and in one of his earliest explicit references to the persona of Moses, he highlighted the movie's theme as "the struggle of Moses, the struggle of his devoted followers as they sought to get out of Egypt." He also asserted the story's universal character: "This is something of the story of every people struggling for freedom. It is the first story of man's explicit quest for freedom. And it demonstrates the stages that seem to inevitably follow the quest for freedom."[7]

Having offered the Exodus narrative as the "basis for our thinking together" (155), King then unfolded the sermon's three main sections. First, he told the "history" of Ghana's independence, recounting its colonization by the British, offering a brief biography of Kwame Nkrumah, who led the independence movement, describing in great detail the transfer of power and concluding with an assessment of the country's future. In the second section, King applied the lessons of Ghana to his own movement. In the third section, King told of his visit to London, the capital of the once-great British Empire and Ghana's former colonizer, stressing that it now symbolized a dying system. King concluded with a rousing, prophetic vision of what he saw as God's plan to bring justice to the entire world.

As King opened his "history" of Ghana's liberation, he prepared his audience to appreciate the country's dramatic reversal of fortune by first highlighting its status as a most unlikely candidate for independence. He offered a seemingly prosaic account of African geography, followed by a description of that continent's indigenous populations as the most oppressed and least powerful in the world, having "suffered all of the pain and the affliction that could be mustered up by other nations" and "all of the lowest standards that we can think about." King then portrayed the Gold Coast itself as the least among these exploited peoples, a "little country" that had been "exploited and dominated and trampled over," a colony that had "suffered all of the injustices, all of the exploitation, all of the humiliation that comes as a result of colonialism" (156). King thus set the stage for recounting Ghana's liberation within the archetypal motif of reversal.

Abruptly, King returned to the mythic-symbolic framework of the Exodus, a return signaled by a shift to a grander style and references to the abstract, universal meaning of the Gold Coast experience: "But like all slavery, like all domination, like all exploitation, it came to the point that the people got tired of it." He spoke of the "throbbing desire . . . for freedom within the soul of every man" (156) that propelled the Ghanaians toward independence from this oppression, a theme he amplified with language from the Exodus story:

> There is something in the soul that cries out for freedom. There is something deep down within the very soul of man that reaches out for Canaan. Men cannot be satisfied with Egypt. They try to adjust to it for awhile. Many men have vested interests in Egypt, and they are slow to leave. Egypt makes it profitable to them; some people profit by Egypt. The vast majority, the masses of people, never profit by Egypt, and they are never content with it. And eventually they rise up and begin to cry out for Canaan's land. (156–57)

Returning to the Ghana "history," King noted how as early as 1844, the country's tribal chiefs had sought independence from Great

Britain, portraying the British response with a clear allusion to Pharaoh's rejection of Moses: "We will not let you go" (157). He then briefly recounted the life of Nkrumah, detailing his early years in Africa, his education in the United States, and his decision to return to his native land. He also described the opposition of some native Africans to Nkrumah's leadership, contrasting them with the "the masses of people" who were "with him," a parallel to the "devoted followers" who had supported Moses in the struggle "to get out of Egypt" mentioned in the sermon's opening paragraph. King recalled Nkrumah's determination to continue the struggle in the face of British resistance, which eventually forced Britain to conclude that "it could no longer rule the Gold Coast" and that it would "release this nation," all because of the perseverance of Nkrumah and "the other leaders who worked along with him and the masses of people who were willing to follow" (158).

King next described in stirring detail the celebrations surrounding the transfer of power, recounting the arrival of dignitaries from all over the world—including leaders of the civil rights movement—gathered to "say to this new nation, 'We greet you and we give you our moral support. We hope for you God's guidance as you move now into the realm of independence'" (158). Here, King shifted his verb tense from past to present, dramatically transporting his hearers into an immediate experience of this momentous occasion:

> And oh, it was a beautiful experience to see some of the leading persons on the scene of civil rights in America on hand to say, "Greetings to you," as this new nation was born. Look over, to my right is Adam Powell, to my lift is Charles Diggs, to my right again is Ralph Bunche. . . . Then you look out and see the vice-president of the United States; you see A. Philip Randolph; you see all of the people who have stood in the forefront of the struggle for civil rights over the years coming over to Africa to say we bid you godspeed. (158–59)

King narrated the ceremonial transfer of power from the colonial parliament to the new, national parliament, punctuating each paragraph with a pronouncement that placed the events within something of a larger "apocalyptic" framework centered on the expectation of a dawning "new age."[8] He described the gathering of five hundred people assembled in the parliament building for the final session of the old parliament, surrounded on the outside by "thousands and thousands and thousands of people" awaiting Nkrumah's arrival: "There was something old now passing away." He recalled Nkrumah's arriving for his closing speech to the old parliament wearing his prison uniform, a sign that "an old Parliament was passing away." He told of how, at midnight that night, a gathering of some five hundred thousand people had crowded into the city's polo grounds to watch the lowering of the Union Jack and the raising of the new flag of Ghana: "This was a new nation now, a new nation being born." Next, he poignantly described Nkrumah's pronouncement, "We are no longer a British colony. We are a free, sovereign people." (159) He recalled the tears that he saw in the eyes of the people around him, and his own tears, noting the repeated cries of the throng throughout the city, "Freedom! Freedom!" in a way that merged Ghana's story with that of black Americans:

> They were crying it in a sense that they had never heard it before, and I could hear that old Negro spiritual once more crying out: "Free at last! Free at last! Great God Almighty, I'm free at last.". . . Everywhere we turned, we could hear it ringing from the housetops; we could hear it from every corner, every nook and crook of the community: "Freedom! Freedom!" This was the birth of a new nation. This was the breaking aloose from Egypt. (160)

Having described Ghana's past and present, King next turned his attention to the challenges that lay ahead for the new nation, again invoking the Exodus experience to explain them: "This nation was now out of Egypt and has crossed the Red Sea. Now it will confront its wilderness. Like any breaking aloose from Egypt, there is a wilderness ahead. There is a problem of adjustment" (160). He detailed several elements of this adjustment related to economic and educational development, frequently calling them the "wilderness." But finally, he expressed his firm hope in the nation's future: "There is a great day ahead. The future is on its side. It's now going through the wilderness. But the Promised Land is ahead" (161).

In the second major section of the speech, King applied the lessons from the Ghana experience, viewed through the lens of the Exodus narrative, to the contemporary struggle for civil rights in the United States, accentuating the "things that we must never forget as we find ourselves breaking aloose from an evil Egypt, trying to move through the wilderness toward the Promised Land of cultural integration." He emphasized, first, that "the oppressor never voluntarily gives freedom to the oppressed. You have to work for it." For this reason, he urged his hearers not to

> go out this morning with any illusions. Don't go back into your homes and around Montgomery thinking that the Montgomery city Commission and that all of the forces in leadership of the South will eventually work this thing out for Negroes. [Do not think that] It's going to work out; it's going to roll in on the wheels of inevitability. If we wait for it to work itself out, it will *never* be worked out. Freedom only comes through persistent revolt, through persistent agitation, through persistently rising up against the system of evil. (161)

Second, he argued, the Ghana story "reminds us of the fact that a nation or a people can break aloose from oppression without violence." Deftly negotiating the paradoxical connection of the language of "revolt" with his commitment to nonviolence, he said, "We've got to revolt in such a way that after revolt is over we can live with people as their brothers and their sisters. Our aim must never be to defeat them or humiliate them." In one of the most arresting illustrations of the entire speech, he described Nkrumah dancing with the Duchess of Kent at the State ball that night, a poignant symbol of "two nations able to live together and work together because the breaking aloose was through nonviolence," the result of which would be "the creation of the beloved community" (162). Third, he told his hearers, the Ghana story reminds them that "freedom never comes on a silver platter." Again he pointed to the story of the Jews leaving Egypt to explain Ghana's experience and, by extension, the ordeals his own followers were undergoing:

> It's never easy. Ghana reminds us that whenever you break out of Egypt you better get ready for stiff backs. You better get ready for some homes to be bombed. You better get ready for some churches to be bombed. You better get ready for a lot of nasty things to be said about you, because you [*sic*] getting out of Egypt, and whenever you break aloose from Egypt the initial response of the Egyptian is bitterness. It never comes with ease. It comes only through the hardness and persistence of life. Ghana reminds us of that.

Merging the identity of his hearers with that of the Jews in the Exodus, he predicted the challenges his movement would face:

> Before you get to Canaan you've got a Red Sea to confront; you have a hardened heart of a pharaoh to confront; you have the prodigious hill-tops of evil in the wilderness to confront. And even when you get up to the Promised Land you have giants in the land. The beautiful thing about it is that there are a few people who've been over in the land. They have spied enough to say, "Even though the giants are there we can possess the land, because we got [*sic*] the internal fiber to stand up amid anything that we have to face.

What challenges his followers did face were to be seen as evidence of their progress toward the ultimate goal:

> And those people who tell you today that there is more tension in Montgomery than there has ever been are telling you right. Whenever you get out of Egypt, you always confront a little tension, you always confront a little temporary setback. If you didn't confront that you'd never get out. (163)

Having subsumed the movement's challenges within the Exodus narrative, King offers the final lesson from the Ghana experience, the fact that "the forces of the universe are on the side of justice." What his own followers, along with their counterparts in Ghana and the rest of the world were experiencing was the dawning of a new age: "An old order of colonialism, of segregation, of discrimination is passing away now, and a new order of justice and freedom and goodwill is being born" (164).

In the third major section of the speech, King offered the second "geographical tour" paralleling the one with which he had begun his sermon. This time, however, his focus was the city of London, center of the vast British Empire—and the colonial exploiter of Ghana. His account, which highlighted Britain's grandeur, provided the counter element to his initial depiction of Ghana as the least powerful nation in the world, thus highlighting the magnitude of the reversal they had achieved. He recalled the awe he felt as he visited Buckingham Palace:

> I looked there at all of Britain, at all of the pomp and circumstance of royalty. And I thought about all of the queens and kings that had passed

through here. Look at the beauty of the changing of the guards and all of the guards with their beautiful horses. It's a beautiful sight. (164)

He told of visiting Westminster Abbey, "this great church, this great cathedral, the center of the Church of England," emphasizing both its architectural grandeur and its historical significance as the burial place of so much of the nation's royalty. As he continued, however, it soon became clear that his account of London's grandeur simply provided a backdrop for his claim that London was a "symbol of a dying system." There had been a day, he reminded his hearers, when "the queens and kings of England could boast that the sun never sets on the British empire." Now even countries as insignificant as Egypt, "a little country, . . . a country with no military power" (165), had successfully thrown off British rule.

As he built toward his sermon's ending, King took on the guise of a prophet: "Somehow I can look out, I can look out across the seas and across the universe, and cry out, 'Mine eyes have seen the glory of the coming of the Lord; He is trampling out the vintage where the grapes of wrath are stored.'" Speaking in the persona of the biblical character of John, he said, "I can look out and see a great number, as John saw, marching into the great eternity." Exhorting his audience to join the "march," he prayed,

> God grant that we will get on board and start marching with God because we got orders now to break down the bondage and the walls of colonialism, exploitation, and imperialism, to break them down to the point that no man will trample over another man, but that all men will respect the dignity and worth of all human personality. And then we will be in Canaan's freedom land.

Coming finally to the climactic moment of the sermon, King took on the identity of Moses himself, dramatically promising that the movement would succeed—whether he was there to see it or not:

> Moses might not get to see Canaan, but his children will see it. He even got to the mountain top enough to see it and that assured him that it was coming. But the beauty of the thing is that there's always a Joshua to take up his work and take the children on in. And it's waiting there with its

milk and honey, and with all of the bountiful beauty that God has in store for His children. Oh, what exceedingly marvelous things God has in store for us. Grant that we will follow Him enough to gain them. (166)

With this stirring language, followed by a final prayer expressing his vision that "we are made to live together as brothers," King concluded his sermon.

AN EVOLVING TRADITION

In his "Birth of a New Nation" address, King interwove his account of Ghana's liberation from British colonialism with references to the Exodus narrative in a way that provided a transcendent perspective on the struggle for racial justice even as it spoke to the immediate challenges he and his hearers faced in their local struggle for civil rights. His strategy appealed to the pervasive human tendency to employ stories, as Bennett observed, "to translate our impressions of a distant event into a form that will allow a listener in an immediate situation to grasp its significance."[9] Further, by juxtaposing Ghana's status as most insignificant and powerless nation within a continent that was itself the poorest and most exploited in the world against Britain's status as the world's most powerful nation, the "Britain that could boast, 'The sun never sets on our great Empire'" (164), he also placed Ghana's story within the archetypal plot of reversal. By repeatedly emphasizing Ghana's independence as representing the dawning of a new age, he also placed Ghana's story within a familiar apocalyptic framework. Both the theme of reversal and the new age possessed the kind of "universality of appeal" that Osborn attributed to archetypal metaphors, which, because they are attached to common human experiences and shared human motives, become "inescapably salient in human consciousness."[10] Most importantly for this study, King's sermon employed the long-standing practice among African Americans of viewing their lives and experiences in terms of the biblical story, a strategy that by this point had become an integral part of the movement's rhetorical tradition. This strategy involved two key components.

First, King closely connected his hearers' experiences with those of the citizens of Ghana. He spoke of "the pain and the affliction" suffered by Africans, recounting their experience of slavery and their history of being "exploited and dominated and trampled over," and he told of how they had finally become "tired of it" (156). That account not only paralleled his audience's experience but also echoed the language he had often used to characterize their history, as in the first mass meeting almost a year and a half previously, in a passage that had evoked thunderous applause: "There comes a time when people get tired of being trampled by the iron feet of oppression."[11] His descriptions of the constant resistance of the white power structure in Africa likewise paralleled their experience in the South. As he came to the close of his account of Ghana's independence, he merged his hearers' identity with that of Ghana's citizens even more closely by describing the Ghanaians' joy at being free from colonial rule in terms of a traditional Negro spiritual that he often quoted to describe African Americans' aspirations: "I could hear that old Negro spiritual once more crying out: Free at last! Free at last! Great God Almighty, I'm free at last!" (160). In this way, King merged the history and identity of the Ghanaians with that of blacks in the United States.

The second component of this overall strategy involved subsuming both "histories" within the larger plot of the Exodus story, which King did by first introducing the biblical narrative in the sermon's opening, highlighting it as a demonstration of the "stages that seem to inevitably follow the quest for freedom" (155), and then returning to that narrative at key moments throughout his account of Ghana's independence. He attributed the Ghanaians' yearning for independence to the fact that "there is something deep down in the very soul of man that reaches out for Canaan" (156), he paraphrased Britain's resistance in the words of Pharaoh, "We will not let you go" (157), he described the transition to independence as the "breaking aloose from Egypt" (160) and the Red Sea crossing, and he portrayed the adjustments that lay ahead for Nkrumah's government as the wilderness. For Ghana, as for blacks in the United States, he assures his listeners, "the Promised Land is ahead" (161).

This basic plot structure had been evolving in King's civil rights rhetoric from its first articulation in his "Death of Evil on the Seashore" sermon, which emphasized the Red Sea crossing symbolized by the *Brown v. Board of Education* ruling as the pivotal event in the story. In his boycott rhetoric, he expanded the signification of the Red Sea to include the successful boycott, and he introduced the wilderness as a crucial stage in the journey. Those elements in the tradition now became included in the "Birth of a New Nation" sermon, which presented the fully articulated, paradigmatic plot structure drawn from the biblical story and applied to both Ghana's liberation and the "liberation" of his own audience, a plot structure that can be schematized in this way:

EXODUS/CIVIL RIGHTS MOVEMENT PLOT STRUCTURE

EXODUS NARRATIVE	GHANA'S LIBERATION	CIVIL RIGHTS MOVEMENT
Stage One: Egyptian captivity	Slavery/Colonialism	Slavery/Segregation
Stage Two: The Red Sea crossing	Ghana's Independence	Montgomery Bus Boycott [*Brown vs. Board of Education*]
Stage Three: Wilderness	Economic/Cultural Challenges	Heightened racial tensions; opposition to the movement's goals
Stage Four: The Promised Land	Ability to "stand in the free world"	"Cultural integration"

Using this basic plot from the Exodus, King situated his hearers at a particular "stage" within a larger, predictable train of events, which he described as the stages through which people seeking freedom inevitably pass. This plot structure coherently explained their past and present, and it foresaw the "ending" of the story, their "arrival" in the Promised Land. In this way, the sermon continued the tradition begun in his "Death of Evil" sermon of inviting blacks to view their identity, history, and present situation through the lens of the ancient myth.

At the same time, King adapted the story in several ways as a response to his changing rhetorical situation, reflecting both his authority as an "interpreter" of the Bible and the movement as well as the elasticity of the cultural myth itself. As with his boycott speeches, first of all, King altered the stage at which he situated his hearers. In the initial sermon, King placed his audience at the point in the story where they had just crossed the Red Sea, so that the address focused on what they saw as they looked back across the water. As anticipated in his "code" references to the Exodus in the boycott speeches, his "Birth of a New Nation" sermon placed the citizens of Ghana, alongside African Americans in the United States, in the wilderness, which he presented as an inevitable stage in the journey. Having left Egypt and crossed the Red Sea, King said, Ghana will "now . . . confront its wilderness. Like any breaking aloose from Egypt, there is a wilderness ahead" (160). Likewise, he described his own people's story of freedom in this way: "Before you get to Canaan, you've got a Red Sea to confront; you have a hardened heart of a pharaoh to confront; you have the prodigious hilltops of evil in the wilderness to confront." He depicted the wilderness experience as one of difficulty and even disappointment: "The road to freedom is a difficult, hard road. It always makes for temporary setbacks." Yet its predictability, he argued, made the experiences of tension and difficulty a sign of the movement's progress: "Whenever you get out of Egypt, you always confront a little tension, you always confront a little temporary setback. If you didn't confront that you'd never get out" (163).

What is perhaps most remarkable about the sermon's depiction of the wilderness is its essentially positive character in King's discourse. Practically speaking, the citizens of Ghana were far beyond African Americans when it came to political power—indeed, from the vantage point of many in the civil rights movement, it might have seemed more accurate to say that Ghana had already entered the Promised Land. King nevertheless placed them in what he called the "wilderness of adjustment," characterizing their travails in terms of adapting themselves to an entirely new political and social order brought about by their dramatic liberation from British control. Blacks in the South were far from achieving that kind of self-determination. By identifying their stories so integrally and depicting Ghana's liberation as the dawning of the new age, however, King was able to cast their own experience of the wilderness as not only a predictable but also a positive stage in the journey, one in which blacks were beginning to see "not an old negative obnoxious peace which is merely the absence of tension, but a positive, lasting peace which is the presence of brotherhood and justice" (164).

A second development involves King's articulation of the agency behind the events that they were witnessing. In his original "Death of Evil" sermon, King depicted blacks' liberation from the Egypt of racial oppression and their passage through the Red Sea, symbolized

by the *Brown v. Board of Education* decision, as entirely a miraculous
work of God carried out through God's "providence." As the boycott
progressed, that agency shifted to include human effort in the quest
for liberation, reflected in the call for protesters to "continue with the
same spirit, with the same orderliness, with the same discipline, with
the same Christian approach."[12] With the "Birth of a New Nation" sermon, King's emphasis became almost entirely one of human agency. In
his opening, he summarized the theme of the recently released movie
The Ten Commandments as the "struggle of Moses . . . [and] his devoted
followers as they sought to get out of Egypt" (155). He described the
Ghanaians' motivation for seeking independence as "the throbbing
desire . . . in the soul that cries out for freedom" (156), attributing their
success in bringing Britain to the point of capitulation to the "continual agitation . . . [and the] continual resistance" of Nkrumah and
the devoted "masses who were willing to follow" (158). The task of
Ghana as it passed through its "wilderness of adjustment" would be to
address the economic, educational, and cultural challenges of a poor,
illiterate citizenry. Applying the lessons of Ghana to his own hearers
who were themselves "trying to move through the wilderness toward
the Promised Land of cultural integration," he stridently proclaimed,
"The oppressor never voluntarily gives freedom to the oppressed. You
have to work for it" (161). Contradicting the formulation of agency in
his original sermon, he urged his hearers not to labor under the illu-
sion that

> it's going to work out; it's going to roll in on the wheels of inevitability. If
> we wait for it to work itself out, it will *never* be worked out. Freedom only
> comes through persistent revolt, through persistent agitation, through
> persistent rising up against the system of evil.

Unlike his "Death of Evil" sermon, in which the story's protagonists
were almost surprised to find themselves on the far side of the Red
Sea, now he attributed the progress toward abolishing "segregation,
discrimination, insult, and exploitation" to the fact that "the Negro has
decided to rise up and break aloose from that" (163–64).

Only as he came to the last of his "lessons" from Ghana, after
he had persistently emphasized the importance of human action, did
King speak of the inevitability of success, expressed in his final application: "Ghana tells us that the forces of the universe are on the side

of justice," a testimony to the fact that "you can't ultimately trample over God's children and profit by it" (164). Similarly, his extended description of London and his indictment of the Church of England for sanctioning Britain's colonial exploitation of Africa culminated in his declaration that "God comes in the picture even when the Church won't take a stand" (165). He could, therefore, urge his hearers in Montgomery "to rise up and know that as you struggle for justice you do not struggle alone, but God struggles with you. And he is working every day," a statement that led to the prophetic, emotionally charged vision with which the sermon ends: "Somehow I can look out, I can look out across the seas and across the universe, and cry out, 'Mine eyes have seen the glory of the coming of the Lord," and then, in the words of Isaiah, to proclaim that "every valley shall be exalted, and every hill shall be made low; the crooked places shall be made straight, and the rough places a plain; and the glory of the Lord shall be revealed, and all flesh shall see it together" (166).

In this way, King continued to negotiate the dialectical tension between assuring his listeners that God was on their side, that God would bring them to victory, even as he repeatedly challenged them to persist in their campaign for racial justice—a dialectic for which the Exodus narrative was particularly well suited. In the biblical narrative, God brought about Pharoah's capitulation to Moses' demands through the ten plagues, miraculously parted the Red Sea, and led Israel through the wilderness. Yet the Israelites would have remained in Egypt had they not obeyed God's orders to leave and persevered in the journey to which God called them. Within the parameters of the biblical story, King could assure his audience that God would bring them success even as he declared that they would never reach the Promised Land without determined effort, a tension he sought to resolve, again using the language of the Exodus, in the closing paragraphs of the sermon:

> God is working in this world, and at this hour, and at this moment. And God grant that we will get on board and start marching with God because we got orders now to break down the bondage and the walls of colonialism, exploitation, and imperialism, to break them down to the point that no man will trample over another man, but that all men will respect the dignity and worth of all human personality. And then we will be in Canaan's freedom land. (166)

Only if they persevered in their resistance to injustice could they be assured of God's victory.

Third, King portrayed the protagonists in the Exodus story in a way that represented a significant development from his previous usage. In his "Death of Evil" sermon, the Israelites are presented as simple, one-dimensional characters, uniformly righteous, innocent sufferers, helplessly "reduced to the bondage of physical slavery under the gripping yoke of Egyptian rule." As the above discussion suggests, by the time he preached his "Birth of a New Nation" sermon, King had transformed the Israelites from the passive recipients of God's gracious actions to agents with the ability to choose to rise up against injustice and who, through their determined efforts, succeed in moving to the Promised Land. But King also shifted the moral character of the story's protagonists in a way that distinguished certain ones among them who were driven by self-interest from the "faithful masses" who followed Moses. After describing Ghana's desolation and then encompassing that desolation within the Exodus motif, with its "throbbing desire . . . that reaches out for Canaan," King acknowledged that some

> men have vested interests in Egypt, and they are slow to leave. Egypt makes it profitable to them; some people profit by Egypt. The vast majority, the masses of people, never profit by Egypt, and they are never content with it. And eventually they rise up and begin to cry out for Canaan's land. (157)

This provides the backdrop for his mention, four paragraphs later, of those who resisted Nkrumah's leadership after he had "worked hard and . . . started getting a following": "The people who had had their hands on the plow for a long time, thought he was pushing a little too fast and they got a little jealous of his influence." The "masses of people," however, "were with him, and they had united to become the most powerful and influential party that had ever been organized in that section of Africa" (158). Although he did not develop this theme further in the sermon, King at least raised the possibility that those who opposed him were driven by jealousy and self-interest, even insinuating that some were more concerned with protecting personal profit than with pursuing racial justice. That they were identified as citizens of Israel cooperating with Egypt in the exploitation of their fellow Hebrews made their crime all the more reprehensible.

A fourth, and related, development in King's sermon, one that is certainly not surprising given his rhetorical situation, has to do with the development of the rhetorical persona of Moses. Because this is a central thread that runs throughout King's rhetoric, continuing through to his final, "Mountaintop" speech, it merits a separate chapter later in this book. At this point, however, King was clearly beginning to identify himself explicitly with that persona in a way he had only suggested in the early months of his leadership of the movement. In his opening lines he condensed the Exodus story to "the struggle of Moses . . . [and] his devoted followers" (155). Later, he identified himself with Nkrumah, even as he cast Nkrumah as a Moses figure. His conclusion included language that would become immortalized in the final speech of his life, his famous "I've Been to the Mountaintop" address. The "Birth of a New Nation" sermon, therefore, clearly shows him consciously beginning to assume the role of one with the prophetic authority to define African Americans' circumstances and, more importantly, to announce their liberation from captivity and lead them to the Promised Land.

A PLAUSIBLE STORY

From the earliest points at which he first attempted to appropriate the Exodus to explain his hearers' circumstances, King showed a concern for making his application of the story believable, for establishing what Fisher called "narrative fidelity," the belief that the account "rings true" with the audience's sense of objective reality.[13] In his original "Death of Evil on the Seashore" sermon, King offered a litany of statistics in support of his claim that he and his audience were witnessing the truths reflected in the Exodus story in their own day. During the boycott itself, he would often connect specific events—the arrest of Rosa Parks, his own arrest for violating Alabama's antiboycott law, the Supreme Court's ruling that segregation in Montgomery's public transportation was unconstitutional—to the cultural myth as a way of demonstrating that blacks were seeing the work of God, that a miraculous, providentially ordained reenactment of the Exodus was unfolding in their midst. In some cases, he cited empirical facts to support his contention that the principles contained in the ancient story held true. In others, he evoked the biblical story to explain why particular events had occurred. What emerged in this rhetorical tradition, then, was a kind of interdependence between the story and historical events such that each shed light on the other, akin to what literary theorists have described as a hermeneutical circle. That strategy received its strongest expression in King's "Birth of a New Nation" sermon.

Traditionally, the hermeneutic circle referred to the reciprocal relationship that exists between the whole and the parts of a literary work. Schleiermacher captured this dual relationship by comparing it to the relationship of a sentence to the words that make up the sentence: "A whole sentence . . . is a unity. We understand the meaning of an individual word by seeing it in reference to the whole of a sentence; and reciprocally, the sentence's meaning as a whole is dependent on the meaning of the individual words."[14] This sense of circularity, of course, was a core tenet of biblical interpretation, prior to the Enlightenment, which posited a fundamental unity to Scripture constituted by the individual passages, but then sought to understand particular passages by reference to the whole.[15] With the rise of philosophical hermeneutics, the hermeneutic circle has alternatively represented a method of historical study, a philosophical problem, and a foundational tenet in the phenomenological study of human behavior.[16] But as Ricoeur noted, something like the hermeneutic circle is also an inescapable dimension in narrative, where the overall plot and the individual events within the plot exist together in just such a reciprocal relationship. The story's plot, even as it is "made up of events," at the same time provides the "configurational dimension . . . [which] transforms the events into a story."[17]

In his "Birth of a New Nation" sermon, King actually created this kind of dual relationship by interweaving his account of Ghana's independence (merged with the "history" of blacks in the United States) with references to the Exodus, creating a reciprocal interpretive relationship between the two, such that Ghana's independence was made intelligible by the Exodus "myth," while the Exodus "myth" was constituted by such events as Ghana's independence. On the one hand, the Exodus myth interpreted the Ghana story, so that what happened in Ghana was made meaningful as another example of the transcendent principles reflected in the ancient biblical narrative. On the other hand, the Ghana story provided the "empirical" evidence that the myth was true—that the dramatic reversal of fortunes narrated in the Bible was actually coming to pass in their own day. Indeed, Ghana's independence reflected a concrete moment in King's hearers' lived experience in which subjugated people of color, against overwhelming odds, had successfully thrown off the yoke of oppression. By recounting his experience of Ghana's freedom within the larger story of the Exodus, therefore, King was able to establish the "truthfulness" of his frequent claims that the "forces of the universe" are on the side of justice.

A crucial element in this dual interpretive relationship between the merged Ghanaian–African American "histories" and the Exodus myth involved King's manipulation of style within the passages devoted to each. As noted previously, King began his account of Ghana's independence by first describing the geography of Africa, punctuating his account with frequent references to the audience's prior knowledge, a rhetorical device that seems to have been intended to establish the verisimilitude of his account, along the lines that Fisher suggested.[18] Reinforcing this sense of objectivity, King employed a style in the sections where he narrated the history of Ghana's independence that was plain and straightforward, characterized by concrete, literal language and simple sentence structure, interspersed with a number of dates and population statistics. In similarly straightforward language, he recounted Nkrumah's arrival in America "with about fifty dollars in his pocket in terms of pounds, getting ready to get an education. And he went down to Pennsylvania, to Lincoln University." In each case, his accounts of Ghana's liberation employed a style that gave the impression that King was simply offering an "empirical" accounting of historical facts, an impression that helped to support his claim that the Exodus motif was truly a recurring historical pattern and that his audience was seeing that recurring pattern unfold both in their own experience and throughout the world.

That style shifted dramatically when King invoked the Exodus. In these passages, he employed the kind of sermonic style for which he was popular, a style characterized by abstract, figurative language, poetic sentence structure, quotations of verse and lyrics, and a variety of other stylistic features that characterized black preaching in its grander form. For example, he initially signaled the shift from the "history" to the myth with an epanaphora consisting of three parallel phrases that captured the motivation behind the Ghanaians' determination to be free: "But like all slavery, like all domination, like all exploitation, it came to the point that the people got tired of it" (156). Using the stylistic scheme known as antimetabole, he told of their "throbbing

desire" for freedom, fueled by their realization that "to rob a man of
his freedom is to take from him the essential basis of his manhood.
To take from him his freedom is to rob him of something of God's
image," a claim he elaborated by quoting Shakespeare's *Othello*:

> Who steals my purse steals trash; 'tis something, nothing;
> 'Twas mine, 'tis his, has been slave to thousands;
> But he who filches from me my freedom
> Robs me of that which not enriches him,
> But makes me poor indeed.

He continued this amplification of the yearning for freedom by invoking the familiar language of the Exodus: "There is something in the
soul of man that cries out for freedom. There is something deep within
the very soul of man that reaches out for Canaan." Later in the speech,
when he enumerated the "lessons" that derived from the history of
Ghana, King again launched into this sermonic style, even using folk
dialect to talk about the challenges faced by those who would seek
freedom:

> Ghana reminds us that whenever you break out of Egypt you better get
> ready for stiff backs. You better get ready for some homes to be bombed.
> You better get ready for some churches to be bombed. You better get
> ready for a lot of nasty things to be said about you, because you get-
> ting out of Egypt, and whenever you break aloose from Egypt the initial
> response of the Egyptian is bitterness. (163)

By shifting to a grander, more sermonic style in his evocations of the
Exodus, King thus imbued the "facts" surrounding the histories of
Ghana and his own hearers with a sense of grandeur, underscoring
the momentous nature of what had happened in Africa and what was
happening in their own experience.

King's "Birth of a New Nation" sermon thus perfected the strategy, present in most of his previous references to the biblical story,
of placing contemporary events and elements of the narrative in a
hermeneutic circle, interweaving a starkly "empirical" presentation of Ghana's history with highly stylized evocations of the Exodus narrative in such a way that the "history" verified the myth even
as the myth interpreted the history. From a broad vantage point, by

creating this reciprocal circle of interpretation King was able to ascribe to the "facts" of Ghana's independence and those of his own hearers the kinds of ideational and emotional associations that they had traditionally connected to the biblical narrative, inviting his hearers, in the words of the prophet Habakkuk, to "look at the nations, and . . . be astonished!" (Hab 1:5).

CONCLUSION

As this chapter has shown, King's "Birth of a New Nation" continued the long-standing tradition of inviting blacks to view their identity, history, and present situation through the lens of the ancient myth, presenting what is perhaps the most complete, paradigmatic application of the ancient story to the struggle for civil rights in the United States. The sermon thus represents in its most complete form the development of what might be called the "Exodus paradigm," which began with King's original "Death of Evil on the Seashore" sermon almost two years previously. At the same time, he was able to reinforce the plausibility of his use of the paradigm by interweaving his account of Ghana's independence and references to the biblical story within a reciprocal interpretive relationship in which each reinforced the other.

Through this paradigmatic use of the Exodus, supported by its connection to Ghana's history, King was able to reinforce his claims about the place his own hearers occupied within the story's plot. As noted previously in this chapter, when the boycott ended, it seem to many that racial tensions were growing worse rather than better and that the movement was further from its goal of racial harmony than when it had begun. Seen from the perspective of the Exodus narrative, these setbacks were not only understandable, they were predictable. God's people had crossed the Red Sea and were now facing the travails of the wilderness. The tensions and setbacks they now faced were actually a sign of their movement toward the Promised Land.

At the same time, King's merging of myth and history also helped to place the local struggle within a global perspective. Viewed within the world of King's sermon, the Montgomery bus boycott that had just concluded was simply one of many such movements happening across the world and throughout history. It was fitting, then, that King's

hearers should set their sights not simply on a fairer seating arrangement on the city's buses but, much more, on the pursuit of racial justice throughout the nation and even the world.

King's use of the Exodus narrative also helped to enhance his ethos
as the movement's leader. His portrayal of Nkrumah's life paralleled
his own, and both recalled the story of Moses. His rousing conclusion
powerfully evoked the story from Deuteronomy 24 where Moses was
granted a vision of the Promised Land. Together, they underscored his
authority as a prophetic leader with the power to proclaim his hearers'
identity as the people of God, to define their present circumstances
and, most importantly, to command the devotion of the "faithful
masses."

Finally, King's account of Ghana's history, viewed from the perspective of the Exodus narrative, provided the participants in the
struggle for racial justice with a powerful sense of hope for the success
of their struggle. Although King's assurances were conditional—his
followers would reach the Promised Land only if they kept moving,
remained a unified people, and endured the travails of the wilderness—the overarching claim of his rhetoric was that God would surely
lead them to victory, a claim demonstrated in the original Exodus and
in its subsequent reenactments. Ghana's story of independence provided empirical support for this hope. Once more the unimaginable
had happened. God had acted decisively in history to overturn power
structures that had seemed unassailable, taking a small, impoverished
people and liberating them from the most powerful empire in the
world. If God could do this for Ghana, surely God would do this for
blacks in the United States. Energized by this hope, King could thus
proclaim, "We will be in Canaan's freedom land. . . . [I]t's there waiting with its milk and honey, and with all the bountiful beauty that God
has in store for His children" (166).

CHAPTER 6

I'VE BEEN TO THE MOUNTAINTOP
King as the Movement's Moses

When he addressed the Montgomery bus boycott's first mass meeting on the night of December 5, 1955, King, just weeks from his twenty-seventh birthday, was virtually unknown outside of his congregation and the small collection of ministers who served the city's other black churches. He had been hastily installed earlier that day as president of the MIA, in part because he was a relative newcomer to the city and had not yet had opportunity to offend any of the major factions in the black community.[1] When he stood before that throng of faces crowded into the Holt Street Baptist Church, he had no real authority to command their respect or cooperation, save what black Christians traditionally accorded to any gospel preacher.

Within little more than a year, King would become a figure of international reputation, fulfilling speaking engagements all over the country, being featured in the national media and gracing the cover of *Time* magazine, and representing the movement across the globe. Given his initial obscurity, King's rise to become the "face" of the civil rights movement in so short a time was nothing less than meteoric.

Certainly, a number of factors can be offered to account for King's emergence as the movement's leader. His status as a member of an elite, educated black middle class was itself a badge of respect in the African American community. He had recently completed a Ph.D. from Boston University and served as minister of one of Montgomery's most well-educated and economically prosperous congregations, the Dexter Avenue Baptist Church. King was also clearly a charismatic orator. Further, once the movement began to receive the attention of the local and then the national media, members of the press naturally looked for a single individual that they could focus on as the campaign's spokesperson and representative, a role that King exploited with remarkable skill.

Central to this process, however, was one critical factor on which these other elements were predicated and to which they all contributed. This factor had to do with the way that King fulfilled his hearers' fervent expectation for the appearance of a black Moses. Given the central place that Moses held in the social knowledge that blacks brought to the protest, it was inevitable that his hearers would seek out characteristics in King that reminded them of the mythical hero. At the same time, within a year of the campaign's start, King began to assume that rhetorical persona explicitly and even self-consciously, using the kind of language about going to the "mountaintop" and seeing the "Promised Land" that would become immortalized more than a decade later in his address to the striking sanitation workers in Memphis on April 3, 1968. His emergence as the movement's leader and symbol thus resulted from something of a reciprocal process through which he and his audience negotiated an identity for King within the biblical narrative that they believed themselves to be reliving. This chapter traces the process through which King assumed the persona of the biblical hero, a process that initially identified King as the faithful, prophetic "narrator" of his audience's modern-day Exodus but that soon positioned him as a central character within the narrative itself, as the Moses who would lead his people to the Promised Land.

The Moses Persona

In ancient theater, the persona referred literally to the mask worn by an actor in a dramatic production and, from this usage, naturally came to denote the character or dramatic role assumed by the actor, as distinct from the identity of the actor himself or herself.[2] By donning the mask, the actor "became the *persona* that the mask symbolized."[3] Working from this understanding of persona as, in Campbell's words, "the imaginary, the fictive being implied by and embedded in a literary or dramatic work,"[4] a number of scholars examining a wide assortment of discourse have highlighted the way that assuming a particular role or identity is a crucial dimension through which rhetors gain a sympathetic hearing among their audiences.[5] Casey, for example, noted that a central rhetorical strategy through which women preachers in colonial America sought to legitimate their own public-speaking practices was to assume the persona of the biblical prophets, a strategy that pitted an assumption of direct divine inspiration against the authority of male preachers, which had been centered in ecclesiastical law and tradition.[6] Similarly, Japp's study of the rhetoric of Angelina Grimké focused on the dilemma that Grimké faced in choosing between two starkly different personae, that of Esther or Isaiah, from which to address society about the rights of women. She argued that the violent reaction of Grimké's audience to her Pennsylvania Hall address on May 14, 1838, ultimately represented a reaction to a persona that posed "a direct challenge to male authority in both religious and political spheres."[7]

As both examples suggest, these "masks" are often already present in culture, awaiting enactment by the rhetor:

> Rhetorical *personae* reflect the aspirations and cultural visions of the audiences from which stems the symbolic construction of archetypal figures.
> . . . [A]n archetypal figure is a classic figure that exists either in history, in myth, or in literature which has gained such prominence in the minds of people that rhetors who remind them of the archetype will gain additional credibility as leaders.

Because they already possess persuasive appeal among the members of an audience, these preexisting personae can be potent sources of ethos when the speaker who evokes the archetypal hero is accorded the hero's authority, a process that Ware and Linkugel described in this way:

> When a speaker's rhetorical self becomes so closely associated with some set of human experiences or ideas that it becomes virtually impossible for auditors to think of one without the other, then that individual stands in a symbolic relationship to those ideas or experiences. The speaker, in such cases, assumes the role of a rhetorical *persona*, . . . that prototype in their psyches whom they imagine will be their deliverer.[8]

In this way, the rhetor "transcends personal identity and becomes a truly charismatic leader."

As we emphasized in chapter 2, no archetypal hero, save perhaps Jesus himself, occupied a more prominent place in African American cultural history than Moses. From the days of slavery forward, in their conversations, songs, and sermons, blacks spoke repeatedly of Moses. When they envisioned God's deliverance from their present circumstances, their hopes found expression as a fervent expectation that God would raise up another Moses. So great was this expectation that at least one African American leader even complained of how easily blacks followed anyone who appeared in the guise of the biblical hero.[9]

The biblical account of Moses' call and leadership, of course, is far more complex than what became the Moses archetype in the black cultural tradition, yet that myth retained many of the overall contours of the biblical story. Moses is born during a period when Pharaoh, threatened by the increasing population of Hebrew slaves in Egypt, orders that all of the males born to Israelite women be cast into the Nile. Moses' mother defies that order by first hiding her infant for three months and then by placing him in a basket among the reeds along the bank of the Nile. At that moment, Pharaoh's daughter comes to the river to bathe, discovers the baby, takes pity on him, and adopts Moses as her own son. Moses is miraculously spared from death and grows up as a member of Pharaoh's household.

When he is a grown man, however, Moses kills an Egyptian taskmaster whom he sees mistreating a Hebrew slave, and he is forced to flee to Midian, where he marries, has children, and spends the next forty years settling into a life of herding sheep. At the end of those forty years, Moses receives a divine call when he encounters a bush that is burning but not consumed, out of which God speaks to him:

> The LORD said, "I have observed the misery of my people who are in Egypt; I have heard their cry on account of their taskmasters. Indeed, I know their sufferings, and I have come down to deliver them from the Egyptians, and to bring them up out of that land to a good and broad land, a land flowing with milk and honey, to the country of the Canaanites, the Hittites, the Amorites, the Perizzites, the Hivites and the Jebusites. The cry of the Israelites has come to me; I have also seen how the Egyptians oppress them. So come, I will send you to Pharaoh to bring my people, the Israelites, out of Egypt." (Exod 3:7-10)

Moses responds with great uncertainty and reluctance, offering God a series of reasons why he is not qualified to carry out this task and finally asking God simply to send someone else (Exod 4:13). In each case, God assures Moses that he will be given what resources he needs to lead the people safely out of Egypt. Thus assured, Moses accepts the task and becomes Israel's deliverer.

Moses returns to Egypt and, in an epic contest of wills with Pharaoh, succeeds in securing the release of Israel, miraculously leading them across the Red Sea, through the wilderness, and toward the Promised Land. Along the way, he is forced to deal with the resistance of other Israelites who, envious of his authority, seek to undermine his leadership, among them Aaron and Miriam, his brother and sister (Num 12), and Korah and his allies (Num 16). In each case God confirms Moses as the true leader of Israel.

Finally, Moses leads the Israelites to the border of Canaan, where they find themselves separated from the Promised Land by the Jordan River. Moses, however, is not able to enter the land himself but, as recorded in Deuteronomy 34, is permitted to ascend Mount Pisgah, from which God gives him a vision of the Promised Land. Having been assured that God would bring Israel safely into Canaan, Moses dies on the mountaintop.

Given the place that that story held in black consciousness, when King appeared before those first mass meetings, speaking of God's deliverance in the familiar language of the Exodus story, it was natural for his hearers to begin to see him in the light of the figure of Moses. As King grew in prominence among the participants in the campaign, those core elements in the story noted previously—Moses' miraculous escape from an early death, his sojourn in a foreign land, his divine call to return and deliver his people from bondage, his leadership in the face of jealous opposition from other leaders, and his prophetic vision of the Promised Land—would all become significant elements in the construction of his own identity. In some cases, those elements of the Moses story would be ascribed to King by those who heard him. In other cases, King would exploit dimensions of the Moses archetype himself. Together, they helped to create among blacks in the South the powerful sense that God had indeed raised up a Moses in their own day.

The Boycott Rhetoric: An Emerging Prophetic Identity

King's initial mass-meeting address, given on December 5, 1955, reflects the clear lack of ethos with which he began as the campaign's leader. Rather than assuming personal agency, he came before his hearers simply as a representative of the people, as "one of them":

> We, the disinherited of this land, we who have been oppressed so long, are
> tired of going through the long night of captivity. And now we are reach-
> ing out for the daybreak of freedom and justice and equality. (*applause*)[10]

As this passage suggests, however, in that capacity as their representative, King implicitly assumed an authority to define what his hearers
were witnessing, which he did by employing the Exodus motif. His
audience responded with fervor and enthusiasm. What followed was
a process through which King and Montgomery's black citizens negotiated a prophetic identity for himself as the movement's leader, an
identity out of which he would later claim his place as their Moses.

This pattern of implicitly enacting the prophetic persona while
avoiding direct claims of authority persisted through the first year
of King's leadership in the emerging movement. One of the striking characteristics of King's rhetoric during this period, in fact, is
his avoidance of the first person pronoun "I" in favor of the plural
"we." A newspaper account of King's address to a mass meeting in
March 1956 recorded King's declaration that "this is the year God's
gonna set his people free, and we want no cowards in our crowd."[11]
Three days later, in a mass meeting address at the Holt Street Baptist
Church, he warned of the tensions that protestors would face in their
quest for justice: "You don't get to the promised land without going
through the wilderness."[12] But, he predicted, "though we may not get
to see the promised land, we know it's coming because God is for it."
Thus could he urge, "Let us continue with the same spirit, with the
same orderliness, with the same discipline, with the same Christian
approach." When he addressed the annual gathering of the NAACP
in June of that year, he spoke of the inevitability that their movement
would succeed: "We believe that, and that is what keeps us going. That
is why we can walk and never get weary because we know that there is
a great camp meeting in the promised land of freedom and equality.
(*applause*)"[13] In his July 1956 address to the convention of the American
Baptist Assembly, he similarly asserted, "We have the strange feeling
down in Montgomery that in our struggle for justice we have cosmic
companionship. And so we can walk and never get weary, because we
believe and know that there is a great camp meeting in the promised
land of freedom and justice."[14] In a particularly moving address, given
on November 14, 1956, to a mass meeting called in response to the

Supreme Court's ruling that segregated transportation was unconstitutional, King likewise spoke as a representative of the people:

> We've got to keep going. We'll keep going through the sunshine and the rain. Some days will be dark and dreary, but we will keep going. Prodigious hilltops of opposition will rise before us, but we will keep going. (*Yes*) Oh, we have been in Egypt long enough (*Well*), and now we've gotten orders from headquarters. The Red Sea has opened for us, we have crossed the banks, we are moving now, and as we look back we see the Egyptian system of segregation drowned upon the seashore. (*Yes*) We know that the Midianites are still ahead. We see the beckoning call of the evil forces of the Amorites. We see the Hittites all around us but, but we are going on because we've got to get to Canaan. (*Yes*) We can't afford to stop. (*Yes*) We've got to keep moving."[15]

As these examples show, King's boycott rhetoric contained almost no claims to explicit, personal authority. We find in these addresses none of the first person, prophetic visions of the Promised Land that characterize his later rhetoric. Indeed, he rarely exhorted his hearers directly, proclaiming instead what "we"—he and they together—must do.[16] His authority derived, instead, from the power that the story itself held for its hearers and the way that King's rhetoric connected them, and himself, to that story.

Part of that authority lay simply in the way that King framed contemporary events within the cultural myth in a way that made sense for his hearers. In other words, his was the ethos of a believable narrator. As emphasized in chapter 3, even before the boycott had begun, King was connecting freedom movements across the world to the story of the Exodus, creating "narrative fidelity"—the connection between events in the story and events in the "real world"—by citing concrete statistics of the number of formerly oppressed peoples who had successfully won their freedom from the Egypt of colonialism. When the boycott actually began, given the obstacles to collective action faced by blacks in the South, the fact that they were able to unite and successfully boycott the city's buses for even one day would have seemed like a miracle, so that King's dramatic pronouncement that they were actually witnessing the story again would have struck his hearers as a real possibility, stirring the fires of hope among them. Later, as the campaign wore on and King depicted the problems protesters continued to face as the travails of the wilderness, his explanation fit the contours of the cultural myth in a way that made his account ring true. King thus established his own credibility by making plausible the connections between the Exodus story and what his hearers were witnessing.

As noted in chapter 4, that process was enhanced by the form in which King cited the ancient story, that of a "code" shared between storyteller and audience. With a word or phrase—the "long night of captivity," the "wilderness," the "Promised Land"—King evoked the larger body of social knowledge that had been such a prominent part of African American cultural history. He thus treated his audience as insiders, with himself, to the cultural code, inviting them to supply the larger body of content and the appropriate emotional reaction, which, as the audience reaction recorded in the transcripts of his speeches demonstrates, they did gladly.

But King's ethos went beyond plausibly identifying protestors' place within the biblical story; his rhetoric also positioned himself within that story as a prophetic voice proclaiming to God's people the "orders from headquarters."[17] In his first mass-meeting address, King assumed the power to speak on behalf of the people, identifying the nature of their internal state of emotion and proclaiming their intentions: "There comes a time when people get tired of being trampled over by the iron feet of oppression." They were tired of enduring the "long night of captivity" and were determined to reach out for the "daybreak of freedom."[18] That first night and throughout the boycott, moreover, he identified the significance of what his hearers were witnessing by proclaiming it to be a miraculous reenactment of the ancient story. When protesters continued to face obstacles in their quest for racial justice, he eloquently proclaimed that they had passed into the wilderness. In none of these passages does King explicitly claim a prophetic identity, attributing his role as leader to a divine call, for example, or articulating a personal prophetic vision of the Promised Land. Nevertheless, without explicitly claiming the role, by naming the significance of blacks' experience within the framework of the Exodus, King clearly performs the prophetic persona.

The expectations of his audience played a crucial role in this process. As chapter 2 argued, the Exodus story had been part of African American cultural history since the days of slavery, constituting a rich and enduring body of social knowledge that they had used to identify themselves and their oppressors, to make sense of their circumstances, to assure themselves that God was aware of their suffering, and to offer each other hope of deliverance. In particular, they longed for a Moses who would lead them to the Promised Land. As the transcripts of King's boycott speeches suggest, his hearers resonated powerfully with his evocations of the Exodus. Indeed, these are precisely the points at which King's audiences responded most vigorously, interrupting him with frequent shouts of "amen" and "yes" and often breaking into applause. In short, the audience reactions suggest that King's hearers were experiencing him in that role and signaling their strong approval in a way that rewarded his enactment of the prophetic persona. Septima Clark, an early, long-time southern activist, would later describe the power of King's evocations in this way: "As he talked about Moses, and leading the people out, and making and getting the people into the place where the Red Sea would cover them, he would just make you see them. You believed it."[19]

This suggests that King's emergence as a prophetic figure occurred through a process of reciprocal influence in which his hearers, steeped in the cultural myth of the Exodus, reinforced King's performance of the role even as King proclaimed that the long-awaited deliverance had begun. His assumption of the prophetic role reflects Hamera's view of persona as "performative in the postmodern sense of processual and relational: it is a system of relations which continually mediates exchanges between the 'self' and the world." Persona is thus a negotiated identity that emerges as a rhetor's words and actions conform to the "mask as audience-mandated artifice."[20] That King would eventually emerge in the role of Moses, in other words, was as much a result of blacks' expectations for a Moses figure as any deliberate attempt on King's part to assume the role of a prophet. At the same time, that emerging prophetic role prepared him and his hearers for his more explicit assumption of the persona of Moses, which would begin shortly after the boycott's conclusion.

THE DEFINING MOMENT

The manner in which King presented himself as leader of the emerging movement shifted dramatically in the early months of 1957. King went from being a prophetic voice among the people, addressing his hearers as one of them, to a divinely appointed leader over the people, their Moses. His assumption of this charismatic role was evidenced in the way that his speeches began to emphasize personal agency, with King speaking directly to them in the first person, and in press accounts that placed him within the predictable biblical story line of Moses' emergence as the leader of Israel. But it is most clear in the way that King's accounts of the Exodus began to highlight the role of Moses in the Exodus narrative and the way that, in his rhetoric, King began explicitly to enact the persona of the biblical hero.

The defining moment in this process, in many ways, occurred on Sunday, January 27, 1957. In the early morning hours, twelve sticks of dynamite had been found on the porch of King's home, unexploded apparently because of a defective fuse that was still smoldering when the bomb was discovered. Later that morning, King spoke to his congregation about what had happened, invoking the Exodus as a frame of reference for explaining the event. Unlike his previous references to the story, however, this one focused explicitly on his role as the movement's leader. Although the original text of the sermon was not preserved, the city's local newspaper, the *Montgomery Advertiser*, in an article titled "King Says Vision Told Him to Lead Integration Forces," carried brief excerpts of the sermon.[21]

As a central part of the sermon, King offered his first public accounting of what he viewed as a divine call to lead the movement, which had occurred almost exactly one year earlier. He told of how, because of the constant threats he and other leaders of the boycott faced in the early days of the campaign, he "went to bed many nights scared to death," and how, "on a sleepless morning in January 1956, rationality left me. . . . Almost out of nowhere," he continued, "I heard a voice that morning saying to me: 'Preach the Gospel, stand up for the truth, stand up for righteousness.'" After narrating his call, King's sermon shifted to a deeply personal prayer recalling this pivotal event. His prayer, ostensibly addressed to God, functioned rhetorically as an apostrophe, placing his audience in the position of "overhearing" the unique, intimate encounter out of which God had called him to lead the movement: "I realize that there were moments when I wanted to give up [leadership of the prointegration movement] and I was afraid but You gave me a vision in the kitchen of my house and I am thankful for it." The most dramatic moment of the sermon, however, came when King spoke these words:

Since that morning I can stand up without fear. So I'm not afraid of
anybody this morning. . . . Tell Montgomery they can keep shooting and
I'm going to stand up to them; tell Montgomery they can keep bombing
and I'm going to stand up to them. . . . If I had to die tomorrow morning
I would die happy, because I've been to the mountain top and I've seen
the promised land and it's going to be here in Montgomery.

Several features of this brief address point to King's assumption
of the persona of Moses. First of all, he narrated his own call to leadership in a way that closely paralleled the call of Moses, a connection
that his hearers would surely have recognized. He presented himself
as a reluctant prophet, one who did not seek the mantle of leadership
and who at times had wanted to give up. But, like Moses, he had had
his own burning-bush experience, hearing the "voice of God" in the
"vision" that he received early that morning in 1956. Assured that
God had called him to "stand up for righteousness," he was no longer afraid. Most obvious, however, was his evocation of the episode at
the end of Moses' life when, from the height of Mount Pisgah, he is
allowed to see the Promised Land and is assured that God will bring
Israel there safely. Echoing that vision, King for the first time spoke
directly in the voice of Moses.

King's sermon that morning thus represented a decisive moment in
a process that had been unfolding throughout the previous year, beginning with his first mass-meeting address, through which he enacted
the prophetic role in the movement by proclaiming that the ancient
story was being relived again. Only now, he was explicitly claiming
the persona of Moses. Given the stature already accorded to him as
a prophetic figure, and in view of the central role of Moses in African American cultural tradition, the associations that King's sermon
established between himself and the deliverer of Israel would have
been unmistakable to his audience. Even a white newspaper account
preserving only excerpts from the sermon detected King's assumption
of that persona, highlighting what it called his "vision," quoting his
prayer, and inserting a subheading titled "Promise Land" immediately before citing King's stirring proclamation that he had been to the
mountaintop.

KING AS MOSES

In the speeches that followed this initial, explicit assumption of the Moses persona, King's discourse reinforced that association in two important ways. First, his references to the Exodus highlighted the work of Moses as a key part of the story, in a way that the previous references had not. Second, King, in the guise of Moses, began to speak with new authority, self-consciously assuming his place as the movement's unquestioned leader in a way that he had not previously done. Both underscore the importance of the character of Moses as another element of the Exodus on which King could draw in his rhetorical leadership of the movement.

MOSES IN THE EXODUS STORY

As this book has emphasized, King had extensively employed the Exodus as a framework for explaining black experience months before any organized collective action had even begun. Once the boycott started, virtually all of King's mass-rally speeches invoked the Exodus as a strategy for exhorting the protestors to continue their efforts. Remarkably, however, the figure of Moses is virtually absent from those early references to the story. King's original "Death of Evil on the Seashore" sermon, which was structured entirely around the Exodus story, did not mention Moses at all. Instead, King told the story in this way:

> [The] Israelites, through the providence of God, were able to cross the Red Sea, and thereby get out of the hands of Egyptian rule. The Egyptians, in a desperate attempt to prevent the Israelites from escaping, had their armies to go in the Red Sea behind them. But as soon as the Egyptians got into the Red Sea the parted waves swept back upon them, and the rushing waters of the sea soon drowned all of them. As the Israelites looked back all they could see was here and there a poor drowned body beaten upon the bank.[22]

The mass-meeting addresses that King gave during the boycott itself likewise contain no mention of Moses. In only one case, in a speech to a mass meeting on March 22, 1956, did King make what might be viewed as an oblique reference to Moses' journey to the mountaintop when he stated, "Though we may not get to see the promised land, we know it's coming because God is for it."[23] But even here, King established the persona as a collective identity shared by all of the protestors who had "seen the promised land."

After the sermon of January 27, 1957, in which King recounted his "mountaintop" vision of the Promised Land, Moses becomes a significant figure in the narrative. In his "Birth of a New Nation" address, the story of the Exodus now became "the struggle of Moses, the struggle of his devoted followers as they sought to get out of Egypt."[24] When, in the same sermon, he told the story of Ghana's independence, he likewise emphasized the role of a single deliverer, an unmistakeable Moses figure, Kwame Nkrumah. He first told of how the British rebuffed efforts of the local chiefs to win independence, using the language of Pharaoh: "We will not let you go." In the next breath, King introduced Nkrumah in a way that pointed to his birth as the critical first step toward Ghana's deliverance and that hinted at divine providence as the source of his call to leadership: "About 1909, a young man was born on the twelfth of September. History didn't know at that time what that young man had in his mind." He described Nkrumah's life in a way that paralleled both the story of Moses and his own story, emphasizing how Nkrumah decided to return from a foreign land to the land of his birth and to his own people to help them find freedom. He told of how other local leaders became jealous of Nkrumah—again, paralleling both King's experience and familiar episodes in the story of Moses. When the Ghanaians finally received their independence, King said, it was because of "the persistent protest, the continual agitation on the part of Prime Minister Kwame Nkrumah and the other leaders who worked along with him and the masses of people who were willing to follow."

Three days later, on April 10, 1957, King addressed a freedom rally where, as he had often done in the past, he told the story of blacks in the United States from the perspective of the Exodus. He recounted how, as a result of the Supreme Court's 1896 "separate but equal" ruling, blacks had been "thrown and left in the Egypt of segregation," noting that, "at every moment there was always some pharaoh with a hardened heart who, amid the cry of every Moses, would not allow us to get out of Egypt."[25] The following year, while King was recovering from a stab wound inflicted by a deranged assailant in New York City, King's wife, Coretta, delivered an address on King's behalf to a Youth March for Integrated Schools, held in Washington, DC, on October

25, 1958. The address emphasized that "walking for freedom has been an integral part of man's struggle for freedom and dignity." It recalled similar marches in India and China, before turning to the story of the Exodus told in this way: "We all know how Moses, inflamed by the oppression of his people, led the march out of Egypt into the promised land."[26]

As these examples show, starting with the January 27, 1957 sermon, King's references to the Exodus now highlighted the character of Moses as a central figure in the story. God's deliverance of Israel was now predicated on the emergence of a single, divinely appointed leader, who leaves the familiarity of an adopted country to return to his people, and who leads them despite the opposition of his jealous detractors. Most importantly, the successful journey to the Promised Land now becomes dependant on the devotion of the faithful masses to his God-ordained leadership.

The focus on Moses as the central figure in the Exodus story in King's rhetoric occurred at precisely the same time that he was emerging as the symbol of the movement in the popular consciousness. As chapter 5 emphasized, in the early months of 1957, King was highly sought after as a speaker and was featured prominently in the national media. What is significant about his identity in the public consciousness was the way that it both reflected and reinforced his assumption of the mantle of the movement's Moses. The *Montgomery Advertiser* article, described previously, with its emphasis on his "divine call" and his prophetic "mountaintop" vision is a clear case in point. A second example is the feature article that appeared in *Time* magazine on February 18, 1957, which attributed the remarkable fact that "Negroes are riding side by side with whites on integrated buses for the first time in history" to "Martin Luther King and the way he conducted a year-long boycott of the transit system." The article offers a brief biography of King, emphasizing his Christian upbringing amidst segregation in the Deep South, describing his education in the North, and recounting his return to the South "to assume the role for which, as if by guess and by God, he had been preparing all his life." The article then narrates the boycott itself, highlighting King's leadership and focusing on the harassment King received from white officials of the Montgomery city government, and particularly on the threats from the "whites' lunatic fringe," leading to an account of King's "divine call" that had been the centerpiece of the January 27 sermon:

"One night," says King, "after many threatening and annoying phone calls, I went into the kitchen and tried to forget it all. I found myself praying out loud, and I laid my life bare. I remember saying, 'I'm here, taking a stand, and I've come to the point where I can't face it alone.'" From somewhere came the answer: stand for truth, stand for righteousness; God is at your side. Says Martin King: "I have not known fear since."

The article concludes by describing a mass meeting before a packed congregation in Montgomery, scheduled for 7:00 p.m. By six o'clock, the church is full, and in the moments before the rally begins, some forty black ministers enter the auditorium and take their places around the altar. But, as the article describes it, the audience is subdued until King himself enters: "Finally, the electric clock on the balcony reaches 7 o'clock. King and his top assistants enter; the crowd rises and applauds wildly."[27]

The sense of King's divine appointment to leadership is particularly underscored in a decidedly hagiographic *New York Post* article about King published on April 8, 1957, titled "Fighting Pastor." The article begins by stating that "the Martin Luther King, Jr., story is a saga which almost ended shortly after it began in Atlanta, Ga.," which it follows with a series of accidents in King's early life in which he faced possible serious injury or even death but was, instead, seemingly delivered as if by divine miracle. The first, which occurred when King was only five years old, is narrated in this way:

> Little Mike . . . was playing alone in the second floor hallway of the comfortable 13-room frame house at 501 Auburn Av. . . . As he leaned over the upstairs banister, he suddenly lost his footing and plunged head first some 20 feet to the ground floor and then catapulted through an open cellar door to the basement.

In bold print, the article then exclaims, "He got up and walked away unscratched." The article then narrates two other such incidents, each ending with similar exclamations, all of which lead to this assertion:

> Some worshipful followers of the 28-year-old minister who was thrust into international fame by his astute leadership of the successful Montgomery bus boycott movement tend to see in these incidents the hand of Divine Providence. "The Lord had his hand on him even then," one elderly Montgomery domestic . . . remarked last May while she and

50,000 other Negroes were trudging to and from work during the bus boycotts. "He was saving him for us. No harm could come to him."[28]

The account, of course, calls to mind the familiar episode when the infant Moses is miraculously delivered from the clutches of Pharaoh.

Later in the same year, the Fellowship of Reconciliation published a comic book titled *Martin Luther King and the Montgomery Story*, again commemorating King as the symbol of the movement. At the bottom of its cover page the comic includes scenes depicting the carpools and blacks and whites boarding a city bus together, but dominating the page is a drawing of King bathed in a stream of light seemingly emanating from heaven, a visual representation of his divine appointment to the leadership of the movement. The comic itself begins by briefly referring to the boycott but then immediately turns its focus to King: "One man's name stood out among the hundreds who worked so hard and unselfishly. That man was 29-year-old Martin Luther King, Jr." It portrays scenes from King's life, again emphasizing his upbringing in Atlanta, his education in Boston, and his determination to return to the South. One scene in particular shows him entering what presumably is the Dexter Avenue church, with this accompanying explanation: "Northern churches were open to the young minister, but in 1954, Martin Luther King and his bride decided to return to the south." The scene depicts King as saying, "It's HERE that God wants me to be, I know." Later, as the comic turns to the boycott itself, King's emergence is again the key to the protest: "A new and important leader had come on the scene—one America would feel proud of."[29] In this way, at the same time that King's rhetoric highlights the role of Moses in the story of deliverance, King himself emerges in the public consciousness as a Moses figure, divinely appointed as the leader of his people.

A VOICE OF AUTHORITY

Both reflecting and reinforcing that identity is the second shift that occurred during this period, a shift that involved the voice with which King addressed the people. As noted previously, in his early addresses King seemed to avoid assuming any authority to speak as a leader over his people, opting instead to speak to them as one of them, a position reflected most clearly in the way he framed his exhortations in terms of what "we" must do. As the boycott drew to a close, however, King began to claim personal agency as a leader, separate from the people, with the authority to exhort them directly. One of the earliest examples of this "voice of authority" occurred in the address he gave to the mass rally called to celebrate the Supreme Court's ruling against segregated public transportation, on November 14, 1956. Perhaps bolstered by the high court's decision in their favor, King told his audience,

> I say to you my friends, in conclusion, that we've been struggling for eleven months, but I want you to know that this struggle has not been in vain. It hasn't been in vain. If it has done one thing in this community it has given us a new sense of dignity and destiny. (*That's right*) And I think that in itself is a victory for freedom and a victory for the cause of justice. It has given us a new sense of dignity and destiny. And I want to urge you this evening to keep on keeping on.[30]

Then, in an exhortation that itself evoked the Exodus journey and that also led into a passage laced with references to the ancient story, King commanded them, "Keep on moving." Of course, in the sermon that he gave on January 27, 1957, hours after the unexploded dynamite was found at his house, King spoke powerfully in the first person, personally defying those who sought to threaten him: "Tell Montgomery they can keep shooting and I'm going to stand up to them; tell Montgomery they can keep bombing and I'm going to stand up to them," for, he announced, "I've been to the mountain top and I've seen the promised land."[31]

Three months later, in his "Birth of a New Nation" sermon, which focused on the Exodus and, in particular, highlighted the central role of Moses in the deliverance of God's people, King spoke with similar authority: "I say to you this morning, my friends, rise up and know that as you struggle for justice, you do not struggle alone. But God struggles with you. And He is working every day."[32] King then explicitly assumed the prophetic persona: "Somehow I can look out, I can look out across the seas and across the universe, and cry out, 'Mine eyes have seen the glory of the coming of the Lord.'" Several lines later, he similarly spoke in the prophetic voice:

> For I can look out and see a great number, as John saw, marching into the great eternity, because God is working in this world, and at this hour,

and at this moment. And God grant that we will get on board and start marching with God, because we got orders now to break down the bondage and the walls of colonialism, exploitation, and imperialism, to break them down to the point that no man will trample over another man, but that all men will respect the dignity and worth of all human personality. And then we will be in Canaan's freedom land.

Having evoked the Exodus and spoken in the guise of the visionary leader, King in his next breath clearly signaled that he envisioned himself as Moses and, what is more, that he expected that his hearers would see him in that role: "Moses might not get to see Canaan," he says, "but his children will see it."

What we find in 1957, then, is a process through which King goes beyond a more generalized prophetic persona to occupying the role of Moses. Several factors reflect and reinforce that identification. Beginning early that year, King's rhetoric began to highlight Moses as central to the Exodus story, even as press accounts and other popular accounts of King depicted him in ways that recalled the archetypal hero. Like Moses, he was miraculously delivered from death as a child, returned from a distant land in order to work for the deliverance of his people, received a direct communication from God to lead that deliverance, and had seen a vision of the destination, the Promised Land. During this period, King also assumed an authority to speak directly and explicitly in the role of the movement's leader. Taken together, these factors point to the same reciprocal process through which King initially assumed a prophetic role in the early months of the movement. His references to the Exodus and, particularly, his allusions to familiar elements in the life of Moses, increasingly associated himself with the archetypal hero. But he also found in his hearers and in the press an audience that was more than ready to cast him in this role.

That King had explicitly assumed this role was clear from a speech that he gave three years later, on April 10, 1960, at a Founders Day celebration for Spelman College, in Atlanta, titled "Keep Moving from this Mountain." Just over two months previously, he had moved to Atlanta, taking a position as a co-pastor with his father at the Ebenezer Baptist Church, so that he could devote more time to the SCLC. Also, just over a month before that, four students had requested and been refused service at the F. W. Woolworth's "whites only" lunch counter in Greensboro, North Carolina, sparking a sit-in movement that eventually spread to over fifty cities in nine states. In his speech, King commended the young people who had undertaken this collective action against segregation, calling the "student movement that has taken place at this time all over our country . . . one of the most significant movements in the whole civil rights struggle."[33] At the same time, he stated many of the same themes he had been articulating from the beginning of the campaign, emphasizing the movement's commitment to nonviolent resistance and the need for protesters to love their enemies.

What is particularly striking about the speech is the way that King began with an extended recounting of the Exodus story just as he had done in his original "Death of Evil by the Seashore" sermon, but in a way that spotlighted Moses as the deliverer of God's people. In language that recalled the original sermon, he said,

> I would like to take your minds back many, many centuries to a group of people whose exploits and adventures have long since been meaningfully deposited in the hallowed memories of succeeding generations. At a very early age in their history, these people were reduced to the bondage of physical slavery. They found themselves under the gripping yoke of Egyptian rule.[34]

In the next breath, King identified the agent of their deliverance: "But soon a Moses appeared on the scene who was destined to lead them out of the Egypt of slavery to a bright and glowing promised land." King went on to describe their journey through a "long and difficult wilderness," recalling how, among several varied reactions to the experience of the wilderness, some Israelites "abhorred the idea of going back to Egypt and yet could not quite attain the discipline and the sacrifice to go on to Canaan." Again placing Moses at the center of the story, King described what follows:

> As Moses sought to lead his people on, he discovered that there were those who would occasionally become emotionally and sentimentally attached to a particular spot so that they wanted to stay there and remain stationary at that point. One day when Moses confronted this problem, he wrote in the book of Deuteronomy, the first chapter and the fifth verse: "You have been in this mountain long enough, turn ye and go on your journey, move on to the mount of the Amorites." This was the message of God through Moses.

Having recounted the Exodus and emphasized Moses as the authoritative voice of God, King then assumed that authority himself, proclaiming that it was time to "move on" from the mountains of moral and ethical relativism, materialism, racial segregation, and "corroding hatred and crippling violence." If they would determinedly pursue racial justice while treating their enemies with love, he promised, they would achieve "not only desegregation, which will bring us together, physically but also integration, which is true intergroup, interpersonal living."

As he moved toward his conclusion, King invoked the Exodus once more, this time speaking directly in the voice of Moses: "I say to you this afternoon as you look ahead to the days to come, always have faith in the possibility of getting over to the promised land."[35] He emphasized the authority out of which he offered this hope:

> I do not stand here as a detached spectator. As I say to you this afternoon, have faith in the future, I speak as one who lives every day amidst the threat of death. I speak as one who has had to stand often amidst the surging murmur of life's restless sea, I speak as one who has been battered often by the jostling winds of adversity, but I have faith in the future. I have faith in the future because I have faith in God and I believe that there is a power, a creative force in this universe seeking at all times to bring down prodigious hilltops of evil and pull low gigantic mountains of injustice.

With this hope, and with his authority as God's voice to the movement, King commanded his hearers, "Keep moving. . . . Move out of these mountains that impede our progress to this new and noble and marvelous land. . . . If you can't fly, run; if you can't run, walk; if you can't walk, crawl; but by all means keep moving."

CONCLUSION

This chapter has argued that King's emergence as the undisputed leader of the civil rights movement resulted not only from his education, social status, or eloquence, but also from the way that those factors, combined with his prophetic invocations of the Exodus story, recalled for his hearers the figure of Moses, the mythical hero in African American cultural history. As we have reconstructed that process,

King at first simply announced that the ancient story was unfolding once again in the lives of his hearers, a claim with which they resonated powerfully. Soon thereafter, King's references to the Exodus began to highlight the central role Moses played in the story, and King himself began to speak directly in the guise of the biblical hero. Again, his audiences clearly welcomed these rhetorical developments. In this way, through a process of mutual reinforcement, King and his hearers, with the help of the press and other media, collaborated to create an identity for King not simply as the movement's spokesperson but as the movement's very "face," its symbolic representation.

As a consequence of this process, participants in the movement now granted King the ethos that had been accorded the mythical hero. In the popular consciousness, King's life had unfolded as if by a divine plan, providentially guided and preserved for this pivotal moment in history. He had been called, almost against his own will, to assume a role for which he felt inadequate. But as the movement's successes and his own testimony demonstrated, God had provided him with the inspiration and wisdom he needed to lead the people.

In the persona of Moses, King found a powerful resource for addressing the movement. He now spoke with the voice of authority, issuing commands and directives to his followers with a confidence and firmness absent from his early boycott rhetoric. He now had a strategy for addressing his detractors and rivals, casting them in the role of those jealous Israelites who opposed Moses in the biblical story, in contrast to the masses who, through their faithful devotion to Moses, safely entered the Promised Land. Most importantly, in the guise of the mythical hero, King could speak as if being transported before their eyes to the mountaintop, from which he could see the land toward which they journeyed. He thus offered emotionally compelling assurance that they would surely reach their goal.

Not surprisingly, as other protests against segregation began to occur in various cities in the South, particularly the sit-in movement and the Freedom Rides, King found himself called on to lend his considerable ethos and authority to these campaigns, which initially had had little connection to King and the SCLC. In each case, King's arrival brought national attention to these often-local efforts, signaling to the larger society that such seemingly isolated campaigns were actually part of a national movement. But much more, his presence conveyed a sense of legitimacy to the local protesters themselves, imbuing their campaigns with an energy and enthusiasm borne out of the sense that they were participating in a tide of social change that was sweeping through the country. Central to that authority was the persona that King now occupied within the movement's overarching narrative as their Moses—a persona that was clearly established by the time he and the other SCLC leaders arrived in Birmingham in early 1963 to launch a large-scale collective action against racial injustice in what was considered by most to be the most segregated city in the country. That he now occupied this role was poignantly captured by Fred Shuttlesworth, a powerful leader in the local black community, as he introduced King to the crowd at the first mass meeting of the Birmingham campaign on April 3, 1963: "Follow him to jail. In the end, he will lead us to freedom."[36]

CHAPTER 7

KEEP THE MOVEMENT MOVING
The Birmingham Protest

In her captivating memoir, *Carry Me Home*, Diane McWhorter pointed to 1963—what she called the "Year of Birmingham"—as "the national turning point" in the history of racial apartheid in the United States. Central to that historical shift, she wrote, were

> the huge nonviolent demonstrations that Martin Luther King Jr. staged in the spring, as school-age witnesses for justice overcame the weapons of the state, including Commissioner Bull Connor's police dogs and fire hoses. The spectacle—something that seemed to belong in the Old Testament rather than the American mid-century—nationalized the faltering civil rights movement and galvanized public opinion behind federal legislation to abolish segregation.[1]

In his study of the civil rights movement, *But for Birmingham*, Glenn Eskew similarly argued that the Birmingham campaign "ended the stalemate in national race relations," forcing the kind of changes needed for "opening the system to African Americans."[2]

As both accounts make clear, what happened in Birmingham in April and May of 1963 represents a climactic moment in the history of the civil rights movement. It brought the power of a well-planned, highly organized mass campaign to bear on one of the chief strongholds of racial oppression in the South.[3] It succeeded in pitting the city's economic establishment against its political leadership, and it evoked the moral outrage of the nation against the South's treatment of its black citizens by provoking the city's virulently racist commissioner of public safety, Theophilus Eugene "Bull" Connor, and his police force into violently attempting to quell the demonstration, which eventually compelled the Kennedy administration to get involved on the side of the protesters.

This chapter argues that the Birmingham campaign also represented a defining moment in the movement's rhetorical history. As this book has shown, a central part of that history was the persistent discursive practice, dating back to the beginning of the movement, of connecting the struggle for racial justice with the biblical story of the Exodus. In Birmingham that use of the Exodus became focused almost exclusively on the theme of movement, a theme that was powerfully reinforced by the "freedom songs" that played such an important role in the nightly mass meetings from which the protesters drew their inspiration. This shift in the use of the Exodus coincided with the emergence of the march as the movement's principal mode of collective action. The march and the Exodus were thus deeply intertwined. The Exodus myth provided the symbolic context out of which the march became the movement's most important means of protest, imbuing the act of marching with significance as a concrete enactment of the story. Because of its connection to the ancient story, the march became more than simply a medium for demanding equal treatment under the law. Instead, it became a ritual through which protesters could, by means of a bodily performance, act out their most deeply held cultural narrative.

THE ROAD TO BIRMINGHAM

In the months following the Montgomery bus boycott, King found himself with a national platform from which to denounce the evils of racism, which he did in a relentless schedule of speeches across the nation and in other parts of the world. At the same time, movement leaders found the transition from a local protest to a national campaign to be far more challenging than expected, and they struggled to maintain any momentum from the Montgomery movement. For the next three years, the newly formed SCLC floundered, struggling to raise enough funds just to meet the payroll for its tiny staff and unable to formulate a coherent strategy for combating segregation in the South.

Two significant events helped to change that situation. The first occurred in early 1960, when groups of young black women and men, most of them college students, began to stage sit-ins at segregated lunch counters in cities throughout the South. These demonstrations, which began in Greensboro, North Carolina, on February 1, 1960, and soon swept across the South, brought new life to the struggle against segregation. Because of his role as the symbol of the fight against racism, King was inevitably drawn into the student-led movement, initially when he answered a plea to address a student rally in Durham, North Carolina, on February 16 and then two months later through his guidance in the formation of what became the Student Nonviolent Coordinating Committee (SNCC), established to bring about greater cooperation among the individual, local protests. But his full involvement came in October of 1960, when students in Atlanta, where King had moved at the beginning of the year to serve as a co-pastor at the Ebenezer Baptist Church, decided to stage a sit-in at the segregated Rich's Department Store and prevailed upon King to join them in the protest. As a result, he and thirty-five others were arrested, and King was eventually sentenced to four months in a state prison for violating conditions of parole from a previous tax-case settlement. The event brought national attention to King once again, and it also secured the involvement of Senator John F. Kennedy, then a candidate for president, whose behind-the-scenes maneuvering helped win King's early release.

The second event was the Freedom Rides, which began in early 1961 under the leadership of the Congress of Racial Equality (CORE) director, James Farmer. The rides, which originated in Washington, DC, on May 4, were intended to challenge segregation in bus terminals throughout cities in the South.[4] After making their way through a number of mid-South cities, the riders arrived in Atlanta on May 13, where King greeted them and gave them his blessing. To this point, they had encountered little resistance and garnered almost no publicity. The next day, however, a violent mob attacked one of the buses as it neared Anniston, Alabama, breaking its windows and setting it on fire, while others boarded the second bus at the Anniston station and severely beat several of the passengers—events all captured in the national press. As Garrow noted, "Pictures of the burning bus and bloodied riders flashed around the world showing the true temper of the white South."[5] After several delays the effort continued days later, and the riders were again viciously attacked by a mob of angry whites as they arrived in Montgomery. Again, King found himself drawn into the protest, as he traveled to Montgomery to address a rally of over one thousand people held at Ralph Abernathy's First Baptist Church.

More importantly, through his previous contacts with John F. Kennedy and his brother Robert, now U.S. attorney general, King was able to help pressure the Kennedy administration to put the weight of the federal government on the side of the fight against segregation, which it did on May 29, 1961, when Robert Kennedy announced that he would ask the Interstate Commerce Commission (ICC) to ban segregation in all facilities that involved interstate travel.

Both protests affected King profoundly. They further underscored his status as the movement's leader and symbol. More importantly, although the SCLC was at this point focusing most of its attention on voter registration and citizenship training for blacks,[6] King came to recognize the importance of direct action:

> The student movement had resolved the debate about civil rights methods in favor of direct action, and had thrust King to new prominence as the principal symbol of the southern movement. The sit-ins, his stay in Reidsville prison, and the Freedom Rides had given King a greater understanding of the challenges the movement faced and the efforts needed to overcome them. Nonviolence could not simply be a tool of persuasion for convincing southern whites of the evilness of segregation, it had to be a political strategy, a means by which the movement could defeat the forces of evil by rallying greater support to its own side. That lesson had been brought home by the Freedom Rides, by the forced activation of a reluctant Kennedy administration, and by the triumph—the ICC order—that eventually emerged from the crisis brought on by the rides.[7]

King further refined his understanding of the role of direct action in what was largely viewed as an embarrassing failure, the "Albany movement," which took place in Albany, Georgia, in 1962. Unlike the sit-in movement and the Freedom Rides, the Albany movement was aimed at ending "all forms of racial domination in Albany. Demonstrations were to be held against segregated buses, libraries, bowling alleys, restaurants, swimming pools, and other facilities."[8] The campaign, however, was hampered by constant infighting between different African American organizations (particularly, resentment among SNCC leaders toward King), by its inability to overcome the shrewd tactics of police chief Laurie Pritchett, who upheld local segregation laws by arresting protesters without resorting to police brutality, and by the naïve assumption of the protesters themselves that they could negotiate in good faith with the white political-power structure. As a result, the movement was unsuccessful in securing any concessions from the city and eventually died out entirely by August of 1962. Nevertheless, for a time, the campaign had succeeded in mobilizing virtually the entire black community in organized, large-scale action against segregation, revealing the protesters' willingness to go to jail for the cause and demonstrating the economic power that the black community could wield through boycotts and mass protests. King and the other SCLC leaders emerged from their experience in Albany, combined with what they had witnessed in the sit-in movement and the Freedom Rides, determined to find a location where there was a highly committed, mobilized black community that could direct its action against economic rather than political leaders, where the SCLC could operate without competition from other organizations, and where the local police force was of such a character that protesters would provoke the kind of violent reaction that would gain the attention of the media and prod the federal government to take action. That place was Birmingham.

MARCHING TO FREEDOM: THE BIRMINGHAM CAMPAIGN

The Birmingham campaign—what McWhorter called the "climactic battle of the Civil Rights Movement"—began in April, 1963, with a series of demonstrations designed to augment a boycott of the city's segregated downtown department stores already in progress. In the first phase of the effort, small groups of protesters would arrive downtown and engage in sit-ins or pickets and would be promptly arrested by Bull Connor's police force. These protests, however, soon gave way to what became the campaign's chief weapon, the march, which sent waves of demonstrators walking toward city hall, only to be arrested and taken to jail.

The first march in the Birmingham campaign, led by Fred Shuttlesworth, a local leader and head of Birmingham's local protest organization, the Alabama Christian Movement for Human Rights (ACMHR), took place on Saturday, April 6, and included some thirty volunteers who were all arrested. The next day, King's brother, A. D. King, led a second small march to the downtown section, this time to be met by Connor's snarling police dogs in a violent confrontation that was covered in the national press, with another two dozen protesters arrested. In the following days, Garrow pointed out, the nightly mass meetings began to be "larger and more enthusiastic."[9] Five days later, on Good Friday, King himself joined about fifty volunteers who were arrested as they made their way downtown. All told, the protesters managed to stage a march every day from the beginning of the campaign until the city leaders finally capitulated to their demands just over one month later.

The campaign's high point occurred on May 2, 1963, when hundreds of young people, some of them children as young as elementary school age, joined the marches. As one leader put it, "On the appointed day, hundreds of teenagers met in Sixteenth Street Baptist Church. As fast as they arrived, they were sent downtown in successive waves, each larger than the last. Before nightfall, more than a thousand were behind bars."[10] With the jails rapidly filling and unable to stem the crowds, Connor attempted to turn back the protesters using water canons and police dogs in violent confrontations that were broadcast in the national and international press.

Just over a week later, on May 10, 1963, under pressure from business leaders and the Kennedy administration, city leaders announced that an agreement had been reached to integrate the city's downtown business establishments, to implement a nondiscriminatory hiring plan for the city's businesses and industry, to release all demonstrators from jail without requiring them to post bond, and to establish a biracial committee to foster continued discussion between the city's black and white communities. More importantly, the protest had far-reaching national implications as well, which Morris described in this way:

> Not only did the SCLC accomplish its specific goals in Birmingham, but it also accomplished its long-range goal by setting in motion hundreds of movements designed to destroy segregation and forced the national government to pass the 1964 Civil Rights Act, which legally prohibited racial segregation. Indeed, within ten weeks following the Birmingham confrontation 758 demonstrations occurred in 186 cities across the South and at least 14,733 persons were arrested.[11]

The marches thus represented the key strategic element in the protest, placing constant pressure on the city's political structure, calling attention to the protest, and reinforcing the boycott.

Not surprisingly, as the surveillance reports prepared by city detectives who attended the nightly mass meetings show, the marches held a central place in the consciousness of the movement participants themselves. As they had from the days of the Montgomery bus boycott, these gatherings, part revival services and part political rallies, typically included songs and prayers, collections of monetary donations, and as many as four or five different addresses, sometimes by local ministers involved in the movement and by King and Abernathy. The speakers would urge support of the boycott, announce upcoming voter registration efforts or other demonstrations, such as sit-ins, "read-ins," in which young black people would occupy segregated libraries, or organized attempts to attend all-white church services. But by far, the marches were the subject of greatest attention in the mass meetings.[12] In some cases, different speakers would announce upcoming marches, inviting volunteers to join them. The following is an example of the kind of announcement that appears numerous times in the police reports, taken from a mass meeting on April 5:

> Reverend Fred Shuttlesworth then spoke about the effectiveness of the downtown boycott, about the Negroes still in jail, and about seeing the Mayor and Commissioner Connor downtown. He said they were going to march on City Hall the next day and that he wanted to drink some of that white water in the City Hall and see if it tasted any better than the colored water. He then announced the next meeting the following morning at 10:00 A. M. at the Thurgood Baptist Church, 7 Avenue and 11 Street North, where they would organize the march on City Hall, to be led by the Reverend Billups and Reverend Shuttlesworth. He called for volunteers for the "freedom march". [sic] 35 people volunteered.[13]

Four days later, on April 9, the mass meeting featured blind jazz vocalist and recording artist Al Hibler, who was recruiting for a similar march the next day. The report of the next day's meeting included this account:

> At this time Al Hibler, Negro singer, sang two songs and told of how he led the march on City Hall and Bull did not arrest him. He said they did not have anything at the City Jail that he could do. He said, Bull asked him, "Boy, what are you doing down here?" Al told him that he came here for freedom. He said he asked him, "Why don't you put me in jail, Bull? He said, "You are blind and can't work." I said I can do anything

> you can do, and then a Sergeant took me back to my motel, but I'll be
> there again tomorrow.[14]

The next day, Abernathy defiantly proclaimed to another audience,
"We ain't afraid of white folks anymore. We are going to march tomorrow. . . . Fred Shuttlesworth and I are marching Good Friday."[15]

In some cases, the speakers would give instructions to marchers
on how to conduct themselves during the marches, as when Andrew
Young urged his hearers, "We have a non-violent movement, but it's
not non violent [*sic*] enough. . . . We must not 'boo' the police when
they bring up the dogs or call them names—we must praise them. The
police don't know how to handle the situation governed by love, and
the power of God."[16] Often, they would report on marches held earlier
that day, as when King's uncle, Joel King, "made a short talk saying he
was glad to be in the Freedom March and was glad to go to jail,"[17] or
Shuttlesworth told of how

> our little folks made it to the City Hall today to pray. Nobody else has
> been able to do it. We asked for permission to come to the City Hall and
> pray. All we want to do is just walk, but everywhere we went the police
> blocked our way. They sure were tired. One policeman said to me, "Hey
> Fred, how many more have you got" and I said at least 1,000 more; and
> the policeman said, "God Almighty."[18]

But always they urged people to keep marching. As Abernathy told
protesters at a rally on May 9 in preparation for a one-day moratorium
on the demonstrations pending the outcome of the negotiations that
were then going on, "We are negotiating at this time with business and
civic leaders and we are not going to back up one bit so I want all of
you to be at the 16th Street Baptist Church in the morning in case we
have to march. I want you to be sure to wear your walking shoes."[19]
The police records thus bear out Wyatt Walker's observation of what
was at the center of the movement: "We just made that [the march]
the focal point and had those marches every day. Day after day. Week
after week."[20]

As Morris emphasized, the "invocation of black church culture"
played a crucial role in sustaining these daily demonstrations by underscoring the need for unity and cohesiveness and bolstering the protesters' courage and determination, particularly in the face of the violent

attempts of Connor's forces to turn them back. Morris described one particularly tense moment in which a throng of protesters faced Connor's angry orders to turn back and his command to the police force, "Dammit. Turn on the hoses!" Suddenly, the protesters dropped to their knees and began to pray:

> The outcome of this event can be explained by examining the church culture. . . . They had sung in church over and over that ninety-nine and a half percent would not do. In this tense situation blacks asked God to give them strength, just as they had during the services of the black church down through the centuries. When confronted by high-power water hoses, blacks reached deep down into their psyches or souls and summoned up that "something extra."[21]

Connor's forces seemed paralyzed, and the protesters rose from their knees and continued their journey. Andrew Young recalled,

> Everybody got up and started walking. We walked right on through. "Bull" Connor was standing there screaming: "Stop them, stop them!" The men with the fire hoses had evidently been caught in all this, and they just dropped them, and the dogs were just as quiet. Walking through the red fire trucks, folks started preaching about the Lord parting the Red Sea again.[22]

At the heart of that "church culture," Young's recollection shows, was the Exodus story.

THE SYMBOLIC CONTEXT OF THE BIRMINGHAM CAMPAIGN

As this book has emphasized, from its earliest days up to the Birmingham campaign, few themes appeared as frequently in civil rights–movement discourse as the biblical story of the Exodus. Months before the first organized campaign had even begun, in his "Death of Evil on the Seashore" sermon, King had applied a creative retelling of the biblical story of the Red Sea crossing—the event that marked for the people of Israel "a joyous daybreak that had come to end the long night of their captivity"[23]—to the experience of blacks in United States. During the Montgomery bus boycott itself, King's speeches frequently contained allusions to the Exodus, drawn, in commonplace fashion, from the paradigmatic application of the narrative to the struggle for civil rights presented in his "Death of Evil on the Seashore" and his "Birth of a New Nation" sermons. Often these references figured prominently in the climactic, emotionally charged appeals with which King would conclude his speeches. When tensions rose during and after the boycott, he equated experiences of opposition with the wilderness experience of ancient Israel: "You don't get to the Promised Land without going through the wilderness."[24] He likewise employed Exodus language to exhort protesters to continue the struggle, using language suggestive of his later appeals during the Birmingham movement:

> Some days will be dark and dreary, but we will keep going. Prodigious hilltops of opposition will rise before us, but we will keep going. (*Yes*) Oh, we have been in Egypt long enough (*Well*), and now we've gotten orders from headquarters. The Red Sea has opened for us, we have crossed the banks, we are moving now, and as we look back we see the Egyptian system of segregation drowned upon the seashore. (*Yes*) We know that the Midianites are still ahead. We see the beckoning call of the evil forces of the Amorites. We see the Hittites all around us but, but we are going on because we've got to get to Canaan. (*Yes*) We can't afford to stop. (*Yes*) We've got to keep moving.[25]

King continued to draw heavily on the Exodus myth in the five years following the boycott, as he crisscrossed the nation delivering speeches aimed at sustaining optimism felt during the protest. In his "Facing the Challenge of a New Age" address, delivered at an NAACP Emancipation Day rally in Atlanta on January 1, 1957, he proclaimed that movements for freedom elsewhere in the world had "broken aloose from the Egypt of colonialism" and were "moving through the wilderness of adjustment toward the promised land of cultural integration."[26] Buoyed by the hope that truth would inevitably triumph over evil, he said, protesters in Montgomery "could walk twelve months and never get weary (*Yeah*), because we know there is a great camp meeting in the Promised Land of freedom and justice. (*applause*)" In an address delivered at the close of a conference on non-violent resistance in Mississippi on September 23, 1959, King warned that "the flight from the Egypt of slavery to the glorious promised land is always temporarily interrupted by a bleak and desolate wilderness, with its prodigious mountains of opposition and gigantic hilltops of evil."[27] Later that year, addressing the annual Institute on Nonviolence and Social Change in Montgomery, he likewise observed that "the road from the Egypt of slavery to the Cannah [*sic*] of freedom is an often lonely and meandering road surrounded by prodigious hilltops of opposition and gigantic mountains of evil."[28] For this reason, he urged in his address to the students of Spelman College in Atlanta on April 10 1960, just over two months after the start of the student-led sit-in movement, to "keep moving. Move out of these mountains that impede our progress to this new and noble and marvelous land. . . . We must keep moving. If you can't fly, run; if you can't run, walk; if you can't walk, crawl; but by all means keep moving."[29]

Although few of the speeches from the Albany campaign have been preserved, what is available indicates that the Exodus story persisted as the backdrop for the movement. At one mass meeting, held on July 16, 1962, one of the local ministers introduced King in this way: "It gives me a good deal of pleasure at this time to again present to Albany one who is now one of us, pledged to stay with us throughout the civil rights struggle, none other than the twentieth-century Moses, Dr. Martin Luther King."[30] Later in the same rally, King's lieutenant, Ralph Abernathy, began an address by leading the congregation in the singing of a song that evoked the biblical story, "Ain't Gonna Let Nobody Turn Me Around":

> I ain't gonna let nobody
> Turn me around! Turn me around! Turn me around!
> Ain't gonna let nobody turn me around,
> I'm gonna keep on a-walkin', keep on a-talkin',
> Marchin' down to freedom's land.
>
> Ain't gonna let Chief Pritchett
> Turn me around! Turn me around! Turn me around!
> I ain't gonna let Chief Pritchett turn me around,
> I'm gonna keep on a-walkin' keep on a-marchin',
> Marchin' down to freedom's land.[31]

He went on to build his address around the Exodus in a way that echoed King's use of the story: "Now when Moses went down to Egypt to lead the children to Canaan, he found three groups of people. And do you know, I'm sorry to tell you, but we still have those three groups to deal with today." The first group, he said, "was the group that did not want to leave Egypt. They wanted to stay in Egypt. They wanted to die in Egypt. And they didn't want to leave because they were caught in the crippling shackles of fear. And they were afraid to venture out." Although the recording ends shortly after this passage, the Exodus story clearly provides the overall structure and content for the address. Abernathy similarly began a speech four days later at Albany's Kiokee Baptist Church by again singing "Ain't Gonna Let Nobody Turn Me Around," a song that depicts the protest's goal as "freedom's land."[32] He then told his audience that there are

> a lot of people in this nation who don't believe that the Negro can get to freedom from where he is now. But we have news for them. I don't care where you are located, you can get to any point if you're willing to go far enough and if you're willing to make enough turns and follow some shortcuts and some detours. So we know we can get to freedom from where we are now. We know that it's going to be a hard struggle, but we can get there.

Although not explicitly citing the Exodus, that story clearly lies behind his depiction of freedom as the destination toward which he and his hearers are traveling. In a rally held several days later, on July 24, 1962, SNCC staffer Charles Jones recalled the confrontation between Moses and Pharaoh as he described a courtroom scene in Albany in which a judge had overruled an injunction against the Albany protests. Jones told of how he was "never more proud, I was never more proud . . . than to be in that courtroom and see black men and women of stature . . . pleading the cause of the Negro, not only in Albany, but throughout this nation, saying, 'Set my people free.'"[33]

These examples indicate that from the beginning of the civil rights movement, African Americans were exposed to a tradition of public address that persistently employed this cultural myth to frame events in their experience in a way that profoundly shaped the movement. In the world view created by this discourse, protesters participated in a collective, symbolic identity as the people of God, long held captive in Egypt but now set free by God's mighty hand, a collective identity that theologically legitimated their demands for justice. Further, this use of the Exodus explained the tensions and problems they faced in their efforts to challenge racial oppression as the predictable travails of the wilderness. It endowed King with the persona of a prophetic leader, the people's Moses. Most importantly, the narrative provided protesters with the promise of eventual success.

"WE ARE ON OUR WAY": BIRMINGHAM AS EXODUS

This rhetorical use of the Exodus narrative continued during the Birmingham phase of the movement, reflecting the persistent salience of the myth within the movement's tradition of oratory. At the same time, Exodus references underwent a marked change from the previous usage, which had applied diverse features of the story to a variety of elements in African Americans' experience. During the Birmingham campaign, that usage was focused in two areas.

The first emphasized King's identity as the movement's Moses.[34] On April 3, 1963, the night that King arrived in Birmingham with Ralph Abernathy to help lead the protest, Shuttlesworth introduced King to a mass meeting at the St. James church in words that clearly placed him in that role: "Follow him to jail. In the end, he will lead us to freedom."[35] Three days later, after King had addressed a mass meeting, Abernathy began his address to the same crowd with these words: "You have just heard our Moses."[36] At a later point in the protest, Abernathy similarly introduced King as "the Moses of our day,"[37] and as the negotiations with the white city leaders were reaching their critical point, on May 9, 1963, he spoke of King in a way that recalled the story: "Two thousand years ago God sent Moses down to Pharaoh to set their people free."[38] Although not referring explicitly to the Exodus, Abernathy also made clear allusion to the story when he told an audience the next day, "There isn't but one Martin Luther King. (*applause*) God sent him to lead us to freedom. (*Amen*) Are you gonna follow him? (*Yes*) Is he our leader? (*Yes*) Then say, 'King.' (*King*) (*sustained applause*)"[39] The rhetoric of the Birmingham campaign thus shows continuity with the tradition, unfolding since the time of the Montgomery bus boycott, of placing King securely in the role of Moses. That most of these references are made by Abernathy likely reflects his desire to overcome the rivalry that other black leaders had felt toward King in previous campaigns.[40] Nevertheless, as the audience reaction suggests, the protesters themselves clearly supported his blatant assertion of King's unique prophetic authority.

Far more striking and significant than these references to King as Moses, however, is the way that the use of the Exodus during the Birmingham protest became drastically compressed into a cluster of words centered on the theme of "movement"—words like *going, moving, rolling, climbing* and *walking, path* and *highway,* and *follow* and *lead.* On April 3, 1963, during the same mass meeting noted previously, in which Shuttlesworth had introduced King as the one who would lead them to freedom, Abernathy reiterated, "I have come with Martin Luther King to help lead you," which he followed with an appeal for volunteers to join the protest.[41] Approximately seventy-five people came forward to begin intensive training for the marches that would soon begin. Three days later, on April 6, some thirty demonstrators were arrested when they attempted to march to the city hall in order to hold a prayer session, beginning what would turn out to be thirty-four straight days of protest marches.

As the Birmingham effort continued, so did this use of the journey motif. Police surveillance records from the mass meetings show that the theme of movement pervaded the speeches during the nightly gatherings. "We are going somewhere," King told a meeting on April 5.[42] "The movement is really moving," he told another crowd several days later.[43] The transcript from the April 9 meeting gives this account of King's address:

> He said it is time to move. "The time is always right when you are moving in the right direction." . . . He said that if the Negroes in Birmingham will stand up that the police dogs, state police and tanks, and city police couldn't stop them. "We are on our way to the freedom land with no violence."[44]

The next night, April 10, as he announced his plan to participate in the Good Friday march two days later, King said, "I can't think of a better day than Good Friday for a move for freedom."[45] The following night he urged, "We must keep on, keep on."[46] From jail, King continued to send messages back to the protesters to "keep the movement moving."[47] Following his release, he returned to the nightly mass meetings and, as recorded by the detectives, "encouraged the people to 'keep moving and don't stop now,'"[48] to "'keep the movement moving.' He said to keep it running; and if you can't run, to keep it walking; and if you can't walk, keep it crawling; but to keep it moving."[49]

Other speakers in these mass meetings echoed King's references to the theme of movement. At a rally held on April 11, Birmingham minister Abraham Woods referred to an injunction issued against the movement by a state judge but then said, "In spite of it, we are still on our way to freedom."[50] Four days later, Dr. Robert Fulton, a white supporter of the movement, told the audience about his experience of "being in the march for freedom this past Friday."[51] On April 12, James Bevel declared, "The Negro has been sitting here dead for 300 years. It is time he got up and walked," after which Edward Gardner, another of the city's black leaders, "took over the meeting and called for volunteers for the freedom march."[52] At an April 23 rally, a Reverend Lindsey announced,

> We want our freedom. We are going to have it. We are on our way. We are not going to be turned around by an injunction. . . . I have never read about an injunction in the Bible. We are going on. We can't stop now. We are on our way.[53]

One month into the protest, on May 2, 1963, after the arrest of some five hundred mostly high-school students who had joined the marches for the first time, Bevel urged a crowded mass meeting, "Let's all meet at the 16th Street Church Friday, Saturday, and Sunday mornings and go from there to freedom."[54] The following day, several hundred more young people began to march toward the downtown area but were met by snarling police dogs and high-powered spray from fire hoses. Hundreds of onlookers began to throw rocks and bottles at the police officers, and a wholesale riot was barely averted. That night King urged a mass meeting audience to "keep going down the paths of nonviolence" for, he said, "we're moving up a mighty highway toward the city of freedom. There will be meandering points. There will be curves and difficult moments."[55] He concluded by calling for the full commitment of everyone in the black community: "We're going on in spite of the dogs and in spite of the hose and in spite of the tanks. We can't stop now. We've gone too far to turn back." Three days later, on May 6, he challenged protesters to "keep this movement moving. (*Amen*) There is power in unity and there is power in numbers. (*Yes*) As long as we keep moving like we are moving, the power structure of Birmingham will have to give in."[56] Later in the speech he promised, "If we go on with the power of unarmed truth, we will be able to keep them disarmed. They just don't know what to do. They get the dogs, and they soon discover that the dogs can't stop us." To thunderous applause, he concluded with this exhortation:

> Keep this movement going. Keep this movement rolling. In spite of the difficulties, and we're going to have a few more difficulties, keep climbing. Keep moving. If you can't fly, run! (*Yeah*) If you can't run, walk. If you can't walk, crawl. But by all means, keep moving.

At that same mass meeting, Abernathy similarly assured his hearers, "All we've got to do is to keep marchin'. Do tomorrow what we did today. And then the next day, we won't have to do it at all."[57] Using the language of two of the movement's most prominent songs, "I'm on My Way" and "Ain't Gonna Let Nobody Turn Me Around," he promised,

> It won't be long before we will march into freedom's land. I'm on my way. I don't know about you, but I'm on my way. And I'm not goin' let anybody turn me around. (*All right*) I'm not goin' let Bull Connor turn me around. (*No*) Not goin' let the city jail turn me around. (*No*) Not goin' let the water hoses turn me around. (*No*) I'm not goin' let the Uncle Toms turn me around. (*No, Amen*) Not goin' let the nervous Nellies turn me around. (*No*) I'm not goin' let Governor Wallace turn me around. (*No*) Because I want to be free. Not only do I want to be free, but I got news for you. I am going to be free. (*Amen*) (*applause*)

In that hope, he urged, "Keep marching to freedom and let no man turn you around. And some day, right here in Birmingham, Alabama, we will walk into freedom's land."

Abernathy's words proved to be prophetic, for the next day, on May 7, when some six hundred young people descended on the downtown area, bringing traffic and commerce to a complete standstill, white business leaders voted to push for a settlement with the campaign leaders. After several days of intense negotiation, on May 10, King announced to a wildly ecstatic audience that they had come "to the climax of a long struggle for justice, freedom, and human dignity in the city of Birmingham."[58] But he warned, the struggle was not over: "For though we have come a long, long way, there is still a strenuous path before us, and some of it is yet uncharted." He gave credit to a number of people who had helped the movement reach its goal, among them Shuttlesworth, who had "walked a long and often lonesome road to reach this day." Later, King enumerated the specific elements of the agreement, noting the speed with which it was to be implemented in comparison with similar agreements in other cities:

> Now, do you know Birmingham is doing something that even the so-called progressive Atlanta didn't do. When we made our agreement, after our sit-ins, to get integration of lunch counters, they were integrated after six months. But here in Birmingham, it's after ninety days. We are moving on the freedom land. (*applause*)

Complementing this use of the journey motif to frame events in the protest was the music that played a central role in the campaign's daily mass meetings. The "freedom songs," as they were called, powerfully heightened participants' sense of emotional involvement in the movement's symbolic world of ideas, a participation reinforced by the interactive character of traditional African American preaching and worship. King himself attributed a great deal of the movement's success to its music:

> In a sense the freedom songs are the soul of the movement. . . . I have stood in a meeting with hundreds of youngsters and joined in while they sang, "Ain't Gonna Let Nobody Turn Me Round." It is not just a song; it is a resolve. A few minutes later, I have seen those same youngsters refuse to turn around before a pugnacious Bull Connor in command of men armed with power hoses. These songs bind us together, give us courage together, help us to march together.[59]

In one rally song, written especially for the Birmingham protest and performed by the ACMHR choir, titled "Ninety-Nine and a Half Won't Do," participants expressed their "one hundred percent commitment" to the cause:

> O Lord, I'm running, running for freedom
> Ninety-nine and a half won't do.
> O Lord, I'm running, running for freedom
> Ninety-nine and a half won't do.[60]

As Morris described it,

> The choir would begin this song in a packed mass meeting by rhythmi-
> cally proclaiming: "Five, ten, fifteen, won't do, twenty, twenty-five, thirty
> won't do." With a quickening tempo, the choir would continue all the
> way to "Ninety-nine and a half won't do." Then the crescendo would
> be reached when the choir and the audience would shout, "A hundred
> percent will do."[61]

In this way, the song proclaimed that the journey to freedom demanded
a total commitment from movement participants.

The police surveillance reports likewise point to the importance
of singing to the mass rallies. Detectives noted in their account of one
rally, for example, that Andrew Young "and a Negro woman named
Mrs. [Dorothy] Cotton led the church in several freedom songs,"[62] and
in another rally, that "Andrew Young led the congregation in several
freedom songs."[63] The report of the April 8 mass meeting noted that
during that evening's collection of donations, the choir sang a spiritual
that clearly evoked the Exodus, "I Am Bound for the Promised Land,"
after which "Martin Luther King made his grand entrance . . . to
a standing ovation."[64] The same report records that, following a call
by Abernathy "for volunteers to go to jail with him on Wednesday,"
the meeting closed with another song that called to mind the familiar
story, "I'm on My Way to the Freedom Land."[65] In one particularly
striking observation that perhaps reflected the detectives' disdain for
blacks as much as it captured the atmosphere of the meeting itself, a
surveillance report described the emotion that singing these freedom
songs aroused in the audience: "At this time, he [James Bevel] led the
church in singing, and the Negroes got all worked up while singing,
stomping their feet and waving their arms and screaming. There were
about 300 standing and marching. The entire attendance was between
1,800 and 2,000."[66]

Judging by the frequency with which both King and Abernathy
alluded to their lyrics, two such freedom songs held special significance
for the Birmingham movement, "I'm on My Way" and "Ain't Gonna
Let Nobody Turn Me Around." In the first, members of the congregation would declare,

I'm on my way to freedom land
I'm on my way to freedom land
I'm on my way to freedom land
I'm on my way, O Lord, to freedom land.[67]

They would follow with such verses as "If you don't go, don't you hinder me," "It's an uphill journey, but I'm on my way," and "There is nothing you can do to turn me around." Toward the end of the song, the congregation would ask, "Are you on your way to freedom land?" which they would follow by singing the opening verse once more. Similarly, "Ain't Gonna Let Nobody Turn Me Around" began with this resolve:

Ain't gonna let nobody
Turn me around! Turn me around! Turn me around!
Ain't gonna let nobody turn me around
I'm gonna keep on a-walkin' keep on a-talkin'
Marchin' down to freedom's land.[68]

The song would continue by proclaiming "Ain't gonna let segregation . . . ," "Ain't gonna let oppression . . . ," "Ain't gonna let your jail cells . . . ," "Ain't gonna let your violence . . . ," and, finally, "Ain't gonna let nobody turn me around." With both songs, movement participants would celebrate their campaign as the reenactment of the ancient story, often as an immediate prelude to the march itself. One observer, recalling an episode from the Albany protest the year before, noted King's jubilance at watching marchers stream from the church singing "Ain't Gonna Let Nobody Turn Me Around. "They can stop the leaders," King remarked, "but they can't stop the people."[69]

    With the exception of a handful of references to King as Moses, during the Birmingham campaign the Exodus thus was almost entirely distilled from a broad application of various elements of the story down to one dominant metaphor, that of the journey. This theme ran throughout the speeches and the songs that challenged protesters to continue their determined crusade in the face of the brutal opposition of Bull Connor's forces. At times, words related to the theme of movement were explicitly connected to the Exodus story while at others, they occurred by themselves. Nevertheless, given the rhetorical tradition that had imposed the narrative on the campaign, even those "movement" words used in isolation functioned as metonymies for the larger story, thereby reinforcing the overall symbolic construction of the campaign. Within this construction, protest actions and successes were represented spatially as steps in a symbolic transit toward "freedom," now symbolized as a "destination." Exhortations in support of the campaign's philosophy of protest and calls to participate in collective action were framed as invitations to join in the journey. Efforts to support King's ethos as the movement leader took the form of pleas to follow one who would lead them to freedom's land. Above all else, this discourse challenged protesters to "keep moving."

This focus on the journey motif occurred at the same time that the protest march was emerging as the movement's principal form of collective action. Walking had, of course, been an important element in the crusade from the days of the Montgomery bus boycott, when it represented the only alternative many blacks had to riding the city's segregated buses. The connection between walking and the Exodus had also been suggested early on, as when King claimed that the "Montgomery story" was about "fifty thousand Negroes . . . willing to substitute tired feet for tired souls," who could "walk and never get weary because we know that there is a great camp meeting in the promised land of freedom and equality." Beyond this vague comparison, however, the explicit connection between the Exodus and the act of marching is notably absent from early movement discourse—despite the fact that the story obviously invites that connection. Further, in the period prior to the Birmingham campaign, protesters had used a number of other forms of collective action besides the march, among them Freedom Rides, lunch-counter sit-ins, and systematic attempts to attend all-white churches. Indeed, the first people arrested in Birmingham on April 4 and 5, 1963, were protesters who sought service at the city's department store lunch counters. Within days, however, these other means of protest were dramatically overshadowed by the marches that began on April 6 and continued daily for over a month.

This distillation of the myth to the theme of movement, coinciding as it did with the emerging prominence of the protest march, thus represented a climactic moment in the campaign's rhetorical history, for it marked the culmination of the symbolic process that merged the movement's collective action with its defining narrative. Of course, the journey motif would have served participants in the same ways that the broader use of the Exodus narrative had done in the campaign's earlier days, reinforcing their sense of collective identity and accounting for the tensions and setbacks they experienced. But what stands out from the Birmingham campaign is the way that the rhetorical use of the myth now became concentrated on a single act of protest, the march. As we noted in chapter 2, the plot of the Exodus narrative was "chronotopic," representing a movement of location and through time. In the African American cultural tradition, the story had often been applied to organized migrations through which, by literally changing locations, blacks saw themselves as reenacting the Israelites' original journey to the Promised Land, a fact that made King's application of the story to a change in social configuration problematic. That inconsistency was resolved in the Birmingham campaign, as the protesters were exposed to a constant stream of rhetoric that highlighted the theme of movement and as they sang about being on their way to the freedom land, all in preparation for the "journey" to freedom that was the march.

Although it might not be possible to argue that the march became the movement's chief mode of collective action *as a result of* the movement's rhetorical tradition, the act of marching, at the least, resonated powerfully with that tradition. It brought a remarkable coherence to the movement's symbolic structure by uniting its narrative and its collective action. The Exodus story, continually recounted in the movement's oratory and its music, gave protesters a powerful motivation for continuing the marches. But it also imbued the act itself with symbolic meaning as the representation of blacks' progress toward the "freedom land." Through their bodily performance, protesters enacted the ancient story in a way that reflected Victor Turner's assertion that rituals communicate "the deepest values of the group" performing them, with the power to generate change and inscribe order "in the minds, hearts and wills of participants."[70] In other words, although the myth certainly provided motivation for continuing the protest, the mode of protest itself actually ritualized the myth.

THE MARCH AS RITUAL

Viewed within the context of the rhetorical tradition out of which it emerged, the act of marching was more than simply a means for paralyzing Birmingham's economy or dramatizing the need for equal treatment under the law. Rather, because it was so deeply rooted in a symbolic context that persistently connected the campaign for racial justice with the Exodus, the protest march itself became a potent form of ritual communication that enacted a salient cultural narrative through explicit, physical action. That union, as Roy Rappaport's theory of ritual suggests, had profound implications for movement participants. Using categories from linguistics, he distinguished between what he called the "canonical" and "self-referential" messages conveyed by ritual, and he explained the distinct relationship of "signifier" (the ritual act itself) to "signified" (the meanings conveyed through the ritual act) through which rituals communicate their messages. Canonical messages, which have to do with abstract beliefs, myths, or social and spiritual ideas or entities, are conveyed through a symbolic relationship, as when, in Christian worship, bread and wine symbolize the body and blood of Christ or, in a secular setting, placing one's hand over one's heart while reciting the Pledge of Allegiance symbolizes loyalty (e.g., pledging one's "heart" to one's country). Self-referential messages, by contrast, "transmit information concerning . . . [ritual performers'] own current physical, psychic or social states to themselves and to other participants." These messages rely on an indexical relationship, in the sense that a sign is "caused by, or is part of . . . that which it signifies,"[71] as when a rash is a sign or index of a medical condition or smoke signifies fire. Applied to ritual, Rothenbuhler observed, the "performative aspect of bodily participation in the ritual" signifies the performer's "relationship vis-à-vis the canon, the liturgy, the meaning of the ritual that is usually carried by symbols."[72]

Viewed from this semiotic perspective, the act of marching, framed by a tradition of speeches and songs that persistently invoked the metaphor of movement, *symbolically* represented a crucial myth from the African American religious "canon," the journey of the children of Israel to the Promised Land. The act of marching, in other words, recalled and reenacted the ancient story. As a *self-referential* act, however, marching also signaled participants' relationship to that story. For the protesters themselves, marching became a concrete, physical way of "doing something" to effect that change. It was an index of their determination to continue the journey, conveying both their resolve to let nothing turn them around and their conviction that they would reach freedom's land.

What is crucial to observe, however, is that marching, as a form of ritual communication, conveyed *both* its symbolic and self-referential meanings through the opposite semiotic process from that of ordinary language. In the typical linguistically encoded message, the "subject matter" (the signified) has weight and substance, whereas the signifier that represents the subject matter, written and spoken words, are "insubstantial" representations of the signified. In ritual, this process is reversed, in that the ritual performance, through its symbolic representation, focuses the abstractions so that they become concrete and tangible. Applied to the protest, abstract ideas related to racial progress, enacted in the performance of marching, now took on concrete physical reality. In Rappaport's words, "Corporeal representation gives weight to the incorporeal and gives visible substances to aspects of existence which are themselves impalpable, but of great importance in the ordering of social life."[73] The result is that the canonical meanings embodied in ritual are no longer experienced as abstractions, but rather, they "daze or dazzle," they "invade" the performer, altering his or her way of seeing the world.[74]

The same inversion of the meaning process also characterizes the self-referential dimension of meaning that protesters communicated through the march. Again, in the typical indexical relationship, the signified is caused by or is in some sense the result of the signifier, as when smoke signifies (is caused by or inherent in) fire, or a rash signifies (is a "symptom" of) a medical disorder. As ritual theorists emphasize, that indexical-meaning process works primarily in the opposite direction in ritual communication. In other words, rituals do more than simply convey preexisting states of consciousness within the performer. Rather, the performance of meaning-laden sequences of action is what actually produces or evokes the emotional and cognitive state within the ritual performer.

From this perspective, the crucial importance of the protest march lay not simply in the way that it functioned as a medium for articulating blacks' demands for racial justice. Rather, if ritual theorists are correct, the act of marching actually may have helped to create or, at least, to reinforce the protesters' consciousness of the reality of the myth. From the beginning of the movement, they had been told repeatedly that the ancient story was unfolding once again in their own day. But now, no longer were they sitting in an auditorium hearing it, nor were they even singing about it. Now, they were embodying the narrative through the concrete act of streaming from the church and walking, step by step, toward downtown Birmingham.

CONCLUSION

Birmingham, Alabama, 1963, witnessed not only the turning point in the history of the civil rights movement, but also what was in many ways the high point in the movement's rhetorical history, the culmination of the process through which the Exodus myth was overlaid on the quest to end racial apartheid in the United States. As this chapter has argued, although the rhetoric of the Birmingham campaign showed continuity with the previous tradition by continuing to place King in the role as the movement's Moses, it also underwent a drastic shift from a broad application of the biblical story down to an almost exclusive focus on the theme of movement. Previous discourse in the movement tradition had included both spatial and temporal elements of the Exodus, as when King, in his 1957 "Birth of a New Nation" sermon, spoke of "something old now passing away" even as he warned of the tensions protesters would face because they were "getting out of Egypt."[75] In Birmingham, that discourse became concentrated almost exclusively around the spatial dimension of the plot—protesters were "climbing," "walking," "going," "moving" along the path that led to the freedom land. As this chapter has also shown, the distillation of the larger myth to the theme of movement coincided precisely with the emergence of the march as the campaign's predominant method of protest. What happened in Birmingham, then, was the fusion of the movement's overarching narrative with its principal mode of collective action into a single, coherent symbolic construction—one that participants in the movement found both meaningful and motivating.

This underscores once again the enduring power and remarkable malleability of the Exodus within the rhetoric of the civil rights movement. In King's hands, the Exodus proved to be the preeminent inventional resource for addressing the needs of the movement at every stage in its history. At the same time, this analysis also illuminates the significance of the march beyond its role as a strategic political or economic act. Viewed within its discursive context, the march provided the unique fusion of canonical and self-referential meaning from which ritual, as a form of communication, derives its power. Through a physical performance, protesters enacted symbolic meanings related to the Exodus even as they came to experience more deeply the reality of those meanings. The march united form and substance in a way that brought what were essentially abstractions—the Exodus myth and the ideals of freedom, equality, dignity and power with which movement rhetoric united the myth—into concrete existence. Shaped by a symbolic context that connected their movement to the biblical narrative, protesters found in the act of marching a way to embody—to give bodily form to and thereby make "real"—the ancient story in a way that made it truly their own.

CONCLUSION

On March 25, 1965, King addressed a gathering of some twenty thousand people crowded around the steps of the Alabama State Capitol to celebrate the successful end to an arduous four-day march from Selma to Montgomery:

> Today I want to tell the city of Selma, (*Tell them, Doctor*) today I want to say to the state of Alabama, (*Yes, sir*) today I want to say to the people of America and the nations of the world, that we are not about to turn around. (*Yes, sir*) We are on the move now. (*Yes, sir*) Yes, we are on the move and no wave of racism can stop us. (*Yes, sir*) We are on the move now. The burning of our churches will not deter us. (*Yes, sir*) The bombing of our homes will not dissuade us. (*Yes, sir*) We are on the move now. (*Yes, sir*) The beating and killing of our clergymen and young people will not divert us. We are on the move now. (*Yes, sir*) The wanton release of their known murderers would not discourage us. We are on the move now. (*Yes, sir*) Like an idea whose time has come, (*Yes, sir*) not even the marching of mighty armies can halt us. (*Yes, sir*) We are moving to the land of freedom. (*Yes, sir*)[1]

His speech poignantly captured the remarkable fusion that had evolved between the civil rights movement's overarching narrative, the Exodus, and its principal means of mass protest, the march, a fusion that occurred in the 1963 Birmingham campaign two years prior. It represented the culmination of a process that began almost a decade previously and that continued throughout King's career, through which he connected the struggle for racial justice in the United States to the biblical story of the Exodus, in which God miraculously delivered the nation of Israel from Egyptian slavery and brought them across the Red Sea, through the wilderness, and into the Promised Land.

163

The purpose of this book has been to trace that process from its earliest point in King's career to its climactic moment in Birmingham, noting the ways that he adapted and applied the story to people and events within the movement's history. It began with King's "Death of Evil on the Seashore" sermon, delivered on July 21, 1955, in which King sought to convince his hearers that they were seeing the ancient story played out once more in their own day. He placed them in the story as the chosen people of God, long oppressed but now set free, yet he fashioned their role as one of sympathetic witnesses to the overthrow of their enemies. Most importantly, he situated them within the story's plot at the far side of the Red Sea, looking back on the "death of evil," as if the journey to the Promised Land had *already* begun— and this, five months before they would begin to engage in any organized collective action.

Throughout the Montgomery bus boycott, King continued to call on the Exodus as a resource for making sense of what his hearers were experiencing, but now with the form and content adapted to the new demands of sustaining a protracted protest against segregation on the city's buses. In his boycott rhetoric, King's references to the biblical story most often took the form of a "code" in which a phrase or even a single word—*the long night of captivity, the Egypt of segregation, the Promised Land of freedom and justice*—called to mind the larger story. During this period, the previously version of the story, which emphasized the Red Sea crossing as a miracle accomplished almost without Israel's being aware that it was happening, and which included no mention of the wilderness, became expanded to include an emphasis on the necessity for human action to complement God's providence. This period also saw the introduction of the wilderness as a predictable and essential element in the journey to freedom's land.

King offered the most complete exposition of the Exodus "paradigm" in his "Birth of a New Nation" sermon, delivered on April 7, 1957, shortly after his return from Ghana. This sermon presented the full plot structure on which references to the story from this point on would be based. It negotiated the tension between the need for human agency and the assurance of God's providence. It presented a more complex version of the character of Israel, distinguishing between the devoted masses who followed Moses and those Israelites who, jealous of God's appointed prophet, undermined his leadership. Most importantly, it underscored King's assertion that a truly miraculous

historical revolution was unfolding across the world. By closely identifying his audience with the Ghanaians who had successfully gained
their independence, and then by interweaving his "empirical" presentation of Ghana's history with references to the myth, King provided a
powerful argument that what his hearers had witnessed in Montgomery was not an isolated event. Rather, it was but one manifestation of a
much larger movement sweeping the globe through which the colored
peoples of the world were gaining freedom.

At the same time that King was developing the paradigm itself,
he was also emerging as the movement's unquestioned leader. Central to his assumption of that role was the way he fulfilled the fervent
expectation for the appearance of a black Moses, a figure who occupied perhaps the preeminent place in their cultural tradition. As we
traced that process in chapter 6, King initially embodied a more general prophetic persona as the faithful "narrator" of his people's history
and destiny, a role that his hearers reinforced in their response to his
pronouncements. In early 1957, however, King began to assume the
role of Moses more explicitly, a shift captured in a passage from his
sermon on January 27, 1957: "I've been to the mountain top and I've
seen the promised land."[2] In that role, he now possessed the authority as God's chosen leader to proclaim to the people the "orders from
headquarters."

Finally, the process through which the campaign for racial justice was aligned with the Exodus narrative reached its high point in
the Birmingham campaign, in early 1963. There, the references to
the larger narrative were distilled down to the theme of movement, a
change that coincided with the emergence of the march as the movement's principal means of collective action. Rhetorically, this theme
of movement, continually recounted in the campaign's oratory and
music, provided a powerful motivation for continuing the marches,
even as the march itself, as a form of ritual, extended the protesters'
experience of the story, a unique and stunning convergence captured
in the passage with which this conclusion began.

In the years following the Birmingham campaign, King would, on
occasion, continue to refer to the Exodus. In his address on August 16,
1967, titled "Where Do We Go from Here?" he spoke of continuing
"our forward stride toward the city of freedom."[3] His famous "Mountaintop" address, on April 3, 1968, immortalized his place as the movement's Moses.[4] But after Birmingham, the story would lose its place as

the primary frame of reference for explaining the movement's identity and purpose. Indeed, by the time of the Selma march, the movement was already undergoing dramatic change and would still change further, with the rise of the Black Power movement and the emergence of a generation of leaders who came not from the pastorate of the black church but rather who had been university students involved in the SNCC.[5] Its focus was shifting from the fight against segregation in the South to a variety of other causes, an evolution that Lentz captured when he described the setting in which King gave his final address in 1968. As he put it, in the five years following Birmingham, King

> had journeyed far afield from the South and the epic campaigns of the old civil rights movement, Montgomery and Selma and Birmingham. He had ventured north, leading an ultimately unsuccessful movement in 1966 against segregation and de facto discrimination in Chicago. He had taken up the anti-war cause a year later, decrying his country's war in Vietnam as but little short of genocide. Now, in 1968, King was preparing to embark on his most ambitious, most radical undertaking, . . . to organize a class-structured social movement.[6]

Not surprisingly, many of King's most well-known speeches from this period contain no mention of the Exodus, and those that do have clearly lost the tight coherence between the biblical narrative, the movement's goal, and its mode of protest. Nevertheless, as this analysis has shown, during the time when the movement was focused exclusively on racial justice in the South, the Exodus was truly its defining narrative.

This conclusion offers a series of reflections on that analysis, in three areas. First, it summarizes the overall process by which the Exodus emerged as the central motif in the movement's overall rhetorical vision. Next, it discusses the broad functions that the narrative served within the movement. Finally, it explores the implications of this study for our understanding of King's place in the movement and, more generally, the role that narrative plays in social movements.

DEVELOPMENT OF THE MOVEMENT'S RHETORICAL VISION

The broad perspective afforded by this analysis, first of all, sheds light on the process through which the Exodus narrative developed as the primary interpretive frame for the civil rights movement. That devel-

opment was certainly due, in part, to King himself. His roots in the tradition of black preaching, with its well-established canons of style and
content, made it virtually inevitable that the biblical story would play
some role in the movement's discourse. That it endured as it did and
proved to be such a malleable resource for addressing so many different events and people in the movement's history also points to King's
genius as a rhetor. Although he clearly struggled to master the organizational and strategic demands of managing an organization like the
SCLC, when it came to public communication, he was sophisticated
and creative, able to craft and deliver dynamic, compelling oratory in
response to an ever-changing political and organizational landscape.
At the same time, however, the black community to which King spoke
also played a key role in this process. They had been steeped in the
same tradition, and they brought to the protests a strong predisposi-
tion for seeing people and events through the lens of the myth and for
resonating with discourse that tapped into the tradition.

As this study has suggested, both King and the black community at
various points seem to have alternated in the role of the primary rhetorical "agent" in the development of the movement's Exodus vision.
At some points in the movement's rhetorical history, King is the agent
who proactively exploits the narrative for what appears to be explicit,
intentional rhetorical aims. His "Death of Evil on the Seashore" seems
intended to create the sense that the watershed moment in black history had already occurred, for an audience who would not have been
accustomed to thinking in such terms. His introduction of the wilderness motif during the boycott, at a time when the campaign was facing unexpected problems and disappointments, likewise seems to have
been an intentional, strategic choice. At the same time, his emergence
as the Moses figure appears to be as much the result of his audience's
determination to place him in that role, expressed in the applause and
other demonstrations of support with which they rewarded his successive approximations of that role as any conscious attempt on King's
part to adopt the persona. When he begins to assume the persona
explicitly, he is as much acceding to the expectations of his hearers
as he is attempting to construct an image for himself. By the time the
campaign comes to Birmingham, the impression left by the records
of the mass meetings is that speakers and audiences are so completely
immersed in the story that it would be difficult to assert a starting point
in the rhetorical process or to determine precisely who is influencing

whom. Rather, in the Birmingham campaign, all of the participants in the movement appear to be equally caught up in their experience of the story, with both rhetor and audience participating in a larger symbolic process that had now taken on a life of its own.

This indicates that the Exodus emerged as the movement's defining narrative through a process of co-creation that involved both King and his hearers. At the least, it would be an oversimplification simply to talk of how King used the Exodus to persuade blacks to believe and act in certain ways. Rather, the biblical story came to define the movement as a result of a dynamic interplay between King and the audiences who heard him, a process of negotiation and mutual reinforcement through which, together, they constructed their symbolic world.

A Transcendent Experience of the Story

This study also allows us to assess more generally the various ways that the Exodus functioned persuasively within the civil rights movement. Simply stated, the Exodus, applied rhetorically to the civil rights movement, provided an overarching narrative structure, rooted in African Americans' religious heritage, from which members of the movement could view themselves and their crusade. It identified in unambiguous terms the central characters within that story. Blacks were the modern-day children of Israel, God's chosen people. Members of the white power structure who resisted calls for reform were Pharaoh, refusing to let God's people go. Those who questioned King's leadership were cast as those rivals to Moses who, in the biblical narrative, had jealously attempted to undermine his authority. King was Moses.

The Exodus narrative also functioned epistemically to make sense of the protesters' past, present, and future. It gave them something of a roadmap that would allow them to chart their precise position and progress at any given moment in the movement's history. It challenged received religious perspectives on social injustice. Viewed from the theological lens of the Exodus, when they engaged in acts of protest and even civil disobedience, blacks were simply responding in faith to God's initiative. God had parted the Red Sea; they were simply passing through. Further, the narrative, applied to their movement, provided a mechanism through which participants could attribute causality to the events that were unfolding around them, a function most clear in King's use of the wilderness to explain difficulties and disappointments. In King's rhetoric, the Exodus transformed these surprises into predictable stages of the journey. Of course, the Exodus provided a source of language through which King and other movement leaders could constantly urge blacks to continue the struggle, to "keep on moving."

Perhaps the most important contribution of the narrative, however, was the way that it connected disparate people and events together into one coherent symbolic framework. In his analysis of the civil rights movement, Eskew emphasized that a crucial reason why the movement succeeded was because the SCLC was able to bring together black masses and the traditional African American leadership in a way that created the appearance to the outside world of a single, unified movement, so that whites saw what they thought was a "monolithic . . . black community," which in actuality was deeply splintered."[7] But as both rhetorical scholars and sociologists studying social movements have insisted, creating this same sense of collective identity, this sense of participating in a "monolithic black community," was just as important for the participants themselves. They needed to be able to see that all of the individual elements—the local organizations and the SCLC, the voter-registration efforts of the NAACP, the Freedom Rides, the lunch-counter sit-ins, the court decisions, the mass rallies—were not isolated, randomly occurring events, but rather were all connected within one grand movement. The Exodus, applied to their cause, provided that coherence by weaving these different threads into a single fabric. The language of the Exodus was a unifying constant across many different locations, protest efforts, and moments in time.

The passages in King's speeches that include what I have called his "code" usages of the Exodus, those times when he evoked the story with a word or short phrase, often in the climactic ending of an address, were particularly important to this process. From the perspective of rhetorical history, the sermons in which King gave detailed expositions of the biblical story's application to the movement provide important insights into that process because they contain the paradigm to which those code references refer. But it is unlikely that they would have had the kind of powerful resonance with the audience that the briefer citations had. Part of this was the result of the setting in which they were originally delivered, that of a Sunday-morning sermon in the more sedate atmosphere of the Dexter Avenue Baptist Church. But more importantly, King presented them in a form, that of an extended analogy, which would have invited hearers to intellectualize about the ways that what they were seeing was like the ancient story, rather than allowing themselves to experience simply being "in" the story. This may account for why King devoted so much attention in those longer sermons to providing "empirical" evidence that the application of the biblical story to their day was valid. The code usages, by contrast, occurred within the highly charged atmosphere of the mass rally. When King entered the room, the crowd would typically rise to its feet in a standing ovation. He usually spoke toward the end, only after the audience had been sufficiently aroused by a series of songs and other speeches. King would evoke the Exodus at the point in the address when emotions were at their highest. Then, with a word or phrase, he would tap into this deeply held reservoir of content and feeling.

What did his hearers experience in those highly charged moments?[28] Although effects are notoriously difficult to posit in a study of historical public address, the record of his audiences' reactions, the first-person accounts of the protesters, even the surveillance reports from the Birmingham campaign, all suggest that his hearers underwent a vivid, immediate, and transformative experience of being "in" the story itself. King's use of literal language (not "This is like the Exodus," but "We are moving to the land of freedom!"), his practice of referring to the Exodus with a single word, in response to which the audience would have supplied the larger content, and the settings in which he would typically evoke the biblical narrative, all would have encouraged the suspension of the tendency to intellectualize or to rationally evaluate the merits of his analogy. Instead, it would have encouraged a largely nonrational state of consciousness through which the audience would have experienced feelings of self-worth and courage, self-efficacy and motivation, and an overwhelming determination to make whatever sacrifices were needed to reach the goal. Indeed, his audiences' responses indicate that they had passed from an intellectual appropriation of the story to a transcendent experience of the story. When they extended this experience during the Birmingham campaign through the act of marching, this would only have served to make their experience of the story that much more real.

All of this highlights the central place that the Exodus narrative held as a source of both meaning and motivation for participants in the civil rights movement. As with no other theme in the movement's rhetorical history, the Exodus paradigm connected their cultural tradition, their religious understandings, and their quest for a better life together within a single, coherent, compelling world view.

King and the Rhetoric of Social Movements

As Carson pointed out in the late 1990s, the historiography of the civil rights movement has undergone a significant turn away from what he described as "simplistic accounts of mass protest leading to moral indignation and finally to national civil rights reform."[9] One of the results of this turn was to challenge accounts that viewed King's emergence and leadership as the primary explanation for why the movement occurred. As Carson noted, "Even biographies . . . now depict King as a leader often reacting to events that he did not initiate" This shift in the historiography of the civil rights movement raises the question of what role King's discourse played in the movement's formation and development.

This analysis of the Exodus narrative in King's civil rights–movement rhetoric provides one answer to that question. It asserts that one of King's signal contributions to the campaign was to connect events the protesters were witnessing with this salient part of their cultural tradition in a way that infused those events with meaning as they were unfolding. In other words, the history of the civil rights movement is not simply a matter of the key events that happened during this period. It also concerns the meaning that those events had for the participants themselves, a meaning that King persistently constructed by invoking the biblical story. Clearly, when he addressed the first mass meeting on December 5, 1955, King was responding to an orchestrated action that had already begun, that shared continuity with previous protests, and that drew on a variety of organizational resources. Even in his most creative uses of the narrative, he was still drawing from a long tradition of social knowledge and in ways that had clear precedent in the history of black oratory. Nevertheless, that first night and thereafter his discourse prophetically "named" the significance of each moment by subsuming it within this paradigmatic story.

Along the lines suggested by social-movement theorists, King's rhetoric imposed a symbolic frame on the emergent protest, offering participants in the struggle a remarkably coherent structure of meaning that explained their circumstances and legitimized their demands for justice. As participants in the Exodus drama, they enacted a collective identity that transcended their divisions and rivalries. They were the children of God, set free from the long night of Egyptian captivity by God's mighty hand. This interpretive frame also identified their opponents, who acted in predictable ways to thwart their efforts to obtain justice, and it explained the tensions they experienced during and after the Montgomery bus boycott. They had crossed the Red Sea and were now in the wilderness. Finally, as King used it, the narrative gave protesters a powerfully emotional conviction that they would succeed, provided they persevered and "kept moving." Despite the troubles they faced, as participants in a symbolic Exodus, protesters were reliving a drama whose outcome they already knew. As he promised in the closing of his "Birth of a New Nation" sermon, "We will be in Canaan's freedom land. . . . It's there waiting with its milk and honey, and with all the bountiful beauty that God has in store for His children."[10]

On a broader level, this study also underscores the potent role that narrative can play in the development of social movements in general, providing the essential point of convergence, the organizing principle, around which individual instances of collective action coalesce into the larger phenomenon that we call a movement. Indeed, if theorists are correct when they describe social movements as "symbolic contests over which meaning will prevail"[11] and when they posit as essential elements in a movement's formation such discursively centered functions as the construction of interpretive frames and the emergence of collective identity, it could be argued that King's use of the Exodus narrative helped constitute the civil rights movement *as a movement*. As a structure of meaning, the Exodus encompassed the protesters' circumstances, gave them a shared identity, brought to their efforts a sense of direction and progress, positioned King as the movement's prophetic leader, and envisioned the goal toward which their journey would inevitably lead. Within that symbolic world, African Americans who joined the movement and who persevered in the struggle for justice were living out the implications of their most cherished story.

NOTES

Introduction

1. Martin Luther King Jr., Montgomery Improvement Association (MIA) Mass Meeting at Holt Street Baptist Church, 5 December 1955, in *The Papers of Martin Luther King, Jr.*, vol. 3: *Birth of a New Age, December 1955–December 1956*, ed. Clayborne Carson, Stewart Burns, Susan Carson, Peter Holloran, and Dana Powell (Berkeley: University of California Press, 1997), 71–72 (hereafter cited as *Papers*, vol. 3); for an analysis of this address, see Kirt H. Wilson, "Interpreting the Discursive Field of the Montgomery Bus Boycott: Martin Luther King Jr's Holt Street Address," *Rhetoric and Public Affairs* 9 (2004): 299–306.

2. King, *Papers*, vol. 3, 72–73.

3. King, *Papers*, vol. 3, 77.

4. Aldon D. Morris, *The Origins of the Civil Rights Movement* (New York: Free Press, 1984), 105.

5. This account is taken from the tribute to Lee's life produced as part of the Southern Poverty Law Center's Civil Rights Memorial, http://www.splcenter.org/crm/memorial.jsp.

6. Morris, *Origins*, 105.

7. Morris, *Origins*, 97.

8. For example, the famous study conducted in the 1930s by Mays and Nickelson found that the majority of sermons had an "other-worldly" focus, in which "the practical aspects of life on earth are secondary or submerged, or . . . in which fear or reward, not in this life but in the world to come, is the dominant note." Benjamin Mays and Joseph Nicholson, *The Negro's Church* (New York: Institute of Social and Religious Research, 1933), 59. Interestingly, King's earliest application of the Exodus story to blacks' circumstances, the subject of chapter 3 of this book, reflects a strand of black preaching that tended to focus on individual growth and development. In that first version, the "Egypt of oppression" is as much a matter of gambling and alcohol addiction, "inordinate" ambition, and sexual promiscuity as it is racial oppression in society. Later versions of the sermon, delivered as the movement was growing, exclude this emphasis on personal morality almost entirely, focusing instead on the "Promised Land" of social and economic justice.

9. Glenn T. Eskew, *But for Birmingham* (Chapel Hill: University of North Carolina, 1997), 137–38.

10. Richard Lischer, *The Preacher King: Martin Luther King, Jr. and the Word that Moved America* (New York: Oxford University Press, 1995), 29.

11. David J. Garrow, *Bearing the Cross: Martin Luther King, Jr. and the Southern Christian Leadership Conference* (New York: William Morrow, 1986), 18. (Italic in original. Note: All subsequent italics are also in original.)

12. Morris, *Origins*, 43.

13. Stephen B. Oates, *Let the Trumpet Sound: The Life of Martin Luther King, Jr.* (New York: Harper & Row, 1982), ix. Other important biographies of King that focus on this period include David L. Lewis's *King: A Biography*, 2nd ed. (Urbana: University of Illinois Press, 1978) and Taylor Branch's *Parting the Waters: America in the King Years, 1954–63* (New York: Simon & Schuster, 1988).

14. See also Stewart Burns, *To The Mountaintop: Martin Luther King Jr.'s Sacred Mission to Save America: 1955–1968* (New York: HarperCollins, 2004).

15. Oates, *Let the Trumpet Sound*, ix.

16. Reflecting the same perspective is Adam Fairclough's *To Redeem the Soul of America: The Southern Christian Leadership Conference and Martin Luther King, Jr.* (Athens: University of Georgia Press, 1987).

17. Morris, *Origins*, xiii, xii.

18. See Adam Fairclough, "The Civil Rights Movement in Louisiana, 1939–54" in *The Making of Martin Luther King and the Civil Rights Movement*, ed. Brian Ward and Anthony Badger (Washington Square: New York University Press, 1996), 15–28; John A. Kirk, "'He Founded a Movement': W. H. Flowers, the Committee on Negro Organizations and the Origins of Black Activism in Arkansas, 1940–57," in Ward and Badger, 29–44; and John White, "Nixon *was* the One: Edgar Daniel Nixon, the MIA, and the Montgomery Bus Boycott," in Ward and Badger, 45–63.

19. J. Mills Thornton III, *Dividing Lines: Municipal Politics and the Struggle for Civil Rights in Montgomery, Birmingham, and Selma* (Tuscaloosa: University of Alabama Press, 2002), 11.

20. Richard Lentz, *Symbols, the News Magazines, and Martin Luther King* (Baton Rouge: Louisiana State University Press, 1990), 2–3.

21. Mary L. Dudziak, *Cold War Civil Rights: Race and the Image of American Democracy* (Princeton: Princeton University Press, 2000), 13–14; see also Philip A. Klinkner and Rogers M. Smith, *The Unsteady March: The Rise and Decline of Racial Equality in America* (Chicago: University of Chicago Press, 1999).

22. Although King has received a great deal of attention from rhetorical scholars, only a handful of studies have explored his use of the Exodus. These include Smylie's essay on King as a biblical interpreter whose message joined thematic elements from the Exodus narrative with an emphasis on Christian love. Although not a rhetorical analysis, his essay did underscore the importance of the biblical story in King's discourse. One of the earliest rhetorical studies to note King's dependence on the Exodus story was Malinda Snow's essay on King's "Letter from Birmingham Jail." Similarly, Miller argued that the prominence of the Exodus in King's preaching points to the profound influence of the tradition of black preaching on King's oratory. Three essays, by Rosteck, Osborn, and Lynch, each examined King's rhetorical use of the Exodus in his final, "Mountaintop" speech from different rhetorical perspectives. My previous essay, "Framing Social Protest," presents a preliminary exploration of the

Exodus narrative in King's boycott rhetoric. James H. Smylie, "On Jesus, Pharaohs, and the Chosen People: Martin Luther King as Biblical Interpreter and Humanist," *Interpretation* 24 (1970): 74–91; Malinda Snow, "Martin Luther King's 'Letter from Birmingham Jail' as Pauline Epistle," *Quarterly Journal of Speech* 71 (1985): 318–34; Keith D. Miller, "Alabama as Egypt: Martin Luther King, Jr., and the Religion of Slaves," in *Martin Luther King, Jr., and the Sermonic Power of Public Discourse*, ed. Carolyn Calloway-Thomas and John Louis Lucaites (Tuscaloosa: University of Alabama Press, 1993), 18–32; Thomas Rosteck, "Narrative in Martin Luther King's 'I've Been to the Mountaintop,'" *Southern Communication Journal* 58 (1992): 22–32; Michael Osborn, "The Last Mountaintop of Martin Luther King, Jr., in Calloway-Thomas and Lucaites, 147–61; Christopher Lynch, "Reaffirmation of God's Anointed Prophet: The Use of Chiasm in Martin Luther King's 'Mountaintop' Speech," *Howard Journal of Communications* 6 (1995): 12–31; and Gary S. Selby, "Framing Social Protest: The Exodus Narrative in Martin Luther King's Montgomery Bus Boycott Rhetoric," *Journal of Communication and Religion* 24 (2001): 68–93.

23. From an address that King gave to a mass meeting on March 19, 1956; quoted in James Booker, " 'God Will Find a Way' Boycotters," *New Amsterdam News* (24 March 1956); cited in *Papers*, vol. 3, 183.

24. Martin Luther King Jr., Address to MIA Mass Meeting at Holt Street Baptist Church, 22 March 1956, *Papers*, vol. 3, 200.

25. This quotation, from King's address to the Annual Meeting of the NAACP Legal Defense and Education Fund on May 17, 1956, is contained in the written version of that speech titled, "The 'New Negro' of the South: Behind the Montgomery Story" in the magazine *Socialist Call*, in *Papers*, vol. 3, 284.

26. Martin Luther King Jr., "Non-Aggression Procedures to Interracial Harmony," Address Delivered at the American Baptist Assembly and American Home Mission Agencies Conference, Green Lake, Wisconsin, 23 July 1956, in *Papers*, vol. 3, 327.

27. Quoted in the press account of King's sermon "King Says Vision Told Him to Lead Integration Forces," *Montgomery Advertiser*, 28 January 1956, 2A, http://nl.newsbank.com/nlsearch/we/Archives?p_action=doc&p_docid=10D160229EF5168&p_docnum=1&p_theme=gannett&s_site=montgomery advertiser&p_product=MGAB (accessed October 12, 2007).

28. Martin Luther King Jr., "Give us the Ballot," Speech at the Prayer Pilgrimage for Freedom, 17 May 1957, in *The Papers of Martin Luther King, Jr.*, vol. 4, *Symbol of the Movement, January 1957–December 1958*, ed. Clayborne Carson, Susan Carson, Adrienne Clay, Virginia Shadron, and Kieran Taylor (Berkeley: University of California Press, 2000), 215 (hereafter cited as *Papers*, vol. 4).

29. Martin Luther King Jr., Address at Youth March for Integrated Schools in Washington, D.C., Delivered by Coretta Scott King, 25 October 1958, in *Papers*, vol. 4, 515.

30. Mass Meeting Surveillance Memorandum, 3 April 1963, Theophilus Eugene "Bull" Connor Papers, Birmingham Public Library, Archives Department (File 268.13.2) (hereafter cited as Connor Papers). All mass meeting transcripts contained in the Connor papers are in the form of memoranda from detectives addressed to police chief Jamie Moore. For consistency, I have cited each as a "Mass Meeting Surveillance Memorandum," followed by the date when the mass meeting took place.

31. Martin Luther King Jr., "Our God is Marching On," 25 March 1965, Martin Luther King, Jr. Papers Project, Stanford University, http://www.stanford.edu/group/King/publications/speeches/Our_God_is_marching_on.html (accessed May 2, 2002).

32. Martin Luther King Jr., "I've Been to the Mountaintop," 3 April 1968, Martin Luther King, Jr. Papers Project, Stanford University, http://www.stanford.edu/group/King/mlkpapers/ (accessed October 12, 2007).

Chapter One

1. Michael Calvin McGee, "'Social Movement': Phenomenon or Meaning?" *Central States Speech Journal* 31 (1980): 242.

2. See, in particular, the response by Lucas, "Coming to Terms," 255–66.

3. Stewart, Smith, and Denton, *Persuasion and Social Movements*, 18.

4. Davis, "Narrative and Social Movements," 8. Rhetorical scholars have long recognized the central role that rhetoric plays in the formation of social movements, an awareness that extends at least as far back as Leland M. Griffin's methodological essay, "The Rhetoric of Historical Movements," *Quarterly Journal of Speech* 38 (1952): 184–88. For an excellent collection of landmark studies in this tradition of scholarship, see Charles E. Morris III and Stephen H. Browne, eds., *Readings on the Rhetoric of Social Protest* (State College: Pa., Strata, 2001).

5. Steven M. Buechler, *Social Movements in Advanced Capitalism* (New York: Oxford University Press, 2000), 40–41.

6. Bert Klandermans, "The Social Construction of Protest and Multiorganizational Fields," in *Frontiers in Social Movement Theory*, ed. Aldon D. Morris and Carol McClurg Mueller (New Haven: Yale University Press, 1992), 77, 79.

7. William A. Gamson, "The Social Psychology of Collective Action," in *Frontiers in Social Movement Theory*, ed. Aldon D. Morris and Carol McClurg Mueller (New Haven: Yale University Press, 1992), 67.

8. Doug McAdam, "The Framing Function of Movement Tactics: Strategic Dramaturgy in the American Civil Rights Movement," in *Comparative Perspectives on Social Movements*, ed. Doug McAdam, John D. McCarthy, and Mayer N. Zald (Cambridge: Cambridge University Press, 1996), 339.

9. Klandermans, "The Social Construction," 80.

10. Gamson, "The Social Psychology," 57.

11. Stewart, Smith, and Denton, "Persuasion and Social Movement," 56, 76–77.

12. Davis, "Narrative and Social Movements," 4, 19.

13. McGee, "Social Movement," 242, 237.

14. Scott, in fact, traced the rise of narrative criticism among rhetorical scholars to Burke's establishment of the dramatism as a principal metaphor for understanding human communication. See Robert L. Scott, "Narrative Theory and Communication Research," *Quarterly Journal of Speech* 70 (1984): 197–204.

15. Kenneth Burke, *Counter-Statement*, 2nd ed. (1953; repr. Berkeley: University of California Press, 1968), 139.

16. Burke, *Counter-Statement*, 31, 145.

17. Kenneth Burke, *A Rhetoric of Motives* (1950; repr. Berkeley: University of California Press, 1969), 58.

18. Kenneth Burke, "Dramatism," in *The International Encyclopedia of the Social Sciences* (1972, repr., New York: MacMillan, 1968), 7:448. See also his discussion of the way that rhetors impose dramatic or literary forms such as epic, tragedy, and comedy on experiences of social disorder in *Attitudes Toward History*, 3rd ed. (Berkeley: University of California Press, 1984).

19. Walter Fisher, "Narration as a Human Communication Paradigm," *Communication Monographs* 51 (1984): 1–22; *Human Communication as Narration: Toward a Philosophy of Reason, Value, and Action* (Columbia: University of South Carolina Press, 1987), 58. In addition to his dependence on Burke (see "Narration," 6), Fisher also acknowledges the influence on his work of Alasdair MacIntyre, who emphasized the "narrative structure of human life" and asserts that the human is "essentially a storytelling animal" in *After Virtue: A Study in Moral Theory* (Notre Dame, Ind.: Notre Dame University Press, 1981), 200–201.

20. For example, see W. Lance Bennett, "Storytelling in Criminal Trials: A Model of Social Judgment," *Quarterly Journal of Speech* 64 (1985): 1–22; William F. Lewis, "Telling America's Story: Narrative Form and the Reagan Presidency," *Quarterly Journal of Speech* 73 (1987): 280–302; Stephen Howard Browne, "Jefferson's First Declaration of Independence: *A Summary View of the Rights of British America* Revisited," *Quarterly Journal of Speech* 89 (2003): 235–52; Robert Wade Kenny, "Thinking about *Rethinking Life and Death*: The Character and Rhetorical Function of Dramatic Irony in a Life Ethics Discourse," *Rhetoric and Public Affairs* 6 (2003): 657–86; Shaul R. Shenhav, "Thin and Thick Narrative Analysis: On the Question of Defining and Analyzing Political Narratives," *Narrative Inquiry* 15 (2005): 75–99.

21. Esther Schely-Newman, "Finding One's Place: Locale Narratives in an Israeli *Moshav*," *Quarterly Journal of Speech* 83 (1997): 401–15.

22. Priscilla Wald, *Constituting Americans: Cultural Anxiety and Narrative Form* (Durham, N.C.: Duke University Press, 1995); Scott R. Stroud, "Narrative as Argument in Indian Philosophy: The Astāvakra Gītā as Multivalent Narrative," *Philosophy and Rhetoric* 37 (2004): 42–71.

23. William G. Kirkwood, "Storytelling and Self-Confrontation: Parables as Communication Strategies," *Quarterly Journal of Speech* 69 (1983): 58–74; "Parables as Metaphors and Examples," *Quarterly Journal of Speech* 71 (1985): 422–40.

24. Charles J. G. Griffin, "The Rhetoric of Form in Conversion Narratives," *Quarterly Journal of Speech* 76 (1990): 152–63.

25. Martha Solomon, "Autobiographies as Rhetorical Narratives: Elizabeth Cady Stanton and Anna Howard Shaw as 'New Women,'" *Communication Studies* 42 (1991): 254–70.

26. Kristin M. Langellier and Eric E. Peterson, "Family Storytelling as a Strategy of Social Control," in *Narrative and Social Control*, ed. Dennis K. Mumby (Newbury Park, Calif.: Sage, 1993), 49–76.

27. Dennis K. Mumby, "The Political Function of Narratives in Organizations," *Communication Monographs* 54 (1987): 113–27.

28. Peter Ehrenhaus, "Cultural Narratives and the Therapeutic Motif: The Political Containment of Vietnam Veterens," in Mumby, *Narrative and Social Control*, 77–96;

Steven R. Goldzwig and Patricia A. Sullivan, "Narrative and Counternarrative in Print-Mediated Coverage of Milwaukee Alderman Michael McGee," *Quarterly Journal of Speech* 86 (2000): 215–31; Troy A. Murphy, "Romantic Democracy and the Rhetoric of Heroic Citizenship," *Communication Quarterly* 51 (2003): 192–208.

29. Lewis, "Telling America's Story," 288.

30. Wayne C. Booth, *The Rhetoric of Fiction* (Chicago: University of Chicago Press, 1983), 274–75.

31. Ronald Bishop, "It's Not Always About the Money: Using Narrative Analysis to Explore Newspaper Coverage of the Act of Collecting," *Communication Review* 6 (2003): 127–28.

32. Kenny, "Thinking about Rethinking Life and Death," 658, 677.

33. Michael Osborn and John Bakke, "The Melodramas of Memphis: Contending Narratives during the Sanitation Strike of 1968," *Southern Communication Journal* 63 (1998): 222–23.

34. Paul Ricoeur, *Time and Narrative* (Chicago: University of Chicago Press, 1984), 1:65.

35. M. M. Bakhtin, *The Dialogic Imagination*, ed. Michael Holquist, trans. Caryl Emerson and Michael Holquist (Austin: University of Austin Press, 1981), 84.

36. Shenhav, "Thin and Thick Narrative Analysis," 94.

37. David M. Boje, *Narrative Methods for Organizational and Communication Research* (London: Sage, 2001), 114.

38. Shenhav noted in particular that political narratives are typically embedded in ongoing discussion so that, although "every act of speaking will obviously end at a particular point, these ending points are part of a continuing discussion, and so concepts such as 'ends' or closures must be arbitrary." However these narratives, on closer examination, typically posit a hypothetical ending and imply what actions will need to be taken to achieve that experience of closure. See Shenhav, "Thin and Thick Narrative Analysis," 83.

39. John Louis Lucaites and Celeste Michelle Condit, "Re-constructing Narrative Theory: A Functional Perspective," *Journal of Communication* 35 (1985): 100.

40. Cited in Davis, "Narrative and Social Movement," 14.

41. Ricoeur, "Time and Narrative," 1: 66–67.

42. Hayden White, "The Value of Narrativity in the Representation of Reality," in *On Narrative*, ed. W. J. T. Mitchell (Chicago: University of Chicago Press, 1981), 22.

43. Lewis, "Telling America's Story," 288. In addition to the examples detailed above, see also Browne, "Jefferson's First Declaration," 245, which emphasizes the attribution of intention as the crucial rhetorical strategy through which Jefferson portrayed Britain's treatment of the American colonies as immoral.

44. Davis, "Narrative and Social Movement," 13.

45. White, "The Value of Narrativity," 22. See especially Mumby's "The Political Function of Narratives," which emphasizes the way that a story's end depicts an outcome that functions to valorize or proscribe particular behaviors within an organization.

46. Sonja Foss, *Rhetorical Criticism: Exploration and Practice*, 2nd ed. (Long Grove, Ill.: Waveland, 1996), 399.

47. Kenneth Burke, *The Philosophy of Literary Form*, 3rd ed. (Berkeley: University of California Press, 1973), 296.

48. Ehrenhaus, "Cultural Narratives," 80. See also Browne, "Jefferson's First Declaration," 237.

49. See Fisher, *Human Communication as Narration*, 47–48, 64.

50. Lewis, "Telling America's Story," 288.

51. Burke, *Counter-Statement*, 145.

52. Fisher, *Human Communication as Narration*, 46–64; see also Griffin, "Conversion Narratives," which explores the strategies through which narrators render dramatic characterological shifts plausible.

53. Lewis, "Telling America's Story," 288.

54. See especially Kenny, "Thinking about Rethinking Life and Death," 677–79.

55. Michael Calvin McGee and John S. Nelson, "Narrative Reason in Public Argument," *Journal of Communication*, 35 (1985): 163. See also Kirkwood, "Storytelling and Self-Confrontation," 65–66, which highlights the evocation of emotional states as a particular function of parables.

56. Rosteck, "Narrative," 23.

57. Griffin, Charles J. G., "The 'Washingtonian Revival': Narrative and the Moral Transformation of Temperance Reform in Antebellum America," *Southern Communication Journal* 66 (2000): 76.

58. Roy A. Rappaport, *Ritual and Religion in the Making of Humanity* (Cambridge: Cambridge University Press, 1999), 24, 107.

59. Victor Turner, "Social Dramas and Stories About Them," *Critical Inquiry* 7 (1980): 161–62. Reflecting the influence of Burke on his understanding of ritual (which he explicitly identifies on p. 149), Turner notes that while rituals may reflect a "syncronization of many performative genres," they are often "ordered by a *dramatic* structure, a plot" (161).

60. Rappaport, *Ritual and Religion*, 31, 37–38.

61. Eric W. Rothenbuhler, *Ritual Communication: From Everyday Conversation to Mediated Ceremony* (Thousand Oaks, Calif.: Sage, 1998), 8.

62. Clifford Geertz, *The Interpretation of Cultures* (New York: Basic Books, 1973), 112.

63. Catherine Bell, *Ritual Theory, Ritual Practice* (New York: Oxford University Press, 1992), 98.

64. Roy A. Rappaport, "Ritual," in *International Encyclopedia of Communications* (New York: Oxford University Press, 1989), 3:469.

65. This and the following quotations are from Rappaport, *Ritual and Religion*, 142, 153.

Chapter Two

1. King, MIA Mass Meeting, 5 December 1955, *Papers*, vol. 3, 73.

2. Martin Luther King Jr., Address to MIA Mass Meeting at Holt Street Baptist Church, 14 November 1956, in *Papers*, vol. 3, 433.

3. Martin Luther King Jr., "The Montgomery Story," 27 June 1956, in *Papers*, vol. 3, 306.

4. King, MIA Mass Meeting, 14 November 1956, *Papers*, vol. 3, 433.

5. Walzer argued more broadly that the Exodus story is a "paradigm of revolutionary thought," foundational to the history of political theory in both Europe and the U.S.: "The Exodus is a story, a big story, one that became part of the cultural consciousness of the West—so that a range of political events . . . have been located and understood within the narrative frame that it provides." Glaude built on that conception to argue that the Exodus narrative provided the grounding for the sense of nationhood that emerged in the black convention movement of the early 1800s. On the one hand, he asserted, blacks read the narrative in a way that identified themselves as the people of God and the United States as the Egypt of oppression, a reading that gave them solidarity, hope, and a motivation to persist in an ongoing struggle for justice. At the same time, the fact the United States developed within a milieu that was itself saturated by the Exodus motif caused blacks to see their fortunes as inextricably linked to the ideal of the identity of the United States, a view that kept them from pursuing a separatist political agenda. Exodus politics, he wrote, can thus "be thought of as a form of criticism that pressures a given society to live up to its ideals. In effect, it is an appeal to principles announced at the nation's inception that somehow have been compromised by the choices of people." Michael Walzer, *Exodus and Revolution* (New York: Basic Books, 1985), 7; Eddie S. Glaude Jr., *Exodus! Religion, Race, and Nation in Early Nineteenth-Century Black America* (Chicago: University of Chicago Press, 2000), 111.

6. Keith D. Miller, *Voice of Deliverance: The Language of Martin Luther King, Jr., and Its Sources* (New York: Free Press, 1992), 19.

7. Bruce Gronbeck, "Narrative, Enactment, and Television Programming," *Southern Speech Communication Journal* 48 (1983): 234.

8. Lewis, "Telling America's Story," 282–83.

9. Browne, "Jefferson's First Declaration," 236, 241.

10. Ehrenhaus, "Cultural Narratives," 78

11. Murphy, "Romantic Democracy," 193, 202.

12. Ehrenhaus, "Cultural Narratives," 82.

13. For an excellent treatment of the recent scholarship of Exodus, see Carol Meyers, *Exodus* (New York: Cambridge University Press, 2005). For a discussion of the history of the interpretation of Exodus, see Brevard S. Childs, *Introduction to the Old Testament as Scripture* (Philadelphia: Fortress, 1979), 161–79.

14. All biblical quotations are from the New Revised Standard Version.

15. Meyers, *Exodus*, xvi.

16. Walter Brueggemann, "The Book of Exodus: Introduction, Commentary, and Reflections," in *The New Interpreter's Bible*, ed. Leander E. Keck (Nashville: Abingdon, 1994), 1:718.

17. Eric J. Sundquist, *Strangers in the Land: Blacks, Jews, Post-Holocaust America* (Cambridge, Mass.: Belknap, 2005), 96. Interestingly, as Hendel observes, elements in the story made it particularly susceptible to this process of appropriation within collective memory, a process that occurs in the Hebrew Scriptures and in early Christianity. See Ronald Hendel, "The Exodus in Biblical Memory," *Journal of Biblical Literature* 120 (2004): 601–22.

18. As Asante pointed out, the actual historical process through which the earliest Africans on the North American continent adopted the Exodus story is uncertain. Further, he noted, the implications of this adoption of a Jewish narrative as a foundational

cultural myth, and the tendency of historians to trace African cultural self-awareness back to the adoption of the biblical narrative are problematic. Nevertheless, an abundance of evidence indicates that at least by the middle of the nineteenth century, the biblical story had become a pervasive source of identity and hope among Africans living in the United States. See Molefi Kete Asante, "Intellectual Dislocation: Applying Analytic Afrocentricity to Narratives of Identity," *Howard Journal of Communications* 13 (2002): 97–110. For an overview of how the story spread and was understood among black slaves, see Albert J. Raboteau, "African-Americans, Exodus, and the American Israel," in *African American Christianity: Essays in History*, ed. Paul E. Johnson (Berkeley: University of California Press, 1994), 1–17.

19. Eugene D. Genovese, *Roll, Jordan, Roll: The World the Slaves Made* (New York: Pantheon, 1974), 253.

20. Langston Hughes and Arna Bontemps, eds., *The Book of Negro Folklore* (New York: Dodd, Mead, 1958), 56.

21. Recorded in George P. Rawick, ed., *The American Slave: A Composite Autobiography*, vol. 18, *The Unwritten History of Slavery (Fisk University)* (Westport, Conn.: Greenwood, 1972), 180.

22. Genovese, *Roll, Jordan, Roll*, 213.

23. Elizabeth Keckley, *Behind the Scenes, or Thirty Years a Slave, and Four Years in the White House* (New York: G. W. Carlton, 1868; http://digital.nypl.org/schomburg/writers_aa19/), 190 (accessed on October 16, 2007).

24. Quoted in Albert J. Raboteau, *Slave Religion: The "Invisible Institution" in the Antebellum South* (New York: Oxford University Press, 1978), 311–12.

25. Molefi Kete Asante, *The Afrocentric Idea* (Philadelphia: Temple University Press, 1987), 89.

26. Lovell's account of the seven recurring biblical places that appear in Negro spirituals lists four from the Exodus (Jordan, Egypt, Red Sea, Canaan). He also notes the prominence of Moses as "one of the spiritual figures" in the songs. See John Lovell, *Black Song: The Forge and the Flame* (New York: MacMillan, 1972), 258–59.

27. Hughes and Bontemps, *The Book of Degro Folklore*, 57.

28. Sterling A. Brown, "The Spirituals," in *The Book of Negro Folklore*, ed. Langston Hughes and Arna Bontemps (New York: Dodd, Mead, 1958), 286.

29. Negrospirituals.com. http://www.negrospirituals.com/news-song/bound_for_canaan_land.htm (accessed September 12, 2005).

30. Negrospirituals.com. http://www.negrospirituals.com/news-song/didn_t_old_pharaoh_get_lost.htm (accessed September 12, 2005).

31. Brown, "The Spirituals," 292.

32. Negrospirituals.com. http://www.negrospirituals.com/news-song/wade_in_the_water.htm (accessed September 12, 2005).

33. Kerran L. Sanger, "Slave Resistance and Rhetorical Self-Definition: Spirituals as a Strategy," *Western Journal of Communication* 59 (1995): 179, 189–90.

34. Absalom Jones, "A Thanksgiving Sermon," in *Lift Every Voice: African American Oratory*, 1787–1900, ed. Philip S. Foner and Robert J. Branham (Tuscaloosa: University of Alabama Press, 1998), 75–77 (hereafter cited as *Lift Every Voice*).

35. Austin Steward, "Termination of Slavery," in *Lift Every Voice*, 107.

36. Frances Ellen Watkins, "Liberty for Slaves," in *Lift Every Voice*, 307.

37. Quoted in Philip S. Foner and Robert J. Branham, eds., *Lift Every Voice: African American Oratory, 1787–1900* (Tuscaloosa: University of Alabama Press, 1998), 454.

38. Lewis Hayden, "Deliver Us from Such a Moses," in *Lift Every Voice*, 456.

39. Keckley, *Behind the Scenes*, 117.

40. Sojourner Truth, *Narrative of Sojourner Truth; A Bondswoman of Olden Time, Emancipated by the New York Legislature in the Early Part of the Present Century; With a History of Her Labors and Correspondence Drawn from her "Book of Life"* (Battle Creek, Mich.: n.p., 1878; http://digital.nypl.org/schomburg/writers_aa19/ (accessed October 15, 2007)), vi–vii.

41. Robert J. Harlan, "Migration Is the Only Remedy for our Wrongs," in *Lift Every Voice*, 601.

42. M. Edward Bryant, "How Shall We Get Our Rights?" in *Lift Every Voice*, 680.

43. William Bishop Johnson, "National Perils," in *Lift Every Voice*, 712–13.

44. W. E.B. Du Bois, *The Souls of Black Folk* (New York: Bantam Books, 1989 [1903]), 6.

45. B. L. Ware and Wil A. Linkugel, "The Rhetorical *Persona*: Marcus Garvey as Black Moses," *Communication Monographs* 49 (1982): 51.

46. Quoted in Miller, *Voice of Deliverance*, 23.

47. Quoted in Miller, *Voice of Deliverance*, 24.

48. Not surprisingly, this connection was reinforced in the discourse of Jewish speakers who addressed participants in the movement. See, for examples, the speeches of Shad Polier and Rabbi Max Davidson, both given to NAACP gatherings, in Davis W. Houck and David E. Dixon, *Rhetoric, Religion, and the Civil Rights Movement, 1954–1965* (Waco, Tex.: Baylor University Press, 2006), 267–70, 325–27.

49. Miller, *Voice of Deliverance*, 20.

50. Miller, *Voice of Deliverance*, 27.

51. Fredrick C. Harris, *Something Within: Religion in African-American Political Activism* (New York: Oxford University Press, 1999), 70, 78, 145. Harris cites examples of this language being used into the 1990s (see 145–53).

52. Miller, "Alabama as Egypt," 22–23.

53. Lischer, *The Preacher King*, 94.

54. Truth, *Narrative of Sojourner Truth*, 196.

55. William H. Crogman, "Negro Education—Its Helps and Hindrances," in *Lift Every Voice*, 628.

56. Truth, Narrative of Sojourner Truth, vi.

57. Henry Highland Garnett, "Let the Monster Perish," in *Lift Every Voice*, 442.

58. Jones, "Thanksgiving Sermon," 76.

59. Johnson, "National Perils," 713.

60. Bryant, "How Shall We Get Our Rights?" 680.

61. Genovese, *Roll, Jordan, Roll*, 253; Watkins, "Liberty for Slaves," 307.

62. Henry Highland Garnett, "An Address to the Slaves of the United States of America," in *Lift Every Voice*, 202.

63. Given the patronizing stance that even more progressive elements of white society held toward blacks, and the pervasive habit among many whites of referring to blacks in diminutive terms (hailing a black man as "boy," for example), King's identification of his hearers with the "children of Israel" risked reinforcing the sense of helplessness and dependency that their society had forced on them.

64. Harlan, "Migration," 600–602.

65. Crogman, "Negro Education," 628.

66. Marcus Garvey, "Speech delivered at Madison Square Garden, New York City," 16 March 1924, in *Philosophy and Opinions of Marcus Garvey*, ed. Amy Jacques Garvey (repr., New York: Arno Press, 1969), 2:21.

67. Marcus Garvey, "Message of Marcus Garvey to Membership of Universal Negro Improvement Association from Atlanta Prison," 1 August 1, 1925, in *Philosophy and Opinions of Marcus Garvey*, ed. Amy Jacques Garvey (repr., New York: Arno Press, 1969), 2:327.

Chapter Three

1. This analysis of King's original "Death of Evil on the Seashore" sermon is based on my transcription of a copy of King's original sermon notes. Unless otherwise noted, all quotations of the original version are from that transcription. I wish to express my gratitude to Clayborne Carson and the Martin Luther King, Jr., Papers Project at Stanford University for making the text available to me.

2. Martin Luther King Jr., "The Death of Evil on the Seashore," 17 May 1956, in *Papers*, vol. 3, 256–65.

3. Martin Luther King Jr., *Strength to Love* (New York: Harper & Row, 1963).

4. Garrow, *Bearing the Cross*, 50. As Garrow notes, although King did join the Montgomery chapter of the NAACP and attended meetings of the Alabama Council on Human Relations, an interracial organization aimed at fostering improved racial relations, "home, church, and writing left King little time for other endeavors" (51). When offered the presidency of the local NAACP chapter, for example, he declined, citing these other pressing responsibilities.

5. Quoted in Garrow, *Bearing the Cross*, 51.

6. The responsibility of religion to address racial oppression was a source of great controversy throughout much of the movement's early history. In particular, as Watson argued, it was a major issue in the 1963 Birmingham campaign, where local clergy sought to "place the controversy in a political arena, ignoring moral issues." A central strategy of King's famous "Letter from the Birmingham Jail," written in reaction to those efforts, was to articulate a comprehensive theological framework for viewing issues of social justice, which made resisting unjust laws the "higher responsibility" of God's people, thus moving the problem of unrest in Birmingham from the political to the theological and moral realm. Martha Solomon Watson, "The Issue is Justice: Martin Luther King Jr.'s Response to the Birmingham Clergy," *Rhetoric and Public Affairs* 7 (2004): 13. See also Snow, "Martin Luther King's Letter."

7. As Carson and others observe, King's creative retelling of the Exodus story is clearly influenced by an earlier sermon of Phillips Brooks titled, "The Egyptians Dead upon the Seashore." See *Papers*, vol. 3, 260, n. 7.

8. For a list of other examples where King uses this kind of statistical argument, see *Papers*, vol. 3, 261, n. 9.

9. Fisher, *Human Communication as Narration*, 105.

10. King, "Death of Evil," *Papers*, vol. 3, 261–62.

11. Martin Luther King Jr., "Birth of a New Nation," 7 April 1957, in *Papers*, vol. 4, 155–67.

12. Booth, *The Rhetoric of Fiction*, 5.

13. In the version of this sermon that King delivered on May 17, 1956, in New York, he actually makes this evocation of compassion toward the vanquished enemies explicit by asserting that the event did not symbolize the drowning of the Egyptians, "for no one can rejoice at the death or defeat of a human person." King, "Death of Evil," *Papers*, vol. 3, 260.

14. King, "Death of Evil," *Papers*, vol. 3, 261.

15. Ricoeur, *Time and Narrative*, 1:65.

16. As Osborn notes, symbolic space is a recurring feature in King's rhetoric. See Michael Osborn, "Rhetorical Distance in 'Letter from Birmingham Jail,'" *Rhetoric and Public Affairs* 7 (2004): 23–36.

17. Ricoeur, *Time and Narrative*, 1:66.

18. For a discussion of the rhetorical power of these processes of formal arrangement, see Burke, *Counter-Statement*, 29–62, and *A Rhetoric of Motives*, 58. For a discussion of the connection of stories to deeper, archetypal plots, see Wallace Martin, *Recent Theories of Narrative* (Ithaca: Cornell University Press, 1986), 89.

19. *Providence* in Christian thought has been traditionally viewed, in Lobstein's words, as "the exercise of God's wisdom, omnipotence, and goodness" and the "guidance of the world toward the end appointed by God." Although in many traditions, that concept entailed a belief that God worked directly and personally in the world, in others providence was viewed more from the perspective of "natural theology" or even deism, where God's purposes in the world are worked out through laws or processes that God has instituted in the universe. Given the way he described the events in the Exodus narrative, King was clearly using the term in this latter, more impersonal sense. P. Lobstein, "Providence," in *The New Schaff-Herzog Encyclopedia of Religious Knowledge*, ed. Samuel M. Jackson and Lefferts A. Loetscher (Grand Rapids: Baker, 1949–50), 9:306.

20. King, "Death of Evil," *Papers*, vol. 3, 261.

Chapter Four

1. King, Address to MIA Mass Meeting, 22 March 1956, *Papers*, vol. 3, 200.

2. Branch, *Parting the Waters*, 149–51.

3. Quoted in Garrow, *Bearing the Cross*, 28, 26.

4. Quoted in Garrow, *Bearing the Cross*, 25.

5. Quoted in Garrow, *Bearing the Cross*, 29.

6. Quoted in Garrow, *Bearing the Cross*, 53.

7. Of the four mass-rally speeches for which texts have been preserved from this period, three, delivered on December 5, 1955, March 22, 1956, and November 14, 1956, include references to the Exodus. All three were given at the Holt Street Baptist Church. (The fourth, delivered on April 26, 1956, at the Day Street Baptist Church, is preserved only as an excerpt.) Other boycott-related speeches that refer to the Exodus include "The 'New Negro' of the South: Behind the Montgomery Story," (a published version of his earlier speech, "A Realistic Look at Race Relations," delivered on May 17, 1956, at a gathering of the NAACP Legal Defense and Education Fund); "The Montgomery Story," delivered on June 27, 1956, at the annual convention of the NAACP in San Francisco; "Non-Aggression Procedures to Interracial Harmony,"

delivered on July 23, 1956, at a conference of the American Baptist Assembly and the American Home Mission Agency, in Green Lake, Wisconsin; "Facing the Challenge of a New Age," delivered on December 3, 1956, at the First Annual Institute on Nonviolence and Social Change at the Holt Street Baptist Church; and "Desegregation and the Future," delivered on December 15, 1956, at the Annual Luncheon of the National Committee for Rural Schools, in New York City. All are published in *Papers*, vol. 3. Of course, the later version of his sermon "The Death of Evil on the Seashore," given in New York City on May 17, 1956, before an audience of some twelve thousand people, is structured entirely around the Exodus story (*Papers*, vol. 3). *Papers*, vol. 4 includes these addresses, which invoke the Exodus: "A Realistic Look at the Question of Progress in the Area of Race Relations," delivered on April 10, 1957, at a freedom rally in St. Louis; "Give Us the Ballot," delivered on May 17, 1957, at the Prayer Pilgrimage for Freedom, in Washington, DC; and "Loving Your Enemies," delivered on November 17, 1957, at the Dexter Avenue Baptist Church, King's home congregation. Given King's practice of delivering the same speech on numerous occasions or repeating stock passages of text in different speeches, the evidence suggests that King's audiences frequently heard allusions to the biblical story applied to their history and present experience. That application was reinforced, of course, by the wide distribution of the later version of his "Death of Evil" sermon.

8. The program of the first mass meeting, on December 5, 1955, is representative of the form that these meetings took. It began with an opening hymn, "Onward Christian Soldiers," followed by a prayer and a reading from the Bible, after which King, Abernathy, and several others addressed the gathering. The meeting concluded with an offering, a closing hymn, "My Country 'Tis of Thee," and a benediction. *Papers*, vol. 3, 70.

9. Garrow, *Bearing the Cross*, 53.

10. King, MIA Mass Meeting, 5 December 1955, *Papers*, vol. 3, 73.

11. King, "Desegregation and the Future," *Papers*, vol. 3, 472.

12. King, "A Realistic Look at the Question of Progress," *Papers*, vol. 4, 171.

13. King, "Facing the Challenge of a New Age," *Papers*, vol. 3, 454; see also "A Realistic Look at the Question of Progress," *Papers*, vol. 4, 176.

14. King, "A Realistic Look at the Question of Progress," *Papers*, vol. 4, 171.

15. King, Address to MIA Mass Meeting, 14 November 1956, *Papers*, vol. 3, 433.

16. King, "A Realistic Look at the Question of Progress," *Papers*, vol. 4, 171.

17. Martin Luther King Jr., Address to Mass Meeting following King's trial before Judge Eugene Carter (quoted in Booker, "'God Will Find Way,'"), in *Papers*, vol. 3, 183.

18. King, Address to MIA Mass Meeting, 22 March 1956, *Papers*, vol. 3, 200.

19. King, "Non-Aggression Procedures," *Papers*, vol. 3, 327.

20. King, "Facing the Challenge of a New Age," *Papers*, vol. 3, 454.

21. King, "Montgomery Story," *Papers*, vol. 3, 303.

22. King, "Death of Evil," *Papers*, vol. 3, 284.

23. King, Address to MIA Mass Meeting, 22 March 22, 1956, *Papers*, vol. 3, 200.

24. King, MIA Mass Meeting, 5 December 1955, *Papers*, vol. 3, 73.

25. King, "Facing the Challenge of a New Age," *Papers*, vol. 3, 454.

26. King, "Montgomery Story," *Papers*, vol. 3, 303.

27. King, Address to MIA Mass Meeting, 22 March 1956, *Papers*, vol. 3, 200–201.

28. King, "Realistic Look at the Question of Progress," *Papers*, vol. 4, 178.

29. This insight comes from Osborn's observations on the "rhetorical determinism" inherent in the "light-dark" metaphor, which presents hearers with "patterned alternatives potential in historical process, depending on a choice specified in the speech." Although King's discourse does not resolve this tension into the kind of "either-or" dichotomy that we find in the light-dark metaphor, his emphasis on choice nevertheless offered his hearers the same sense that they were "playing an important role in an elemental conflict." Michael Osborn, "Archetypal Metaphor in Rhetoric: The Light-Dark Family," *Quarterly Journal of Speech* 53 (1967): 118.

30. King, Address to MIA Mass Meeting, 22 March 1956, *Papers*, vol. 3, 200.

31. King, "Death of Evil," *Papers*, vol. 3, 261.

32. King, Address to MIA Mass Meeting, 14 November 1956, *Papers*, vol. 3, 433.

33. King, "Facing the Challenge of a New Age," *Papers*, vol. 3, 454.

34. King, "A Realistic Look at the Question of Progress," *Papers*, vol. 4, 176.

35. King, "Give Us the Ballot," *Papers*, vol. 4, 215.

36. King, "Loving Your Enemies," *Papers*, vol. 4, 323.

37. King, Address to MIA Mass Meeting, 22 March 1956, *Papers*, vol. 3, 199–201.

38. King, Address to MIA Mass Meeting, 22 November 1956, *Papers*, vol. 3, 425, 432–33.

39. See chapter 3, n. 1, above.

40. Indeed, given both the story's place in African American culture and King's frequent references to it in connection with the Montgomery campaign, the Exodus in King's boycott speeches took on a similar function to what Osborn and Ehninger called "metaphoric stereotypes," which they defined as "conventionalized stimuli" that "not only make for ease and rapidity of comprehension, but may also be an effective means of arousing emotion." Michael M. Osborn and Douglas Ehninger, "The Metaphor in Public Address," *Speech Monographs* 29 (1962): 233.

41. Kirkwood, "Storytelling and Self-Confrontation," 64. Although Kirkwood clearly problematizes rigid distinctions between exemplary and metaphorical narratives, he nevertheless does agree that narratives as metaphors invite hearers to "participate" in the story rather than simply "hear" it. See his "Parables as Metaphors and Examples," 434. For a general account of the power of metaphor to structure experience, see Mark Johnson, "Introduction: Metaphor in the Philosophical Tradition," in Mark Johnson, ed., *Philosophical Perspectives on Metaphor* (Minneapolis: University of Minnesota Press, 1981), 3–47.

42. Davis, "Narrative and Social Movements," 16.

43. Kirkwood, "Storytelling and Self-Confrontation," 66.

44. King, Address to MIA Mass Meeting, 14 November 1956, *Papers*, vol. 3, 433.

45. Lawrence W. Levine, *Black Culture and Black Consciousness* (New York: Oxford University Press, 1977), 30–31.

46. Quoted in Lischer, *The Preacher King*, 138.

47. Quoted in Lischer, *The Preacher King*, 138–39.

48. King, MIA Mass Meeting, 5 December 1955, *Papers*, vol. 3, 73.

49. King, Address to MIA Mass Meeting, 14 November 1956, *Papers*, vol. 3, 433. In his original "Death of Evil" sermon, King represented the Red Sea crossing as the Supreme Court's 1954 ruling that the "separate but equal" policy in public schools was unconstitutional.

50. King, "Non-Aggression Procedures," *Papers*, vol. 3, 327.

51. A view of social change that emphasized blacks' agency almost exclusively emerged very early in the civil rights movement, ironically, in the discourse of Ralph David Abernathy. See Gary S. Selby, "Scoffing at the Enemy: The Burlesque Frame in the Rhetoric of Ralph David Abernathy," *Southern Communication Journal* 70 (2005): 134–45. Of course, it becomes full blown in the Black Power movement. See Charles Stewart, "Evolution of a Revolution: Stokely Carmichael and the Rhetoric of Black Power," *Quarterly Journal of Speech* 83 (1997): 429–46.

52. Morris, *Origins*, 98.

53. King, MIA Mass Meeting, 5 December 1955, *Papers*, vol. 3, 73.

Chapter Five

1. Carson et al., *Papers*, vol. 4, 7.

2. King, "Facing the Challenge of a New Age," *Papers*, vol. 3, 452.

3. Oates, *Let the Trumpet Sound*, 123.

4. Oates, *Let the Trumpet Sound*, 108.

5. Garrow, *Bearing the Cross*, 87.

6. Garrow, *Bearing the Cross*, 88, 90.

7. King, "Birth of a New Nation," *Papers*, vol. 4, 155. Subsequent citations from this speech in chapter 5 will be indicated in parentheses in the text.

8. The theme of the two ages (i.e., the passing of the old order and the dawning of the new) is a central theme in Jewish and Christian apocalyptic eschatology. Examples in the New Testament include Romans 13:11-14; 1 Corinthians 7:29-31; 1 John 2:17; 2 Peter 1:19. Particularly noteworthy is Revelation 21:4, a strongly consolatory text that offers a vision of freedom from suffering and want in these terms: "the old order of things has passed away" (NIV). For a rhetorical analysis of this language in the New Testament, see Gary S. Selby, "'Blameless at His Coming': The Discursive Construction of Eschatological Reality in 1 Thessalonians," *Rhetorica* 17 (Fall 1999): 385–410. For an exploration of this form in contemporary discourse generally, see Barry Brummett, *Contemporary Apocalyptic Rhetoric* (New York: Praeger, 1991). For an analysis of this form in several different King speeches, see David Bobbitt and Harold D. Mixon, "Prophecy and Apocalypse in the Rhetoric of Martin Luther King, Jr.," *Journal of Communication and Religion* 17 (1994): 27–38.

9. Bennett, "Storytelling in Criminal Trials," 3.

10. Osborn, "Archetypal Metaphor in Rhetoric," 116. As Martin noted, "Even in recent history, one can find examples of rather commonplace events that have been transformed, in the course of oral transmission, into archetypical stories; such changes offer further evidence that there are narrative patterns, innate or acquired, that shape

our perception of experience." *Recent Theories of Narrative*, 89. The reversal archetype is pervasive in the Bible. Examples include the story of Jacob's "election" over Esau (Gen 27), the "Song of Moses" (Exod 15), the "Song of Mary" (Luke 1), and Paul's assertion that in the gospel, God has confounded the "wisdom of this age" (1 Cor 2:6 NIV).

11. King, MIA Mass Meeting, 5 December 1955, *Papers*, vol. 3, 71.

12. King, Address to MIA Mass Meeting, 22 March 1956, *Papers*, vol. 3, 200–201.

13. Fisher, "Narration as a Human Communication Paradigm," 1–22.

14. Quoted in Richard E. Palmer, *Hermeneutics: Interpretation Theory in Schleiermacher, Dilthey, Heidegger, and Gadamer* (Evanston, Ill.: Northwestern University Press, 1969), 87.

15. For a discussion of the hermeneutic circle in biblical interpretation, see Hans-Georg Gadamer, *Truth and Method*, ed. and trans., Garrett Barden and John Cumming (New York: Seabury, 1975), 155–56.

16. See Palmer, *Hermeneutics*, 77, 120–21; and Joseph Bleicher, *Contemporary Hermeneutics: Hermeneutics as Method, Philosophy, and Critique* (London: Routledge & Kegan Paul, 1980), 98–103.

17. Ricoeur, *Time and Narrative*, 1:66.

18. Fisher, "Narration as a Human Communication Paradigm," 1–22. Although his focus is to offer more a descriptive than a critical account of the speech, Sunnemark's observation that King employs a rhetorical strategy of moving from the known to the unknown is helpful here. See Fredrik Sunnemark, *Ring Out Freedom! The Voice of Martin Luther King, Jr., and the Making of the Civil Rights Movement* (Bloomington: Indiana University Press, 2004), 170–71.

Chapter Six

1. See especially Garrow's account of King's selection as an alternative to either of the two dominant rival leaders in Montgomery, E. D. Nixon and L. Roy Bennett, in *Bearing the Cross*, 20–21.

2. Ware and Linkugel, "The Rhetorical *Persona*," 50.

3. Ware and Linkugel, "The Rhetorical *Persona*," 50.

4. Paul N. Campbell, "The *Personae* of Scientific Discourse," *Quarterly Journal of Speech* 61 (1975): 391.

5. Based on his study of the relationship between the personae and the substantive arguments in the works of Plato, Kauffman concluded that the characters themselves function "as another level of argument with the same logical status as the discursive statements"; Charles Kauffman, "Enactment as Argument in the *Gorgias*," *Philosophy and Rhetoric* 12 (1979): 128; Ware and Linkugel, "The Rhetorical *Persona*," 50.

6. Michael W. Casey, "The First Female Public Speakers in America (1630–1840): Searching for Egalitarian Christian Primitivism," *Journal of Communication and Religion* 23 (2000): 1–28.

7. Phyllis M. Japp, "Esther or Isaiah?: The Abolitionist-Feminist Rhetoric of Angelina Grimké," *Quarterly Journal of Speech* 71 (1985): 343.

8. Ware and Linkugel, "The Rhetorical *Persona*," 50.

9. Crogman, "Negro Education," in *Lift Every Voice*, 628.

10. King, MIA Mass Meeting, 5 December 1955, *Papers*, vol. 3, 73.

11. King, Address to Mass Meeting, 19 March 1956, *Papers*, vol. 3, 183.

12. King, Address to MIA Mass Meeting, 22 March 1956, *Papers*, vol. 3, 200.

13. King, "Montgomery Story," *Papers*, vol. 3, 306.

14. King, "Non-Aggression Procedures," *Papers*, vol. 3, 327.

15. King, Address to MIA Mass Meeting, 14 November 1956, *Papers*, vol. 3, 433.

16. King's November 14 address is an exception to this, including numerous direct exhortations (e.g., "I want to urge you this evening to keep on moving."). This reflects King's emerging personal ethos, resulting from both his leadership of the movement over the previous eleven months and the perception, marked by the Supreme Court ruling, that the campaign had been successful.

17. King, Address to MIA Mass Meeting, 14 November 1956, *Papers*, vol. 3, 433.

18. King, MIA Mass Meeting, 5 December 1955, *Papers*, vol. 3, 73.

19. Morris, *Origins*, 98.

20. Judith Hamera, "Loner on Wheels as Gaia: Identity, Rhetoric, and History in the Angry Art of Rachel Rosenthal," *Text and Performance Quarterly* 11 (1991): 38.

21. All excerpts are from the press account of King's sermon, "King Says Vision Told Him to Lead Integration Forces," *Montgomery Advertiser*, 28 January 1956, 2A.

22. See chapter 3, n. 1.

23. King, Address to MIA Mass Meeting, 22 March 1956, *Papers*, vol. 3, 200.

24. King, "Birth of a New Nation," *Papers*, vol. 4, 155, 157–58.

25. King, "Realistic Look at the Question of Progress," *Papers*, vol. 4, 171.

26. Coretta Scott King, Address at Youth March for Integrated Schools on October 25, 1958, in *The Papers of Martin Luther King, Jr.*, vol. 5, *Threshold of a New Decade, January 1959–December 1960*, eds. Clayborne Carson, Tenisha Armstrong, Susan Carson, Adrienne Clay, and Kieran Taylor (Berkeley: University of California Press, 2005), 515 (hereafter cited as *Papers*, vol. 5).

27. "Attack on Conscience," *Time* (18 February 1957), www.time.com/time/archive/preview/0,10987,809103,00.html (accessed May 11, 2006).

28. Ted Poston, "Fighting Pastor," *New York Post* (8 April 1957), reprinted in *Papers*, vol. 5, 227.

29. *Martin Luther King and the Montgomery Story* [Reprint] (New York: Fellowship of Reconciliation, 1957).

30. King, Address to MIA Mass Meeting, 14 November 1956), *Papers*, vol. 3, 432.

31. "King Says Vision Told Him," *Montgomery Advertiser*, 28 January 2956, 2A.

32. King, "Birth of a New Nation," *Papers*, vol. 4, 166.

33. Martin Luther King, Jr., "Keep Moving from this Mountain," Address at Spelman College on 10 April 1960, in *Papers*, vol. 5, 415.

34. King, *Papers*, vol. 5, 410, 415–16, 418.

35. King, *Papers*, vol. 5, 418–19.

36. Mass Meeting Surveillance Memorandum, 3 April 1963, Connor Papers.

Chapter Seven

1. Diane McWhorter, *Carry Me Home; Birmingham, Alabama: The Climactic Battle of the Civil Rights Movement* (New York: Simon & Schuster, 2001), 15.

2. Eskew, *But for Birmingham*, 17.

3. For discussions of racial oppression in Birmingham before the Birmingham campaign, see McWhorter, *Carry Me Home*; also Garrow, *Bearing the Cross*, 231–32.

4. For an excellent treatment of the public discourse surrounding this campaign, see John M. Murphy, "Domesticating Dissent: The Kennedys and the Freedom Rides," *Communication Monographs* 59 (1992): 61–78.

5. Garrow, *Bearing the Cross*, 157.

6. For a discussion of the SCLC's Citizenship Education Program, see Morris, *Origins*, 237–39.

7. Garrow, *Bearing the Cross*, 172.

8. Morris, *Origins*, 241.

9. Garrow, *Bearing the Cross*, 241.

10. Quoted in Morris, *Origins*, 267.

11. Quoted in Morris, *Origins*, 274.

12. Of the thirty-two surveillance reports covering the Birmingham movement included in the Connor Papers, twenty-three deal with the marches in some form, and in many cases, they are mentioned several times or are discussed at length.

13. Mass Meeting Surveillance Memorandum, 5 April 1963, Connor Papers.

14. Mass Meeting Surveillance Memorandum, 10 April 1963, Connor Papers.

15. Mass Meeting Surveillance Memorandum, 11 April 1963, Connor Papers.

16. Mass Meeting Surveillance Memorandum 3 May 1963, Connor Papers.

17. Mass Meeting Surveillance Memorandum, 5 May 1963, Connor Papers. The reporting detectives misidentify King's uncle as "Joseph King."

18. Mass Meeting Surveillance Memorandum, 2 May 1963, Connor Papers.

19. Mass Meeting Surveillance Memorandum, 9 May 1963, Connor Papers.

20. Morris, *Origins*, 264.

21. Morris, *Origins*, 268.

22. Quoted in Morris, *Origins*, 268.

23. See chapter 3, n. 1.

24. King, Address to MIA Mass Meeting, 22 March 1956, *Papers*, vol. 3, 200.

25. King, Address to MIA Mass Meeting, 14 November 1956, *Papers*, vol. 3, 433.

26. King, "Facing the Challenge of a New Age," *Papers*, vol. 4, 76, 83.

27. Martin Luther King, Jr., Address at Public Meeting of the Southern Christian Ministers Conference of Mississippi, 23 September 1959, in *Papers*, vol. 5, 281.

28. Martin Luther King, Jr., Address at the Fourth Annual Institute on Nonviolence and Social Change at Bethel Baptist Church, 3 December 1959, in *Papers*, vol. 5, 338.

29. King, "Keep Moving from this Mountain," *Papers*, vol. 5, 418–19.

30. Mass Meeting at Shiloh Baptist Church, 16 July 1962 (audiocassette), Archives of the Attorney General's Office, Georgia Department of Archives and History, Atlanta (transcribed by the author).

31. Ralph David Abernathy, Address to Mass Meeting at Shiloh Baptist Church, 16 July 1962 (audiocassette), Archives of the Attorney General's Office, Georgia Department of Archives and History, Atlanta (transcribed by the author.)

32. Ralph David Abernathy, Address to Mass Meeting at Kiokee Baptist Church, 20 July 1962 (audiocassette), Archives of the Attorney General's Office, Georgia Department of Archives and History, Atlanta (transcribed by the author.)

33. Mass Meeting at Shiloh Baptist Church, 24 July 1962 (audiocassette), Archives of the Attorney General's Office, Georgia Department of Archives and History, Atlanta (transcribed by the author).

34. One exception to this is Ralph Abernathy's assurance to a mass-meeting audience, when he and King first arrived in the city to help lead the protest, that he was not an outsider: "Some people may call us outsiders and outside agitators, but Alabama is my home. I came up from a cotton field in Georgia. The Lord called me from that cotton field just as he called Moses and said go down into Egypt land and set my people free. I heard something was going on in Birmingham. I have heard that the movement was rolling, so I came here." Mass Meeting Surveillance Memorandum, 3 April 1963, Connor Papers.

35. Mass Meeting Surveillance Memorandum, 3 April 1963, Connor Papers.

36. Mass Meeting Surveillance Memorandum, 6 April 1963, Connor Papers.

37. Mass Meeting Surveillance Memorandum, 29 April 1963, Connor Papers.

38. Mass Meeting Surveillance Memorandum, 9 May 1963, Connor Papers.

39. Ralph David Abernathy, Speech to Birmingham Mass Meeting, 10 May 1963 (audiocassette), "'A Happy Day in Birmingham: Birmingham, Testament of Nonviolence' Radio Program, Part 1," Donald H. Smith Tape Recordings Collection, State Historical Society, Wisconsin (transcribed by the author).

40. The surveillance transcript of one other meeting records Rev. Ed Gardner opening the rally with these words: "The Lord said to Moses, 'Go down to Egypt and set my people free.'" However the account does not make clear whether he is referring to King or simply evoking the Exodus more generally; Mass Meeting Surveillance Memorandum, 5 April 1963, Connor Papers.

41. Mass Meeting Surveillance Memorandum, 3 April 1963, Connor Papers.

42. Mass Meeting Surveillance Memorandum, 5 April 1963, Connor Papers.

43. Mass Meeting Surveillance Memorandum, 8 April 1963, Connor Papers.

44. Mass Meeting Surveillance Memorandum, 9 April 1963, Connor Papers.

45. Mass Meeting Surveillance Memorandum, 10 April 1963, Connor Papers.

46. Mass Meeting Surveillance Memorandum, 11 April 1963, Connor Papers.

47. Mass Meeting Surveillance Memorandum, 15 April 1963, Connor Papers.

48. Mass Meeting Surveillance Memorandum, 22 April 1963, Connor Papers.

49. Mass Meeting Surveillance Memorandum, 23 April 1963, Connor Papers.

50. Mass Meeting Surveillance Memorandum, 11 April 1963, Connor Papers.

51. Mass Meeting Surveillance Memorandum, 15 April 1963, Connor Papers.

52. Mass Meeting Surveillance Memorandum, 12 April 1963, Connor Papers.

53. Mass Meeting Surveillance Memorandum, 23 April 1963, Connor Papers.

54. Mass Meeting Surveillance Memorandum, 2 May 1963, Connor Papers.

55. Martin Luther King, Jr., Speech to Birmingham, Alabama, Mass Meeting, 3 May 1963, Archives Collection, box 5, Birmingham Public Library.

56. Martin Luther King, Jr., Speech to Birmingham Mass Meeting, 6 May 1963 (compact disc), "Birmingham, Alabama, 1963: Mass Meeting," *Lest We Forget*, vol. 2 (Washington, DC: Smithsonian Folkways Recordings, 2001) (transcribed by the author).

57. Ralph D. Abernathy, Speech to Birmingham Mass Meeting, 6 May 1963 (compact disc), "Birmingham, Alabama, 1963: Mass Meeting," *Lest We Forget*, vol. 2 (transcribed by the author).

58. Martin Luther King, Jr., Speech to Birmingham Mass Meeting, 10 May 1963 (audiocassette), "'A Happy Day in Birmingham: Birmingham, Testament of Nonviolence' Radio Program, Part 1," Donald H. Smith Tape Recordings Collection, State Historical Society of Wisconsin (transcribed by the author).

59. Quoted in Morris, *Origins*, 257. Morris also records the recollection of one leader in the Albany protest, William Kunstler, who noted that demonstrators would march out of the church singing "I Ain't Gonna Let Nobody Turn Me Around" (248).

60. Transcribed by the author from original recordings included in the collection titled, "Movement Soul: Sounds of the Freedom Movement in the South, 1963–1964" *Lest We Forget*, vol. 1 (Washington, DC: Smithsonian Folkways Recordings, 2001).

61. Morris, *Origins*, 256.

62. Mass Meeting Surveillance Memorandum, 5 April 1963, Connor Papers. The reporting detectives misidentify Young as "Reverend Robert Young."

63. Mass Meeting Surveillance Memorandum, 12 April 1963, Connor Papers.

64. Mass Meeting Surveillance Memorandum, 8 April 1963, Connor Papers.

65. Mass Meeting Surveillance Memorandum, 8 April 1963, Connor Papers.

66. Mass Meeting Surveillance Memorandum, 2 May 1963, Connor Papers.

67. "Movement Soul," *Lest We Forget*, vol. 2.

68. Department of History, University of Houston, http://vi.uh.edu/pages/buzzmat/aintgonna.html

69. Quoted in Morris, *Origins*, 248.

70. Turner, "Social Dramas," 163.

71. Rappaport, *Ritual and Religion*, 52.

72. Rothenbuhler, "Ritual Communication," 62.

73. Rappaport, *Ritual and Religion*, 141.

74. Rothenbuhler, "Ritual Communication," 19.

75. King, "Birth of a New Nation," *Papers*, vol. 4, 159, 163.

Conclusion

1. Martin Luther King, Jr., "Our God is Marching On," 25 March 1965, Martin Luther King, Jr. Papers Project, Stanford University, http://www.stanford.edu/group/King/publications/speeches/Our_God_is_marching_on.html

2. "King Says Vision Told Him," *Montgomery Advertiser*, 28 January 1956, 2A.

3. Martin Luther King, Jr., "Where Do We Go from Here?" in *The Voice of Black America: Major Speeches by Negroes in the United States*, 1797–1971, ed. Philip S. Foner (New York: Simon & Schuster, 1972), 1077.

4. King, "I've Been to the Mountaintop."

5. For a discussion of this shift, see Stewart, "Evolution of a Revolution," 432–36.

6. Lentz, *Symbols*, 1.

7. Eskew, *But for Birmingham*, 16.

8. I am indebted for this critical perspective to William G. Kirkwood's insightful analysis into this experiential function of narrative in "Storytelling and Self-Confrontation."

9. Clayborne Carson, Book Reviews, *Journal of American History* 85 (1998): 1155.

10. King, "Birth of a New Nation," *Papers*, vol. 4, 166.

11. Gamson, "The Social Psychology," 67.

BIBLIOGRAPHY

Primary Sources (Archival Materials, Manuscript Collections, etc.)

Archives of the Attorney General's Office. Georgia Department of Archives and History. Atlanta.

Archives Collection. Birmingham Public Library. Birmingham.

Booker, James. "'God Will Find a Way' Boycotters." *New Amsterdam News*, March 24, 1956. Quoted in *The Papers of Martin Luther King, Jr. Vol. 3, Birth of a New Age, December 1955–December 1956*. Edited by Clayborne Carson, Stewart Burns, Susan Carson, Peter Holloran, and Dana Powell, 183. Berkeley: University of California Press, 1997.

Bryant, M. Edward. "How Shall We Get Our Rights?" In *Lift Every Voice: African American Oratory, 1787–1900*, edited by Philip S. Foner and Robert J. Branham, 676–80. Tuscaloosa: University of Alabama Press, 1998.

Crogman, William H. "Negro Education—Its Helps and Hindrances." In *Lift Every Voice: African American Oratory, 1787–1900*, edited by Philips S. Foner and Robert J. Branham, 623–33. Tuscaloosa: University of Alabama Press, 1998.

Department of History. University of Houston. http://vi.uh.edu/pages/buzzmat/aintgonna.html.

Donald H. Smith Tape Recordings Collection. State Historical Society. Wisconsin.

Fellowship of Reconciliation. "Martin Luther King and the Montgomery Story." Reprint, New York: Fellowship of Reconciliation, 1957.

Foner, Philip S., ed. *The Voice of Black America: Major Speeches by Negroes in the United States, 1797–1971*. New York: Simon & Schuster, 1972.

Foner, Philip S., and Robert J. Branham, eds. *Lift Every Voice: African American Oratory, 1787–1900*. Tuscaloosa: University of Alabama Press, 1998.

Garnett, Henry Highland. "An Address to the Slaves of the United States of America." In *Lift Every Voice: African American Oratory, 1787–1900*, edited by Philip S. Foner and Robert J. Branham, 198–205. Tuscaloosa: University of Alabama Press, 1998.

———. "Let the Monster Perish." In *Lift Every Voice: African American Oratory, 1787–1900*, edited by Philip S. Foner and Robert J. Branham, 432–43. Tuscaloosa: University of Alabama Press, 1998.

Garvey, Amy Jacques, ed. *Philosophy and Opinions of Marcus Garvey*. Vol. 2. Reprint, New York: Arno Press, 1969.

Harlan, Robert J. "Migration is the Onl Remedy for our Wrongs." In *Lift Every Voice: African American Oratory, 1787–1900*, edited by Philip S. Foner and Robert J. Branham, 599–602. Tuscaloosa: University of Alabama Press, 1998.

Hayden, Lewis. "Deliver Us From Such a Moses." In *Lift Every Voice: African American Oratory, 1787–1900*, edited by Philip S. Foner and Robert J. Branham, 454–56. Tuscaloosa: University of Alabama Press, 1998.

Houck, Davis W., and David E. Dixon, eds. *Rhetoric, Religion, and the Civil Rights Movement, 1954–1965*. Waco, Tex.: Baylor University Press, 2006.

Johnson, William Bishop. "National Perils." In *Lift Every Voice: African American Oratory, 1787–1900*, edited by Philip S. Foner and Robert J. Branham, 708–713. Tuscaloosa: University of Alabama Press, 1998.

Jones, Absalom. "A Thanksgiving Sermon." In *Lift Every Voice: African American Oratory, 1787–1900*, edited by Philip S. Foner and Robert J. Branham, 73–79. Tuscaloosa: University of Alabama Press, 1998.

Keckley, Elizabeth. *Behind the Scenes, or Thirty Years a Slave, and Four Years in the White House*. New York: G. W. Carlton, 1868. http://digital.nypl.org/schomburg/writers_aa19/.

King, Martin Luther King, Jr. *Strength to Love*. New York: Harper and Row, 1963.

———. *The Papers of Martin Luther King, Jr.* Vol. 3, *Birth of a New Age, December 1955–December 1956*. Edited by Clayborne Carson, Stewart Burns, Susan Carson, Peter Holloran, and Dana Powell. Berkeley: University of California Press, 1997.

———. *The Papers of Martin Luther King, Jr.* Vol. 4, *Symbol of the Movement, January 1957–December 1958*. Edited by Clayborne Carson, Susan Carson, Adrienne Clay, Virginia Shadron, and Kieran Taylor. Berkeley: University of California Press, 2000.

———. *The Papers of Martin Luther King, Jr.* Vol. 5, *Threshold of a New Decade, January 1959–December 1960*. Edited by Clayborne Carson, Tenisha

Armstrong, Susan Carson, Adrienne Clay, and Kieran Taylor. Berkeley: University of California Press, 2005.

Lest We Forget. Vol. 1, "Birmingham, Alabama, 1963: Mass Meeting." Vol. 2, "Movement Soul: Sounds of the Freedom Movement in the South, 1963-1964." Washington, DC: Smithsonian Folkways Recordings, 2001 (2 compact discs).

Martin Luther King, Jr., Papers Project. Stanford University. http://www. stanford.edu/group/King/mlkpapers/.

Montgomery Advertiser. "King Says Vision Told Him to Lead Integration Forces," January 28, 1956, 2A. http://nl.newsbank.com/nl-search/ we/Archives?p_action=doc&p_docid=10D160229EF51068&p_ docnum=1&p_theme=gannett&s_site=montgomeryadvertiser&p_ product=MGAB.

Negrospirituals.com. http://www.negrospirituals.com/.

Rawick, George P., ed. *The American Slave: A Composite Autobiography.* Vol. 18, *The Unwritten History of Slavery (Fisk University).* Westport, Conn.: Greenwood, 1972.

Steward, Austin. "Termination of Slavery." In *Lift Every Voice: African American Oratory, 1787–1900,* edited by Philip S. Foner and Robert J. Branham, 104–109. Tuscaloosa: University of Alabama Press, 1998.

Theophilus Eugene "Bull" Connor Papers. Archives Department, Birmingham Public Library.

Truth, Sojourner. *Narrative of Sojourner Truth; A Bondswoman of Olden Time, Emancipated by the New York Legislature in the Early Part of the Present Century; With a History of Her Labors and Correspondence Drawn from her "Book of Life."* Battle Creek, Mich.: n.p., 1878. http://digital.nypl. org/schomburg/writers_aa19/.

Watkins, Frances Ellen. "Liberty for Slaves." In *Lift Every Voice: African American Oratory, 1787–1900,* edited by Philip S. Foner and Robert J. Branham, 305–307. Tuscaloosa: University of Alabama Press, 1998.

Secondary Works

Asante, Molefi Kete. *The Afrocentric Idea.* Philadelphia: Temple University Press, 1987.

———. "Intellectual Dislocation: Applying Analytic Afrocentricity to Narratives of Identity." *Howard Journal of Communications* 13 (2002): 97–110.

Bakhtin, M. M. *The Dialogic Imagination*. Edited by Michael Holquist. Translated by Caryl Emerson and Michael Holquist. Austin: University of Texas Press, 1981.

Bell, Catherine. *Ritual Theory, Ritual Practice*. New York: Oxford University Press, 1992.

Bennett, W. Lance. "Storytelling in Criminal Trials: A Model of Social Judgment," *Quarterly Journal of Speech* 64 (1985): 1–22.

Bleicher, Joseph. *Contemporary Hermeneutics: Hermeneutics as Method, Philosophy, and Critique*. London: Routledge & Kegan Paul, 1980.

Bishop, Ronald. "It's Not Always About the Money: Using Narrative Analysis to Explore Newspaper Coverage of the Act of Collecting." *Communication Review* 6 (2003): 117–35.

Bobbitt, David, and Harold D. Mixon. "Prophecy and Apocalypse in the Rhetoric of Martin Luther King, Jr." *Journal of Communication and Religion* 17 (1994): 27–38.

Boje, David M. *Narrative Methods for Organizational and Communication Research*. London: Sage, 2001.

Booth, Wayne C. *The Rhetoric of Fiction*. Chicago: University of Chicago Press, 1983.

Branch, Taylor. *Parting the Waters: America in the King Years, 1954–63*. New York: Simon & Schuster, 1988.

Brown, Sterling A. "The Spirituals." In *The Book of Negro Folklore*, edited by Langston Hughes and Arna Bontemps, 279–89. New York: Dodd, Mead, 1958.

Browne, Stephen Howard. "Jefferson's First Declaration of Independence: *A Summary View of the Rights of British America* Revisited." *Quarterly Journal of Speech* 89 (2003): 235–52.

Brueggemann, Walter. "The Book of Exodus: Introduction, Commentary, and Reflections." In *The New Interpreter's Bible*, edited by Leander E. Keck, 1:675–981. Nashville: Abingdon, 1994.

Brummett, Barry. *Contemporary Apocalyptic Rhetoric*. New York: Praeger, 1991.

Buechler, Steven M. *Social Movements in Advanced Capitalism*. New York: Oxford University Press, 2000.

Burke, Kenneth. *Attitudes Toward History*. 3rd ed. Berkeley: University of California Press, 1984.

———. *Counter-Statement*. 2nd ed. Berkeley: University of California Press, 1953. Reprinted, 1968.

———. "Dramatism." In *The International Encyclopedia of the Social Sciences*, 7:445–52. New York: MacMillan, 1968. Reprinted, 1972.

————. *The Philosophy of Literary Form*. 3rd ed. Berkeley: University of California Press, 1973.

————. *A Rhetoric of Motives*. Berkeley: University of California Press, 1950. Reprinted, 1969.

Burns, Stewart. *To The Mountaintop: Martin Luther King Jr.'s Sacred Mission to Save America: 1955–1968*. New York: HarperCollins, 2004.

Campbell, Paul N. "The *Personae* of Scientific Discourse." *Quarterly Journal of Speech* 61 (1975): 391–405.

Carson, Clayborne. Book Reviews. *Journal of American History* 85 (1998): 1155–1156.

Casey, Michael W. "The First Female Public Speakers in America (1630–1840): Searching for Egalitarian Christian Primitivism." *Journal of Communication and Religion* 23 (2000): 1–28.

Childs, Brevard S. *Introduction to the Old Testament as Scripture*. Philadelphia: Fortress, 1979.

Davis, Joseph E. "Narrative and Social Movements: The Power of Stories." In *Stories of Change: Narrative and Social Movements*, edited by Joseph E. Davis, 3–29. Albany: State University of New York Press, 2002.

Du Bois, W. E. B. *The Souls of Black Folk*. 1903. Reprint, New York: Bantam Books, 1989.

Dudziak. Mary L. *Cold War Civil Rights: Race and the Image of American Democracy*. Princeton, N.J.: Princeton University Press, 2000.

Ehrenhaus, Peter. "Cultural Narratives and the Therapeutic Motif: The Political Containment of Vietnam Veterens." In *Narrative and Social Control*, edited by Dennnis K. Mumby, 77–96. Newbury Park, Calif.: Sage, 1993.

Eskew, Glenn T. *But for Birmingham*. Chapel Hill: University of North Carolina, 1997.

Fairclough Adam. "The Civil Rights Movement in Louisiana, 1939–54." In *The Making of Martin Luther King and the Civil Rights Movement*, edited by Brian Ward and Anthony Badger, 15–28. Washington Square: New York University Press, 1996.

Fisher, Walter. *Human Communication as Narration: Toward a Philosophy of Reason, Value, and Action*. Columbia: University of South Carolina Press, 1987.

————. "Narration as a Human Communication Paradigm." *Communication Monographs* 51 (1984): 1–22

Foss, Sonja. *Rhetorical Criticism: Exploration and Practice*. 2nd ed. Long Grove, Ill.: Waveland, 1996.

Gadamer, Hans-Georg. *Truth and Method*. Edited and translated by Garrett Barden and John Cumming. New York: Seabury, 1975.

Gamson, William A. "The Social Psychology of Collective Action," in *Frontiers in Social Movement Theory*, edited by Aldon D. Morris and Carol McClurg Mueller, 53–76. New Haven: Yale University Press, 1992.

Garrow, David J. *Bearing the Cross: Martin Luther King, Jr. and the Southern Christian Leadership Conference*. New York: William Morrow, 1986.

Geertz, Clifford. *The Interpretation of Cultures*. New York: Basic Books, 1973.

Genovese, Eugene D. *Roll, Jordan, Roll: The World the Slaves Made*. New York: Pantheon, 1974.

Glaude, Eddie S. *Exodus! Religion, Race, and Nation in Early Nineteenth-Century Black America*. Chicago: University of Chicago Press, 2000.

Goldzwig, Steven R., and Patricia A. Sullivan. "Narrative and Counternarrative in Print-Mediated Coverage of Milwaukee Alderman Michael McGee." *Quarterly Journal of Speech* 86 (2000): 215–31.

Griffin, Charles J. G. "The Rhetoric of Form in Conversion Narratives." *Quarterly Journal of Speech* 76 (1990): 152–63.

———. "The 'Washingtonian Revival': Narrative and the Moral Transformation of Temperance Reform in Antebellum America." *Southern Communication Journal* 66 (2000): 66–78.

Griffin, Leland M. "The Rhetoric of Historical Movements." *Quarterly Journal of Speech* 38 (April 1952): 184–88.

Gronbeck, Bruce. "Narrative, Enactment, and Television Programming." *Southern Speech Communication Journal* 48 (1983): 234.

Hamera, Judith. "Loner on Wheels as Gaia: Identity, Rhetoric, and History in the Angry Art of Rachel Rosenthal." *Text and Performance Quarterly* 11 (1991): 77–94.

Harris, Fredrick C. *Something Within: Religion in African-American Political Activism*. New York: Oxford University Press, 1999.

Hendel, Ronald. "The Exodus in Biblical Memory." *Journal of Biblical Literature* 120 (2004): 601–22.

Hughes, Langston, and Arna Bontemps, eds. *The Book of Negro Folklore*. New York: Dodd, Mead, 1958.

Japp, Phyllis M. "Esther or Isaiah?: The Abolitionist-Feminist Rhetoric of Angelina Grimké." *Quarterly Journal of Speech* 71 (1985): 335–48.

Johnson, Mark. "Introduction: Metaphor in the Philosophical Tradition." In *Philosophical Perspectives on Metaphor*, edited by Mark Johnson, 3–47. Minneapolis: University of Minnesota Press, 1981.

Kauffmann, Charles. "Enactment as Argument in the *Gorgias*," *Philosophy and Rhetoric* 12 (1979): 114–29.

Kenny, Robert Wade. "Thinking about *Rethinking Life and Death*: The Character and Rhetorical Function of Dramatic Irony in a Life Ethics Discourse." *Rhetoric and Public Affairs* 6 (2003): 657–86.

Kirk, John A. " 'He Founded a Movement': W. H. Flowers, the Committee on Negro Organizations and the Origins of Black Activism in Arkansas, 1940–57." In *The Making of Martin Luther King and the Civil Rights Movement*, edited by Brian Ward and Anthony Badger, 29–44. Washington Square: New York University Press, 1996.

Kirkwood, William G. "Parables as Metaphors and Examples." *Quarterly Journal of Speech* 71 (1985): 422–40.

———. "Storytelling and Self-Confrontation: Parables as Communication Strategies." *Quarterly Journal of Speech* 69 (1983): 58–74.

Klandermans, Bert. "The Social Construction of Protest and Multiorganizational Fields." In *Frontiers in Social Movement Theory*, edited by Aldon D. Morris and Carol McClurg Mueller, 77–103. New Haven: Yale University Press, 1992.

Klinkner, Philip A., and Rogers M. Smith. *The Unsteady March; The Rise and Decline of Racial Equality in America*. Chicago: University of Chicago Press, 1999.

Langellier, Kristin M., and Eric E. Peterson. "Family Storytelling as a Strategy of Social Control." In *Narrative and Social Control*, edited by Dennis K. Mumby, 49–76. Newbury Park, Calif.: Sage, 1993.

Lentz, Richard. *Symbols, the News Magazines, and Martin Luther King*. Baton Rouge: Louisiana State University Press, 1990.

Levine, Lawrence W. *Black Culture and Black Consciousness*. New York: Oxford University Press, 1977.

Lewis, David L. *King: A Biography*, 2nd ed. Urbana: University of Illinois Press, 1978.

Lewis, William F. "Telling America's Story: Narrative Form and the Reagan Presidency." *Quarterly Journal of Speech* 73 (1987): 280–302.

Lischer, Richard. *The Preacher King: Martin Luther King, Jr. and the Word that Moved America*. New York: Oxford University Press, 1995.

Lobstein, P. "Providence." In *The New Schaff-Herzog Encyclopedia of Religious Knowledge*, edited by Samuel M. Jackson and Lefferts A. Loetscher, 9:306–12. Grand Rapids, Mich.: Baker, 1949–50.

Lovell, John. *Black Song: The Forge and the Flame*. New York: MacMillan, 1972.

Lucaites, John Louis, and Celeste Michelle Condit. "Re-constructing Narrative Theory: A Functional Perspective." *Journal of Communication* 35 (1985): 90–108.

Lucas, Stephen E. "Coming to Terms with Movement Studies." *Central States Speech Journal* 31 (1980): 255–66.

Lynch, Christopher. "Reaffirmation of God's Anointed Prophet: The Use of Chiasm in Martin Luther King's 'Mountaintop' Speech." *Howard Journal of Communications* 6 (1995): 12–31.

MacIntyre, Alasdair. *After Virtue: A Study in Moral Theory.* Notre Dame, Ind.: Notre Dame University Press, 1981.

Martin, Wallace. *Recent Theories of Narrative.* Ithaca, N.Y.: Cornell University Press, 1986.

Mays, Benjamin, and Joseph Nicholson. *The Negro's Church.* New York: Institute of Social and Religious Research, 1933.

McAdam, Doug. "The Framing Function of Movement Tactics: Strategic Dramaturgy in the American Civil Rights Movement." In *Comparative Perspectives on Social Movements,* edited by Doug McAdam, John D. McCarthy, and Mayer N. Zald, 338–56. Cambridge: Cambridge University Press, 1996.

McGee, Michael Calvin. "'Social Movement': Phenomenon or Meaning?" *Central States Speech Journal* 31 (1980): 233–44.

McGee, Michael Calvin, and John S. Nelson. "Narrative Reason in Public Argument," *Journal of Communication* 35 (1985): 139–55.

Meyers, Carol. *Exodus.* New York: Cambridge University Press, 2005.

McWhorter, Diane. *Carry Me Home: Birmingham, Alabama:, The Climactic Battle of the Civil Rights Movement.* New York: Simon & Schuster, 2001.

Miller, Keith D. "Alabama as Egypt: Martin Luther King, Jr., and the Religion of Slaves." In *Martin Luther King, Jr., and the Sermonic Power of Public Discourse,* edited by Carolyn Calloway-Thomas and John Louis Lucaites, 18–32. Tuscaloosa: University of Alabama University Press, 1993.

———. *Voice of Deliverance: The Language of Martin Luther King, Jr., and Its Sources.* New York: Free Press, 1992.

Morris, Aldon D. *The Origins of the Civil Rights Movement.* New York: Free Press, 1984.

Morris III, Charles E., and Stephen H. Browne, eds., *Readings on the Rhetoric of Social Protest.* State College, Penn.: Strata, 2001.

Mumby, Dennis K. "The Political Function of Narratives in Organizations." *Communication Monographs* 54 (1987): 113–27.

Murphy, John M. "Domesticating Dissent: The Kennedys and the Freedom Rides." *Communication Monographs* 59 (1992): 61–78.

Murphy, Troy A. "Romantic Democracy and the Rhetoric of Heroic Citizenship." *Communication Quarterly* 51 (2003): 192–208.

Oates, Stephen B. *Let the Trumpet Sound: The Life of Martin Luther King, Jr.* New York: Harper & Row, 1982.

Osborn, Michael. "Archetypal Metaphor in Rhetoric: The Light-Dark Family." *Quarterly Journal of Speech* 53 (1967): 115–26.

———. "Rhetorical Distance in 'Letter from Birmingham Jail.'" *Rhetoric & Public Affairs* 7 (2004): 23–36.

———. "The Last Mountaintop of Martin Luther King, Jr." In *Martin Luther King, Jr., and the Sermonic Power of Public Discourse*, edited by Carolyn Calloway-Thomas and John Louis Lucaites, 147–61. Tuscaloosa: University of Alabama University Press, 1993.

Osborn, Michael, and John Bakke. "The Melodramas of Memphis: Contending Narratives during the Sanitation Strike of 1968." *Southern Communication Journal* 63 (1998): 220–34.

Osborn, Michael M., and Douglas Ehninger, "The Metaphor in Public Address." *Speech Monographs* 29 (1962): 223–34.

Palmer, Richard E. *Hermeneutics: Interpretation Theory in Schleiermacher, Dilthey, Heidegger, and Gadamer.* Evanston, Ill.: Northwestern University Press, 1969.

Raboteau, Albert J. "African-Americans, Exodus, and the American Israel." In *African American Christianity: Essays in History*, edited by Paul E. Johnson, 1–17. Berkeley: University of California Press, 1994.

———. *Slave Religion: The "Invisible Institution" in the Antebellum South.* New York: Oxford University Press, 1978.

Rappaport, Roy A. "Ritual." In *International Encyclopedia of Communications*, edited by Erik Barnouw, George E. Gerbner, Wilbur Schramm, Tobia L. Worth, and Larry Gross, 3:467–73. New York: Oxford University Press, 1989.

———. *Ritual and Religion in the Making of Humanity.* Cambridge, UK: Cambridge University Press, 1999.

Ricoeur, Paul. *Time and Narrative.* Vol. 1. Chicago: University of Chicago Press, 1984.

Rosteck, Thomas. "Narrative in Martin Luther King's 'I've Been to the Mountaintop.'" *Southern Communication Journal* 58 (1992): 22–32.

Rothenbuhler, Eric W. *Ritual Communication: From Everyday Conversation to Mediated Ceremony.* Thousand Oaks, Calif.: Sage, 1998.

Sanger, Kerran L. "Slave Resistance and Rhetorical Self-Definition: Spirituals as a Strategy." *Western Journal of Communication* 59 (1995): 177–92.

Schely-Newman, Esther. "Finding One's Place: Locale Narratives in an Israeli Moshav." *Quarterly Journal of Speech* 83 (1997): 401–15.

Scott, Robert L. "Narrative Theory and Communication Research." *Quarterly Journal of Speech* 70 (1984): 197–204.

Selby, Gary S. "'Blameless at His Coming': The Discursive Construction of Eschatological Reality in 1 Thessalonians." *Rhetorica* 17 (1999): 385–410.

———. "Framing Social Protest: The Exodus Narrative in Martin Luther King's Montgomery Bus Boycott Rhetoric." *Journal of Communication and Religion* 24 (2001): 68–93.

———. "Scoffing at the Enemy: The Burlesque Frame in the Rhetoric of Ralph David Abernathy." *Southern Communication Journal* 70 (2005): 134–45.

Shenhav, Shaul R. "Thin and Thick Narrative Analysis: On the Question of Defining and Analyzing Political Narratives." *Narrative Inquiry* 15 (2005): 75–99.

Smylie, James H. "On Jesus, Pharaohs, and the Chosen People: Martin Luther King as Biblical Interpreter and Humanist." *Interpretation* 24 (1970): 74–91.

Snow, Malinda. "Martin Luther King's 'Letter from Birmingham Jail' as Pauline Epistle." *Quarterly Journal of Speech* 71 (1985): 318–34.

Solomon, Martha. "Autobiographies as Rhetorical Narratives: Elizabeth Cady Stanton and Anna Howard Shaw as 'New Women.'" *Communication Studies* 42 (1991): 254–70.

Stewart, Charles. "Evolution of a Revolution: Stokely Carmichael and the Rhetoric of Black Power." *Quarterly Journal of Speech* 83 (1997): 429–46.

Stewart, Charles J., Craig A. Smith, and Robert E. Denton Jr. *Persuasion and Social Movements.* 2nd ed. Prospect Heights, Ill.: Waveland, 2001.

Stroud, Scott R. "Narrative as Argument in Indian Philosophy: The *Astāvakra Gītā* as Multivalent Narrative." *Philosophy and Rhetoric* 37 (2004): 42–71.

Sundquist, Eric J. *Strangers in the Land: Blacks, Jews, Post-Holocaust America.* Cambridge, Mass.: Belknap, 2005.

Sunnemark, Fredrik. *Ring Out Freedom! The Voice of Martin Luther King, Jr., and the Making of the Civil Rights Movement.* Bloomington: Indiana University Press, 2004.

Thornton, J. Mills, III. *Dividing Lines: Municipal Politics and the Struggle for Civil Rights in Montgomery, Birmingham, and Selma*. Tuscaloosa: University of Alabama Press, 2002.

Turner, Victor. "Social Dramas and Stories About Them." *Critical Inquiry* 7 (1980): 141–68.

Wald, Priscilla. *Constituting Americans: Cultural Anxiety and Narrative Form*. Durham, N.C.: Duke University Press, 1995.

Walzer, Michael. *Exodus and Revolution*. New York: Basic Books, 1985.

Ware, B. L., and Wil A. Linkugel. "The Rhetorical *Persona*: Marcus Garvey as Black Moses." *Communication Monographs* 49 (1982): 50–62.

Watson, Martha Solomon. "The Issue is Justice: Martin Luther King Jr.'s Response to the Birmingham Clergy." *Rhetoric and Public Affairs* 7 (2004): 1–22.

White, Hayden. "The Value of Narrativity in the Representation of Reality." In *On Narrative*, edited by W. J. T. Mitchell, 1–24. Chicago: University of Chicago Press, 1981.

White, John. "Nixon *was* the One: Edgar Daniel Nixon, the MIA, and the Montgomery Bus Boycott." In *The Making of Martin Luther King and the Civil Rights Movement*, edited by Brian Ward and Anthony Badger, 45–63. Washington Square: New York University Press, 1996.

Wilson, Kirt H. "Interpreting the Discursive Field of the Montgomery Bus Boycott: Martin Luther King Jr.'s Holt Street Address." *Rhetoric and Public Affairs* 8 (2004): 299–306.

INDEX

Aaron (brother of Moses), 31, 33, 119

Abernathy, Ralph David: and Birmingham campaign, 143-54; 187n51, 191n34; and Freedom Rides, 139; and Montgomery bus boycott, 73, 75, 185n8; as King's confidant, 52; as target of bombing, 94

abolition, 38

"Address to the Slaves of the United States of America," 47

Africa, 107–12

African American church. *See* black church

"Ain't Gonna Let Nobody Turn Me Around," 147–48, 152–55, 192n59

Alabama Christian Movement for Human Rights (ACMHR), 6, 141, 153

Alabama Christian Movement for Human Rights choir, 153

Alabama state troopers, 6

Albany campaign, 55, 47–48, 140–41, 192n59

Amalekites, 40

American Baptist Assembly, 77, 120

American Home Missions Agency, 175n26, 185n7

Amorites, 30, 80, 84, 118, 121, 133, 146

Anniston, 139

anticolonialism. *See* colonialism

antimetabole, 111

apocalyptic, 97, 102, 187n8

apostrophe, 124

archetype, 28, 63, 117–19, 184n18, 188n10; Exodus narrative as, 10, 41; good vs. evil as, 63; metaphors as, 102; dramatic persona as, 117, 132; reversal as, 92, 102

Asante, Molefi K., 35, 180n18

Atlanta: boyhood home of Martin Luther King, 129–30; segregation in, 153; location of Marcus Garvey's imprisonment, 48; location of King's first involvement with sit-in movement, 139; location of King's NAACP Emancipation Day Rally Speech, 146; location of King's Spelman College Founder's Day address, 132, 147

Bakhtin, M. M., 20

Bakke, John, 19

Beard, Rev. Luke, 4

Bell, Catherine, 24

Bennett, L. Roy, 118n1

Bennett, W. Lance, 102, 117n20

Bevel, James, 151, 154

Billups, Rev. Charles, 143

Birmingham: as nation's most racially oppressive city, 2, 36; as high point of civil rights movement, 7, 10–11, 137–38, 141, 163–65, 167–68; campaign in, 2, 6, 9, 136–61, 170, 191n43; church bombing in, 5; industrialists' funding of black

191n34; related to oppression of blacks in U.S., 9, 51–68, 75–77, 80–82, 84, 87, 89, 95–101, 103–5, 121, 126–28, 133, 146–48, 160, 163–64, 172; related to colonialism, 54, 57, 60–61, 81, 88, 95–101, 103–8, 112, 121, 146

Egyptians. *See* Egypt

Ehninger, Douglas, 85, 186n40

Ehrenhaus, Peter, 29, 177n28, 179n48

Emancipation Day Rally, 146

Emancipation Proclamation, 40

emplotment, 52, 63

epanaphora, 111

eschatology. *See* apocalyptic

Eskew, Glenn T., 4, 137, 169

Exodus: applied to Ghana, 95–102; biblical account of, 30–34, 46, 146; in African American cultural tradition, 34–42, 43–49; in broader U.S. and European political thought, 180n5; overview of King's usage of, 8–10; plot structure of, 104; rhetorical function in civil rights movement of, 168–72

Ezekiel (biblical character), 41

"Facing the Challenge of a New Age," 81, 93, 146

Fairclough, Adam, 174n16, 174n18

faith. *See* religion

Farmer, James, 139

Fellowship of Reconciliation, 130

First Baptist Church (Atlanta), 139

Fisher, Walter, 17, 22, 55, 109, 111, 177n19

Flowers, W. H., 174n18

form. *See* Burke, Kenneth: psychology of form

Forster, E. M., 20

Foss, Sonja, 178n46

Franklin, C. L., 41

Freedom Rides. *See* protests

Fulton, Dr. Robert, 151

Gadamer, Hans-Georg, 188n15

Gamson, William A., 14, 176n10, 193n11

Gardner, Rev. Ed, 151, 191n40

Garnett, Henry Highland, 44, 47

Garrow, David J., 5, 75, 94, 139, 142, 183n4, 188n1, 190n3

Garvey, Marcus, 40, 47

Gayle, W. A., 74

Geertz, Clifford, 24

Genovese, Eugene D., 34

Ghana: King's visit to, 91–92, 94; subject of King's "Birth of a New Nation" sermon, 95–114, 127, 164–65

"Give Us the Ballot," 175n28, 185n7

Glaude, Eddie S., 180n5

God: Abernathy called by, 191n34; as attentive to suffering of blacks, 38, 43, 123; as "clockmaker," 67; as coworker with blacks to overcome racial oppression, 37, 57, 67, 79, 88–89, 101, 107–8, 164, 168; as directly intervening in overthrow of racial oppression, 34, 39, 41–42, 44, 47, 49, 58–59, 63, 66, 145; blacks as chosen people of, 10, 37, 41, 43, 52, 59–63, 77, 86, 114, 148, 172, 180n5; in songs and spirituals, 36–37, 153, 155; King as unique, divinely-appointed agent of, 11, 44, 88, 122–36, 165; providence of 54–55, 64–69, 76–78, 87–89, 105, 184n19; role in biblical account of Exodus, 30–34, 45–47, 118–19

Gold Coast. *See* Ghana

Goldzwig, Steven R., 178n28

Goodgame, Rev. John W., 4

gospel. *See* religion

Gray, Fred, 74

Greensboro, 132, 139

Griffin, Charles J. G., 23, 177n24,